THE X LIST

THE X LIST

The National Society of Film Critics'

Guide to the Movies That Turn Us On

EDITED BY

JAMI BERNARD

DA CAPO PRESS
A Member of the Perseus Books Group

Designed by Jeff Williams
Set in 11-point Berkeley Book by the Perseus Books Group

Cataloging-in-Publication data for this book is available from the Library of Congress.

First Da Capo Press edition 2005
ISBN 0-306-81445-5
ISBN-13 978-0-306-81445-7

Published by Da Capo Press
A Member of the Perseus Books Group
www.dacapopress.com

Da Capo Press books are available at special discounts for bulk purchases in the U.S. by corporations, institutions, and other organizations. For more information, please contact the Special Markets Department at the Perseus Books Group, 11 Cambridge Center, Cambridge, MA 02142, or call (800) 255-1514 or (617) 252-5298, or e-mail special.markets@perseusbooks.com.

1 2 3 4 5 6 7 8 9—09 08 07 06 05

For Sam Bernard, 1921–1995
His favorite thing: staying up late
watching movies until the networks signed off

Contents

Introduction

I KNOW IT WHEN I SEE IT.

Better yet, I know it when I feel it. To sidestep Supreme Court Justice Potter Stewart for the moment in favor of quoting Conrad Birdie from the movie musical *Bye Bye Birdie*: You gotta feel it *here!*

Movies uplift us, educate us, thrill us, move us, and make us laugh until we snort. They also turn us on. That turn-on can come from the innocent tilt of your favorite star's head, or from the less innocent pleasures of gratuitous nudity in an otherwise forgettable picture you nevertheless keep adding to your Netflix queue. The turn-on can come from a porn flick whose title makes you giggle, or from the exquisite sensuality of a chaste Hollywood classic.

When, how, and why a movie turns us on is the subject of this book. In essays on particular titles and sidebars on themes, techniques, even personal crushes, the members of the National Society of Film Critics discuss the movies that changed, challenged, enhanced, or perverted our notions of screen sexuality. Here we delve into the history, artistry, spectacle, and, above all, the pleasures of movies that rocked the world. Or rocked *our* worlds; in many cases, we lift the veil of critical distance and bravely go naked before you with our personal turn-ons.

Our choices may surprise you. You'll find classics here—*Wuthering Heights, Last Tango in Paris, The Unbearable Lightness of Being, Ecstasy.* But there's also Charles Taylor on the perverse eroticism of *The Mummy* and Sheila Benson on the charms of Mark Ruffalo's potty-mouth in *In the Cut.* And I might be the only critic in the group who faints with pleasure over *Bye Bye Birdie,* but I have my reasons. We all do, which is why *The X List* can be seen as a pleasure-centered rejoinder to Jean Renoir's dictum in *The Rules of the Game:* "There is one terrible thing in this world, and that is that everyone has their reasons."

Several critics write about the first movie to unleash their libido (*The Servant* for David Ansen, *Hercules* for Armond White, *Persona* for Michael Wilmington, *The Horror of Dracula* for David Edelstein). Nathan Lee has a surprising confession to make after salivating over *O Fantasma*. Others celebrate the movies that celebrate good sex between married partners: Charles Taylor on *Tarzan and His Mate,* Sheila Benson on *Don't Look Now.*

We have our erotic weaknesses. Everyone seems to agree on Julie Christie. Peter Keough has a thing for nuns. Peter Travers and Gerald Peary duke it out over Drew Barrymore, while Desson Thomson is frankly surprised by his sudden tenderness toward Jane Fonda in *Klute.*

There's bad sex (Ella Taylor on *Twentynine Palms*), too much sex (Peter Brunette on *In the Realm of the Senses*), unforgivable sex (David Sterritt on *Irréversible*), vindictive sex (Desson Thomson on *Contempt*), weird sex (Andy Klein on *Blue Velvet*), and transgressive sex (James Verniere on *Black Sunday*).

Oh, and sex involving breasts, big breasts (Roger Ebert on *Beyond the Valley of the Dolls*).

But this book is not just about sex. Movies that turn us on also introduce us to an almost spiritual transcendence (Peter Rainer on *The Makioka Sisters*), the zeitgeist of an era (Stephanie Zacharek on *Shampoo,* Emanuel Levy on *Picnic*), the idea of sex itself (Rob Nelson on *In the Mood for Love*), the paramount importance of emotional intensity (Michael Sragow on *Splendor in the Grass*). There is movie history—both cultural and economic—to be gleaned from what separates hard-core from soft-core porn, why *Deep Throat* crossed over from "dirty movie" to must-see, and how a calculated production like *Troy* squandered its erotic resources.

In the ongoing dialogue over how movies advance or erode our notions of men, women, and sexuality, there remains one hard-core fact: Movies turn us on for reasons we can't always intellectualize. Why should we, anyway? Will there ever be a way—or need—to dryly deconstruct art into calibrated components to be filed away in dusty lab drawers? This book discusses sexuality in film, but also celebrates the way movies stir our senses beyond reason.

When Justice Stewart famously said of porn, "I shall not today attempt further to define the kinds of material I understand to be embraced . . . [b]ut

I know it when I see it," his taste-test became part of the Supreme Court ruling that let Louis Malle's *The Lovers* off the hook on obscenity charges.

In truth, there is no neat divide when it comes to subjective views of filmed sexuality. Most of what turns us on in movies falls somewhere along a sinuous, sneaky continuum of titillation, from the mildly suggestive to the kind of thing that makes Supreme Court justices scratch their heads and give up.

What turns us on in movies? We know it when we see it, when we feel it, when it haunts us in our dreams, when we come back to it again and again. We may not always be able to put a finger on it, but we embrace it.

JAMI BERNARD
New York City, 2005

The Age of Innocence
Torn between two lovers

Directed by Martin Scorsese; starring Daniel Day-Lewis,
Michelle Pfeiffer, Winona Ryder (1993)

by Amy Taubin

LOVINGLY ADAPTED FROM EDITH WHARTON'S NOVEL ABOUT
manners, marriage, and missed opportunities, Martin Scorsese's *The Age of
Innocence* stars Daniel Day-Lewis as Newland Archer, an eligible bachelor
with vague intellectual leanings who meets the love of his life, the enigmatic,
slightly scandalous Countess Ellen Olenska (Michelle Pfeiffer), just hours
after proposing to her conventional cousin May Welland (Winona Ryder).
The novel and the film are set in the rigidly coded, upper-class New York society of the 1870s. When Scorsese announced his intention to adapt *The Age
of Innocence*, the media gasped in snobbish amazement at the thought of the
goodfella invading Wharton's drawing rooms. But despite class differences,
there are striking parallels between the director and the novelist—in their
lives and their art.

In their signature works, Scorsese (*Mean Streets*, *Raging Bull*) and Wharton
(*The House of Mirth*, *The Age of Innocence*) examine the culture in which they
came of age from the fictional perspective of insiders, when they themselves
were outsiders. Ambivalence is central to their style. Aware even as children
that they were unsuited to the gender ideals prescribed for them, each found
an identity in art. Scorsese grew up in the ethnic working-class enclave of
Manhattan's Little Italy. Exempted by his asthma from the male rites his films
eroticize and critique, he escaped by going to the movies and drawing

1

comics. Wharton was born into a no less rigid culture—that of the nine-teenth century upper-class descendants of New York's original Dutch and German settlers. Her adolescent nicknames included both "Pussy" and "John." Confined by a social order that regarded literary achievement with suspicion, if not contempt, she nevertheless devoured her father's library and began writing stories when she was twelve. When her first engagement was broken off, the *Newport Daily News* speculated that the cause was "an alleged preponderance of intellectuality on the part of the intended bride."

By the time Wharton wrote *The Age of Innocence* (a 1921 Pulitzer Prize winner), she had decamped to Paris. The distance of an ocean, the turning of a century, and a war allowed her to infuse her satiric depiction of the society she fled with a romantic yearning for the past—specifically for the novel's leading character, Newland Archer. That impossible love, whose consumma-tion is an act of the imagination, is mirrored in the desire Newland feels for the mysterious, alluring, yet vulnerable Countess Olenska. Writing in the third person, Wharton devotes herself exclusively to Archer—what he thought, wanted, did, didn't do. Archer's is the only subjectivity to which Wharton gives us direct access. That is to say, our perception and under-standing of the two women in his life—exotic Ellen and traditionalist May—is mediated by his views of them.

I first read *The Age of Innocence* when I was fourteen. Lying on the porch of my family's house, I read it, wept, read it again. I had some inchoate un-derstanding of the subterranean depths of Wharton's feelings for the male character she created—that she at once loved him, identified with him, and wanted to rescue him. I couldn't have admitted then that those feelings cor-responded to mine for my father, whom I wanted to rescue from everything I found oppressive in suburban family life, beginning with my mother.

I hope I don't need to add that my shy, decorous father would have been horrified by the unconscious fantasy I projected onto Wharton's novel. Psy-choanalysis, however, counsels that all triangular love stories are Oedipal in origin. Wharton called the jargon of Freudianism "sewerage," but she left un-finished at her death *Beatrice Palmato*, a novel that would have been about father-daughter incest. I have no idea what part, if any, reality played in the conception of this novel, or the reason Wharton never got far with it. But there is considerable biographical evidence to suggest that the characters of Newland and May resemble Wharton's father and mother, and that there is much of Edith in Ellen, the Europeanized bohemian, the only successfully independent female character Wharton ever created.

When I interviewed Scorsese when *The Age of Innocence* was released, he spoke about his desire "to recreate for the viewing audience the experience he had reading the book." He had read many novels from or about the nineteenth century, but he never felt about them the way he felt about *The Age of Innocence*. "For me," he explained, "it had to do with Archer's relationship to Ellen and his not being able to fulfill it as he *thinks* he would like to. That's what's so moving—the things you miss in life with people, or think you miss."

Despite the differences of class and historical circumstances, Archer shares with some of Scorsese's other protagonists the guilt and repression that make it impossible for him to act on his desires, and that make him desire only the impossible. Trapped between duty (doing what he has been bred to do) and rebellion (longing to break free from his claustrophobic society and discover other worlds to which Ellen holds the key), he vacillates, dashing from one woman to the other, until the "tribe," rallying around the seemingly guileless May, decides for him.

What's different here for Scorsese is that the gap between desire and action cannot be bridged by physical violence—not by the carnage of Travis Bickle or the head-banging of Jake LaMotta. The repressed does not return in this film; it merely produces the anxiety of ambivalence. In the scenes between Archer and Ellen and Archer and May, Scorsese charts that ambivalence—the barely perceptible oscillations of desire—frame by frame. Here, rather than in the obsessively researched, baroque displays of decoration and architecture, costumes and artifacts, fruit and flowers, is where the filmmaking brilliance is located.

The most expressive element in *The Age of Innocence* is the acting, and in particular, Day-Lewis's interpretation of Archer. In the highly coded society of *The Age of Innocence*, people rarely speak their minds or act on their feelings. So skilled is Archer in keeping up appearances that he fools even himself. He doesn't realize until halfway through the film that his initial feelings of pity for Ellen (because she was the victim of a bad marriage) and envy (for her freedom to come and go) have coalesced into full-fledged *amour fou*. Day-Lewis's performance is most extraordinary when he lets us know things about Archer that Archer doesn't know himself. Early in his relationship with Ellen, Archer goes to a flower shop to fulfill his daily ritual of sending lilies of the valley to May and finds his hand wandering to some yellow roses, then writing a card addressed to Countess Olenska to accompany them. The gestures are of a man sleepwalking through a decision that will change his life. And what is moving for us—for me—is precisely the intensity of the denial.

Scorsese has always communicated a taste for denial and anxiety, but never so much as in this film—the suffocating anxiety of waiting for the sign on which one believes one's life depends, wanting it to come and at the same time fearing it. Scorsese plays with the rhythms of desire, denial, anxiety, and sexual guilt the way Hitchcock did in *Vertigo* (it's hardly accidental that Saul Bass's title sequence for *The Age of Innocence* raises the specter of the one he did for *Vertigo*) and Wong Kar-wai would, a decade later, in *In the Mood for Love*. These are films in which yearning and the memory of yearning are more intense than consummation could possibly be—at least within the world projected on the screen. Of these three films, *The Age of Innocence* is the most pure in that there is no implication that the lovers have a moment of intimacy beyond what we're permitted to see. It is from beginning to end a mindfuck, and more exquisite than any I could have imagined on my own.

Anatomy of Hell
Tea for two

Directed by Catherine Breillat; starring Amira Casar,
Rocco Siffredi (2004)

by Stephanie Zacharek

THE DESCRIPTIVE WORD MOST OFTEN DRAPED AROUND FRENCH
filmmaker Catherine Breillat, almost like apologetic bunting, is *provocateur*.
Both admirers and detractors must acknowledge that she likes to push the
infinitely stretchy skin of the envelope. Who else would show us a bloodsoaked tampon used as a tea bag, turning a glass of water into a pinkish elixir
that two characters drink in order to cement their own holy communion?

That's the image that almost everyone who sees *Anatomy of Hell* remembers most vividly, perhaps with revulsion, perhaps with puzzlement or admiration—or any combination of the three. But to describe the scene so
baldly negates the wonder and audacity of it. The beauty of the sequence
isn't that it's so gracefully presented we forget to be queasy, it's that Breillat re-
spects our queasiness as an allowable response that's as much evidence of our
humanity as is the bloody tincture of the water.

Breillat is a provocateur, but she's the plain-brown kind, her brand of
provocation markedly lacking in showmanship. She doesn't serve up that
bloody tampon as an existential shockeroo, left to lie there, limply, at a philo-
sophical dead end. She wouldn't insult us by being so maddeningly vague.

To put it another way: What could be less abstract than a used tampon?

In *Anatomy of Hell*, a young woman is brought back from the brink of suicide by a gay man who catches her just as she's slicing her wrist with a razor.

("Why did you do that?" he asks with blank incredulity. "Because I'm a woman," she replies, as if he'd asked why she'd raised her umbrella in a rainstorm.) Recognizing him as an impartial audience—in other words, a man who has no interest in her sexually—she invites him to spend four nights at her house perched on a cliff overlooking the ocean, the kind of desolate locale more likely to foster desperation than romance. She wants him to "watch me where I'm unwatchable." She'll even pay him for it. Her instructions: "Just say what you see."

The woman, the luminous Amira Casar, and the man, Rocco Siffredi (the Italian porn star who was so touching in Breillat's 1999 *Romance*), spend most of their time in a bedroom, although not necessarily in bed. We never learn their names, although we become intimately familiar with their bodies.

What unfolds during those four nights—on each night, the man arrives at the appointed hour in a rippling oyster-colored suit, each time looking slightly less like a spectator and more like a suitor—is a peculiar kind of intimacy that transcends sexual preference. It transcends sex. The woman reveals herself to him in ways that she herself can't even see. She shows him how she responds to his curious, if unenthusiastic, touch; she shows him how easily she can accommodate, and expel, a large stone dildo; and she shows him how she bleeds. Her purpose is to reveal to him, and to articulate for herself, the revulsion that women's bodies can incite in men—revulsion founded in the fact that women's bodies, with all their hidden though penetrable corridors, are the ultimate plumbable-yet-not-knowable mystery.

The woman reclines on the bed, an all-powerful odalisque, a nude drawn with two parallel hill-and-valley strokes. The man is unmoved by this bride stripped bare, in fact goes out of his way to berate her. He lectures her about her own vulnerability. ("The fragility of female skin inspires disgust or brutality. Women depend on one or the other.")

But the more time he spends with her—not just looking at her and touching her, but listening to her—the more he begins to understand her. *Anatomy of Hell* isn't a meditation on misogyny—that's its most obvious reading and, frankly, its laziest. Breillat uses this man and woman on a bed (sometimes only he is clothed, and sometimes the two of them are naked) as a way of exploring the meaning of women's bodies from social, political, and personal angles, instead of purely sensual ones.

Breillat frequently shows us the woman's pubis in glistening close-up. The opening credits explain that a body double was used for the most explicit scenes, but it doesn't matter whose parts we're seeing: The intimacy of these close-ups is stifling at first, but we learn to relax into them.

Still, that kind of directness is bound to make some people uncomfortable. One gay critic had this to say: "Eeeuw." I wouldn't call that a misogynist response—maybe femmephobic. But while I don't think *Anatomy of Hell* has anything so clumsy as a thesis, I do think that critic's response proves Breillat's point exactly—that the sexual essence of women is so foreign to men that revulsion is part of their response to it. (That may be the very response she's hoping for.)

But Breillat is aware that that revulsion is felt by women as well, and not solely because of social conditioning. Our parts are mysterious to us too: We can't get a good look at them without a mirror. (And I'll bet there are plenty of us who thought "Eeeuw" the first time we saw what we really look like.) Our lovers are often more intimately acquainted with our hidden parts than we are.

Maybe that's why Siffredi's performance here is so moving. He and the woman have intercourse on the first night—he's aroused in spite of himself—and afterward, we see her sound asleep while he weeps quietly at the foot of the bed. We don't really know what his tears are for. They could be a simple release, or perhaps he feels moved by her vulnerability (or identifies with it) in ways he can't articulate.

Even so, his feelings for her and her womanhood are anything but tidy. At one point, his simmering resentment toward her causes him to retrieve a gardening tool from the shed and prop its stubby handle in her vagina as she sleeps—maybe an acknowledgment that, even with his magnificent manhood, he's all too easy to replace.

The surprise of *Anatomy of Hell* is that Siffredi's character is ultimately more vulnerable than the woman, because while she knows exactly what to expect from him, he's susceptible to her in ways he never could have predicted. Siffredi's performance is lovely, partly because of the languid expressiveness of his slightly droopy eyes. He's such a securely masculine presence that he doesn't need any phony macho affectations. (The performances he delivers for Breillat are the polar opposite of his rough porn persona.) The purity of Siffredi's sexual confidence hovers far outside any socially prescribed notion of what a man should be. He's so masculine he's almost feminine.

Although *Anatomy of Hell* at first seems to present women as aggrieved souls, it ultimately asserts the certainty of their power. There's something queenly about the way Casar drapes herself along the length of her bed. Even as she speaks of the vulnerability of womankind, she looks ready to rule the world. Breillat and her camera crew (Yorgos Arvanitis, Guillaume Schiffman, Miguel Malheiros, and Susana Gomes) light Casar as if they'd wanted to paint her: Her skin has an unreal lunar glow, a visual metaphor for feminine sexual allure. The ocean that rages practically outside her door may be rushing to get to her, or to escape her.

Catherine Breillat is less a feminist filmmaker than an aggressively feminine one. I'm sure she does want to shock us with that bloody tampon cocktail. But she also reminds us that that blood—which men of many cultures have used as evidence that women are "unclean"—is the source of all human life.

À nos amours
Home schooling

Directed by Maurice Pialat; starring Sandrine Bonnaire,
Maurice Pialat (1983)

by David Edelstein

SANDRINE BONNAIRE, THE SEVENTEEN-YEAR-OLD STAR OF
Maurice Pialat's *À nos amours*, has a disruptive erotic power. During the credit
sequence, scored with Henry Purcell's woeful "Cold Song," her character,
Suzanne, stands at the prow of a yacht, her back to the camera, and the wind
lifts her already short skirt high in the air. Even her brother remarks how
provocative she looks—and smells. She's punishingly desirable, the way certain junior-high-school girls—the mere sight of them—can be punishing to
young boys swept up in that first tidal wave of sexual longing.

The movie's hook is its heroine's allure, but its real subject is her family's
rage at her burgeoning sexuality, as if she secretes something—that smell—
that drives them mad and threatens to bring down the house. At fifteen,
Suzanne is semi-oblivious to her own budding powers of attraction, even as
men ogle her and cars pull over and honk. But she's increasingly flirtatious
with her father (played by Pialat) and brother (Dominique Besnehard). And
she's clearly competing with her mother (Evelyne Ker), who is exhausted
keeping the men from alternately abusing or fondling the girl.

Most films about teens coming of age take pains to separate the horny
highjinks of youth from the households that produced them: Parents are
often turned into boobish authority figures or omitted altogether. But the
feelings for one's parents and siblings are often worked out in sex. Over the

9

course of *À nos amours*, Suzanne transforms from a needy young woman into a passionless sex object. She's not heartless. But promiscuity is the only way to break loose from those unmanageable family bonds.

À nos amours moves in a kind of trance, with months and years elapsing between scenes, the only thread being the slow burn of its protagonist's flame as she clings to people and then pushes them away. In an early scene, she slips off for a spot of heavy petting with her boyfriend, Luc (Cyr Boitard). As he fondles her breasts she stiffens and freezes him out, and he pulls away, wounded. A short time later she meets a smarmy American and decides on a whim to surrender her virginity. He says, "Thanks a lot" when he's had his way, and she replies, in English, "You're welcome. It's free." The encounter leaves a horrible taste, but it's also liberating. She can now have sex with anyone—except Luc, for whom she cares. "I'll never, never do it with you," she tells him. "You disgust me."

Why so squirmy about commitment? The clues are in the increasingly harrowing episodes at home. Her father gives her a hard time when she asks to go to the movies, although she protests that she's already made the date, obviously a sexual liaison. "You do it once more and I'll strangle you," he says. She smiles, the way girls smile before they say something like "Oh dad, you just *act* tough," and *whap!*—we barely see the hand that shoots out and smacks her hard on the face. She recoils, stunned, and then goes out to get fucked, hard.

"You think parents have no imagination?" asks her father when she creeps in after a bout of sex with yet another beau. He tells her he's leaving home—he can't take it anymore. What he can't take he doesn't articulate. The characters have little idea themselves about what they're acting out, and the loose script isn't full of problem-drama signposts. As the mother, Ker crosses into a twilight zone where you're not sure where the character ends and the honest-to-goodness seizure begins. She wails that she wants to die; she throws herself on the ground; she has convulsions. The script doesn't spell it out, but the mother resents Suzanne so intensely that—because mothers aren't supposed to hate their daughters—she turns those sentiments on herself, feeling them as Suzanne's contempt for *her*. But Ker orients us in her first scene, when she tries to keep the peace yet can't help measuring herself against this smooth-skinned beauty. When the explosion comes, we're prepared.

Often, the actors don't seem to be acting. When the father moves out and the mother and brother start shrieking at Suzanne and slapping her around, the blows don't look faked. These are the most difficult scenes in *A nos amours*—scenes that some in the audience have to laugh at to endure. Like John Cassavetes, Pialat simply aims his camera at the hysterics and films without cuts. The brother, in the guise of defending his mother, strikes Suzanne and orders her down on her knees to beg forgiveness. The girl responds with a posture of bewilderment, anger, and finally slutty defiance. The real horror is that as she squirms and fights off her brother, she's sexier to him still. Pialat has captured the erotic component of domestic violence, and because the brother has no insight into his own motives, the scenes are never cathartic. They're a ritual of abuse that's reenacted again and again, until at last Suzanne goes away to school, meets a nice young man, and marries. She doesn't love him, of course. But he "stabilizes" her, and that, she asserts, is the sort of match she needs to escape the pain of her unbearable lightness of being. Guess how many minutes the marriage lasts.

À nos amours, which means "to our loved ones," says sex education really does begin at home. In the sad final scene between father and daughter, he tells her she's never learned the difference between loving and needing to be loved, and she asks, "Isn't everyone like that?" The expression on Pialat's face is not just the despair of a parent who knows his child is destined to be unhappy. It's also the shame of a parent who knows that he has unwittingly helped to mold whatever his child has become.

It must have taken a lot of courage for Pialat to make *À nos amours*. In person, he was both hostile and self-flagellating; at one New York Film Festival appearance (with *Loulou*), he had nothing but harsh words for his own movie. In *À nos amours*, you can feel his compulsion to bare his forbidden impulses and expose his failings as a parent and a man; you also feel his misanthropy. Near the end, there's a scene in which the father baits and excoriates some dinner guests. The scene does little for the plot but is shockingly effective, as if the director's poisons had accumulated to such an intolerable degree that he was forced to inject them into someone or he'd die. (The scene was reportedly improvised, and genuinely appalled the participants.)

À nos amours isn't a bitter, puritanical work about the horror of sex; it's the work of someone too much in the world—a family man. Pialat must have put his actors through hell, but they came back with things I've never seen in a movie. This is one of the most eviscerating films about sex ever made.

Ayn Rand: A Sense of Life
The erotics of Objectivism

Directed by Michael Paxton (1997)

by Jonathan Rosenbaum

WHEN AYN RAND'S NAME COMES UP, I USUALLY SCOFF. PART of my scoffing is intellectual and part is political, but a third part is emotional, which I suspect is closely allied with why many Americans scoff at Jerry Lewis: Like Rand, he's come to stand for a stage in our adolescence we'd rather forget. Rand's vibrant appeal to adolescents is profoundly sexual: a sense of exalted fantasy tied up with raging hormones that resolves the vexing need to reconcile self-interest with social and ethical duties. Rand's message that selfishness is empowering and self-sacrifice destructive can pierce teenage confusion like a comforting ray of light, as penetrating as Rand's own gaze, and make the blood race in the bargain.

Indeed, the sexiness of *The Fountainhead* and *Atlas Shrugged* is an integral part of their utopianism, making them blood sisters of Leni Riefenstahl's *Triumph of the Will* and *Olympia* in their kitschy splendor and sexual lift (if not in their political programs). The American dream of untrammeled freedom and glittering self-realization can at times be boiled down to a compulsive desire to relive and rewrite our adolescent traumas, giving them a happier outcome. If Jerry Lewis represents the implied hell of adolescence, Rand ushers us into the implied heaven, for which her phallic skyscrapers are always reaching. Moreover, since she fled communist Russia to script Hollywood movies when she was twenty-one, surely her own American adventure was a protracted postadolescent episode, for better or worse.

To its credit, Michael Paxton's *Ayn Rand: A Sense of Life* acknowledges the snobbish impulse to scoff. But to its discredit, it attributes that skepticism almost exclusively to the culture's supposed ideology of collectivism, without taking other factors into account.

Rand's taste in literature and the other arts is an obstacle when it comes to accepting her as a world-class intellectual, as this film clearly does: She revered others besides Aristotle, Victor Hugo, Frank Lloyd Wright, and the Fritz Lang of *Siegfried* and *Metropolis*. Paxton's film alludes to Rand's touching celebration of the utopian spirit of Marilyn Monroe, offered shortly after the actress's death, but it excludes her appalling defense of the early novels of Mickey Spillane and his hero Mike Hammer. (Spillane eventually became Rand's friend, and she wrote with admiration in *The Romantic Manifesto* that "he gives me the feeling of hearing a military band in a public park"—one indication of her musical taste.) Page through the index of her *Letters* in search of the giants of literary modernism, and you find most are absent, though she does link James Joyce to the "beatniks" as an example of the sort of junk that's "admired in English courses."

Paxton is attentive to the romantic side of Rand's legacy but skimps on the sexual side. For that story, one needs to turn to Barbara Branden's 1986 biography, which stretches all the way from a Petrograd friend named Leo (a traumatic infatuation that he didn't reciprocate) to Nathaniel Branden, the biographer's former husband and Rand's key acolyte for the better part of two decades. For fourteen years—starting in the mid-'50s, when he was twenty-four and Rand nearly fifty—they were lovers, with the full knowledge (and tortured approval) of their spouses but almost no one else. The affair came to a cataclysmic end when Rand discovered Nathaniel had been sleeping with another Rand acolyte for several years. He was violently excommunicated, an action accounted for only by Rand's announcement that he'd been involved in a series of personal and professional deceptions.

Leo isn't mentioned in this purportedly intimate documentary, and Nathaniel is accorded a stretch of about three-and-a-half minutes (out of 145). Meanwhile, brave Barbara Branden—who remained a passionate Rand disciple before, during, and after, and one of her closest friends until shortly after her husband's excommunication—barely figures at all. The complex spiritual links between Ayn, Nathaniel, and Barbara are perhaps rooted in the fact that they all adopted hard-sounding goy replacements for their original Jewish names: Alice Rosenbaum, Nathaniel Blumenthal, and

Barbara Weidman. Neal Gabler's provocative thesis in *An Empire of Their Own: How the Jews Invented Hollywood*—that Hollywood's version of the American Dream was largely the dopey creation of Jews in flight from their ethnicity—can probably be applied to the founding gospel of Rand's Objectivism, which was in turn guided by Hollywood.

Given Rand's monstrous behavior when scorned, it's understandable that Paxton leapfrogs over this episode and omits the painful story of Leo. But the crushing irony of Paxton's massive act of repression—made in deference to Rand and her own self-representations after her bitter break with the Brandens—is how close it comes to the historical elisions of Stalinism. This is a paradox to reckon with, because it's difficult to think of a twentieth-century writer who hated communism in general and Stalinism in particular more than Rand did. But even if this movie dutifully, eloquently articulates that hatred while (probably unconsciously) enacting a Freudian return of the repressed, the history of the Cold War was full of such unnerving mirror effects—like the ideological boomerang that turned America and the Soviet Union into grotesque twins at the height of their mutual opposition.

One might assume that Rand would have welcomed Ronald Reagan and his economic reforms with open arms, especially after one of her disciples, Alan Greenspan, became a top Reagan adviser. But as she wrote to a fan in 1981, "I did not vote for any of the Presidential candidates. I do not approve of Mr. Reagan's mixture of capitalism and religion." Because her atheism ran neck and neck with her economics, she refused to condone potential boondoggles and convenient alliances. (That same inflexibility could be found in some of her heroes; informed gossip tells me that the reason Frank Lloyd Wright set impossible conditions for designing the sets for *The Fountainhead* was that he regarded Rand as a screwball.) In fact, the only political campaigning she ever did was for Wendell Willkie in 1940, and she became so disillusioned by what she regarded as his betrayal of capitalism in his speeches that she wound up declaring him "the guiltiest man of any for destroying America, more guilty than Roosevelt, who was only the creature of his time, riding the current." Betrayals were as vital to her erotic program as projected matches on Mount Olympus.

Rand's inability to compromise undoubtedly produced a kind of tragic heroism, and Paxton's affectionate portrait amply illustrates her unswerving idealism. In her later years, after the death of her beloved husband, Frank

O'Connor, she was asked on a national TV show if she wouldn't entertain the possibility of joining him in an afterlife. Her poised and firm reply was that if she could, she would kill herself immediately. One of the film's final quotations from her is for me the most memorable, encapsulating her art and her metaphysics in a single sentence: "Death isn't important; eternity is important, and eternity is now."

Baby Doll
Cribbing

Directed by Elia Kazan; starring Carroll Baker,
Karl Malden, Eli Wallach (1956)

by Michael Sragow

THE COMEDY OF SEXUAL VULNERABILITY ANIMATES ELIA
Kazan's *Baby Doll* like dirty Disney. Ruined by a spanking new cotton gin at
a large Delta plantation, old-time gin owner Archie Lee Meighan (Karl
Malden) burns down his competition. The scorched plantation manager,
Silva Vacarro (Eli Wallach), discovers who's responsible and seeks revenge—
partly by seducing Archie's child bride, Baby Doll (Carroll Baker).

Baby Doll's father gave her to Archie when she was eighteen on the condition that Archie would support her in comfort and she'd stay a virgin until
her twentieth birthday. The poor slob feels he's honored half his vow by setting the two of them up in a haunted mansion—and he'd like nothing better
than to break the other half. Since everybody in town has learned of this
agreement, Archie Lee lives in shame. The straw that breaks the cracker's
back comes when the Ideal Pay As You Go Plan Furniture Company removes
his five rooms full of goods the day before Baby Doll reaches the magic birthday. That's what impels Archie to commit arson during the Syndicate Plantation's first anniversary party.

Although you feel sorry for the white-trash schlub, you feel sorrier for the
literally crib-bound Baby Doll, who sleeps in her own nursery furniture in
part because it's the only stuff the couple actually owns. She has to put up
with her legal husband's playing Peeping Tom or barging into her bath.

When Archie Lee complains of his public humiliation, Baby Doll responds, "Private humiliation is just as painful." Kazan doesn't overplay the line. He has Baby Doll deliver it while lapping up a single-dip ice cream cone and envying a little girl who's enjoying a double-dip. Kazan once said, "The fact that [Baby Doll] sucks her thumb doesn't mean she wants a penis in her mouth. . . . There's no indication of actual sex. All that Silva does is lay in her crib and take a nap." But this is an extremely oral, hilariously horny movie. (Tennessee Williams wrote the script from two of his short plays, *Twenty-Seven Wagons Full of Cotton* and *The Long Stay Cut Short, or The Unsatisfactory Supper.*)

Silva Vacarro ("like in 'silva lining,'" suggests Archie) is a Sicilian from Corpus Christi who dresses in natty black suits or Western outfits complete with Stetson, riding crop, and a belt with a showy silver buckle. This seething yet self-contained figure can't help breaking into Italian gestures, biting his thumb, or hacking the air with the edge of his hand like a meat chopper. And there's something archetypally Sicilian about the way that Silva exacts his revenge: bringing his cotton to Archie Lee's gin and then using his charm to pressure Baby Doll into signing a letter attesting to her husband's guilt. Sad-sack Archie, balding, chunky, and putty-nosed, adrift in family and business troubles, is no match for a sleek polecat like Silva.

One of the miracles of the movie is that Silva's seduction of Baby Doll is sexy and touching as well as darkly humorous. What arouses her sensuality—what awakens her from adolescence into womanhood—isn't just Silva's relatively graceful roughhousing but his insinuating intimacy. Unlike the bogus, insecure Archie, Silva gives Baby Doll the minute attentions she craves. He praises her refinement for refusing a pecan he's cracked open in his mouth. He sympathizes with her irritation over the cotton lint in the atmosphere. Silva plants every caress squarely but precisely, even when he uses his riding crop. And Baby Doll needs a man with a slow whip hand. Gradually, this girl who berates herself for dropping out of school because she cried over long division gets some sense of her value and allure as a woman. But the film never loses its comic ring. Emboldened by her sex play with Silva, she defends her intelligence to Archie by saying, "I've been to school in my life, and I'm—a magazine reader!"

Costume designer Anna Hill Johnstone dresses the heroine in baby-doll pajamas, and Kenyon Hopkins's music brings back the time when sax-y meant sexy. Sometimes the score is Mickey Mouse, but more often it's ripplingly effective. Hopkins gives the stylized sequences—such as the lovers' game of hide-and-seek through the empty mansion—some of the snap and funk of a good '50s Jerome Robbins ballet. Kazan once instructed Dartmouth students to study the cinematography in this movie to see "a master, Boris Kaufman, making a great use of white on white to help describe the washed-out Southern whites." Kaufman's work is so textured that you can almost *feel* the cotton lint. And when he shows you the mansion in a dusky long shot on the day of the fire, as Archie splashes his rattletrap car through a patch of muck that picks up the distant house lamps, the scene is haunted by demons of desire.

As with any of Kazan's peak films, though, the glory of *Baby Doll* is its acting. Archie Lee may be an embarrassing character, but Karl Malden does blubbery wonders with him—he's a Rodney Dangerfield who doesn't have to make jokes because he knows his soul is a joke. Eli Wallach is sharp and flashy in the best sense, like a knife blade. You can catch the twenty-five-year-old Rip Torn in a beaming cameo as a dentist who's tempted to give Baby Doll work as a receptionist. Most of all, you get to see Carroll Baker seizing her one great chance and giving an astonishing performance. Sucking her thumb and wiggling her toes when she's dozing in her crib, she looks as malleable as a child. When she wakes up, she's a fierce young animal who can be as imperious as any belle, though she mostly wears a slip instead of a ball gown.

Baker's tour de force outdoes Sue Lyon's Lolita (a part Baker's daughter would later play on stage). Baker expresses both the trembling eroticism and the growing maturity of a girl on the brink of womanhood. At the end, Baby Doll is stranded without either man—forlorn and confused, but also glad to be free of Archie Lee and determined to take the next days as they come. Baker's strength and comic timing help turn her into a skewed, dirt-poor relation of Henrik Ibsen's Nora—and help transform this movie into *A Baby Doll's House.*

Baby Face
The unkindest cuts

Directed by Alfred E. Green; starring Barbara Stanwyck (1933)

by Dave Kehr

HISTORIANS OF FILM CENSORSHIP CITE ALFRED E. GREEN'S *Baby Face,* a Warner Bros. melodrama from 1933, as one of the movies that helped to bring down the enforcement of the Production Code in 1934. Even today, *Baby Face* is startling. The script, from a story by Warner's head of production Darryl F. Zanuck, tells the presumably cautionary tale of Lily Powers (Barbara Stanwyck, twenty-six and satin slinky), an enterprising young woman raised in her father's two-story speakeasy (and, the film not so subtly implies, gambling den and brothel) in a working-class neighborhood of Erie, Pennsylvania.

Apparently, Lily's father (Robert Barrat) has long been offering her companionship to the local steelworkers (one of whom, a shirtless laborer played by professional thug Nat Pendleton, keeps imploring her to "go for a walk over by the quarry"). But when the old man trades her services to a corrupt politician (Arthur Hohl) in exchange for a greasy wad of bills, Lily has had enough. When the politician tries to caress her thigh, she pours hot coffee on his hand; when he tries to grab her breasts from behind, she knocks him cold with a beer bottle. All of this happens in the first ten minutes, in the breathless style typical of early '30s Warner Bros. films.

Lily packs a bag and hops a freight train for New York City, accompanied by Chico (Theresa Harris), the young black woman who is her best friend, coconspirator, and (thanks to the conventions of the time) personal maid.

She gets a job as a file clerk at the Gotham Trust Company by performing a lewd, off-screen favor for a tubby office manager and begins her climb up the corporate ladder. Her rise is symbolized by a camera pan up an exquisite miniature of the Gotham Trust skyscraper, counting off a floor for each of her conquests until, several firings, a broken home, a murder, and a suicide later, Lily reaches the boardroom in the building's phallic pinnacle.

The version of *Baby Face* that has been astounding audiences for seventy years is a heavily censored one. Although the film industry's self-policing Hays Office was set up in 1922 (as a reaction to the Fatty Arbuckle scandals), it had lost most of its teeth by the early '30s. But the local censor boards, often staffed by influential clerics, the widows of policemen, and other representatives of civic order, had not lost their power. The New York censor board was among the strongest; it could even ban films outright, and if a title couldn't play in New York State, its chances of turning a profit were compromised. So when Warner Bros. received the one-word reaction of the New York board on April 28, 1933—"REJECTED"—the studio removed some ten minutes of material and reworked other scenes to reduce their impact and even alter their sense. It is this version that has been in circulation ever since.

In the summer of 2004, Michael Mashon, a curator at the Motion Picture Division of the Library of Congress, made a remarkable discovery. Asked by the London Film Festival to strike a new print of *Baby Face,* Mashon found two negatives. One was the original camera negative; the other, though identified as a duplicate negative, looked as if it might be longer.

It was. What Mashon had discovered was *Baby Face* in its raw state—very likely the version that had been submitted to the New York censors. A comparison shows that some of the changes were superficial—a steelworker describes Lily as "the sweetheart of the night shift," which became "the sweetheart of the night" in the censored version—but others were fundamental, and not just when it came to sex. The film's philosophy, morality, and even politics had been completely transformed.

Baby Face may well be unique in surviving in both prerelease and postcensorship versions. As such, it has a lot to tell us about the priorities of the censorship bodies during that period.

The Production Code of the Motion Picture Industry, as it was formally adopted by the Motion Picture Producers and Distributors of America on March 31, 1930 (and enforced only after June 13, 1934), was largely a list of subjects to be approached with caution, if at all: "Crimes against the law . . .

shall never be presented in such a way as to throw sympathy with the crime," "The use of liquor in American life, when not required by the plot for proper characterization, shall not be shown," "Excessive and lustful kissing, lustful embraces, suggestive postures and gestures, are not to be shown."

Baby Face, like many films of the period, blithely ignored those restrictions. The sweaty patrons of Pop's speakeasy merrily order bootleg beers, and the camera lingers over Stanwyck in her lacy slips and silk dressing gowns. The film is nothing if not sympathetic to Lily as she seduces and betrays her bosses. The story is told almost entirely from Lily's point of view, suggesting that she is only using her feminine wiles as a man would use his fists or a gun.

It seems likely that Zanuck conceived *Baby Face* as a sort of female variation on his studio's successful gangster films—Mervyn LeRoy's *Little Caesar* and William Wellman's *Public Enemy,* both released in 1931. Though these films offered a moralizing ending—Edward G. Robinson's Rico is gunned down in a gutter, James Cagney's Tom is executed by a rival gang, his body propped up like a mummy outside his mother's door—their sympathy toward their antiheroes was otherwise undisguised. At a time of uncertainty and fear, gangsters represented a perverse kind of hope, strong men for hard times.

Lily, in fact, shares a last name with the protagonist of *Public Enemy,* and it hardly seems an innocent one: Powers. The gangster film depicts individuals who tap into their personal power. They were, in the early years of the Depression, radical individualists who took their lives in their own hands, prompted by the massive failure of the social system. The films may have carried finger-wagging warnings—the 1930s equivalent of "Don't try this at home"—yet they freely invited the audience to share the fantasies of power and domination that the gangster heroes embodied. What harm could there be in indulging the daydreams of the disenfranchised?

Plenty, or so the authorities of the time seemed to think. Here was a most dangerous idea: that the individual could liberate himself from the constraints and responsibilities of a corrupt social order and shape his own destiny. It was a notion that smacked of the philosophies of Friedrich Nietzsche, whose rhetoric was being used by the political movements of Hitler and Mussolini.

There is a curious character in the censored version of *Baby Face:* Cragg (Alphonse Ethier), a not-so-kindly German cobbler who encourages Lily to try her luck in New York. He is the film's Jiminy Cricket, periodically popping up to issue moral bromides. Late in the film, when Lily has been installed in a Park Avenue apartment by the bank's elderly vice president (Henry Kolker), she receives a Christmas gift from old Cragg: a book in which he's inserted an angry letter of rebuke. "You have chosen the wrong way," he writes. "You are still a coward. I send you this book hoping that you will allow it to guide you right." Though we aren't shown the title, we're allowed to understand that it's something morally improving. As it turns out, that scene represents the single most drastic concession to the censors—the book is Nietzsche's *Thoughts Out of Season,* and instead of calling her back to the straight and narrow, Cragg's letter originally urged Lily to "Face life as you find it, defiantly and unafraid! Waste no energy yearning for the moon! Crush out all sentiment!"

Other changes softened the movie's sexually suggestive content. The corrupt politician's first look at Lily was originally a leering panning shot that begins with Stanwyck's legs and rises slowly, almost reluctantly, to her face. She spent a bit more time behind closed doors with the tubby office manager, and a scene in which she has an apparent sexual encounter with an early mentor (Douglas Dumbrille) was both longer and clearly located in the "Ladies' Powder Room."

Still, more than enough risqué material remains to suggest that the censors had more than mere sex on their minds. What they wanted to repress was the notion of sex as empowerment, a woman's weapon in a man's world.

Even in the precensorship *Baby Face,* Lily Powers pays the price for her transgressions: She is ready to sacrifice her hard-earned savings to rescue the reputation of the man she loves (George Brent). The censored cut goes further, adding a scene in the bank's boardroom in which we learn that Stanwyck and Brent have returned to Pennsylvania, where Brent's character has found work as a poor but honest laborer. Lily has been sent back to the beginning of her journey, there to pick things up as a properly constrained wife, her sexuality in check. For much of its running time, the original cut of *Baby Face* was a call to anarchy and adventure, a revolution based on a woman's refusal to accept the life laid out for her. The revised *Baby Face* is a call to come home.

Bad Education

Pedro-philia

Directed by Pedro Almodóvar; starring Gael García Bernal, Fele Martínez (2004)

by Andy Klein

IN PEDRO ALMODÓVAR'S EARLY MOVIES, FEMALE PROTAGONISTS usually provided all or part of the narrative point of view. In the new millennium, however, women have all but disappeared from his films while paradoxically remaining central. It's not merely that *Talk to Her* (2002) stuck rigorously to the POV of its male characters, but that its two important females spent most of their screen time literally comatose, functioning less as characters than as mysterious objects of desire.

In *Bad Education*, they function as objects of emulation. Aside from two brief conversations with a mother, the largest female part in *Bad Education* belongs to classic Spanish movie star Sara Montiel, who is not even *in* the film, technically speaking. During a scene set in a movie theater, Montiel appears on the screen in Mario Camus's 1969 *A Woman*, and twice we see drag performers dressed like her and lip-synching to her recordings.

Almodóvar's films invariably include either gay or bi- characters and/or transvestites or transsexuals. *Bad Education* includes nothing but. The protagonist here is a film director, Enrique Goded (Fele Martinez), and while Almodóvar says the film is not literally autobiographical, he strongly associates himself with Enrique from the start: The opening credits end with "Written and directed by Pedro Almodóvar" superimposed over a movie poster, then dissolving into the poster's inscription, "Written and directed by Enrique Goded."

It is 1980, and Enrique's young career has already hit a snag. Stuck for a story, he spends his days with his assistant (Juan Fernández) seeking inspiration in newspaper clips about grotesque events. One day, a gorgeous actor (Gael García Bernal) walks in, identifying himself as Enrique's old school chum Ignacio Rodriguez, now performing under the name Angel Andrade. He insists on giving Enrique a story he has written called "The Visit," based in part on their experiences in school.

We quickly learn that Ignacio is more than an old chum; he was, in fact, the first love of Enrique's life. Their adolescent romance is at the heart of "The Visit."

It's here, about ten minutes in, that the narrative gets tricky. As Enrique reads "The Visit," we hear it in a voice-over by Angel/Ignacio, and we see the story onscreen (helpfully distinguished by a narrower image than the outer film's CinemaScope frame) . . . or, perhaps more accurately, we see the story as envisioned as a movie by Enrique. "The Visit" is about a female impersonator named Zahara (but originally called Ignacio), who, while performing in his old hometown, decides to blackmail Father Manolo (Daniel Giménez Cacho), the boarding-school priest who molested him and jealously broke up his relationship with a classmate named Enrique. He presents Father Manolo with a story he has written called "The Visit," which describes the priest's vile behavior seventeen years earlier. We see *that* story onscreen as well—a story within a story within the film itself.

These various stories called "The Visit" take up at least 30 of *Bad Education*'s first 45 minutes. Yet those are the easiest of the movie's narrative contortions, with the varying image widths to help keep track of where you are.

Enrique is determined to turn "The Visit" into a film, until Angel/Ignacio insists on playing "himself," Ignacio/Zahara. Surprisingly, Enrique dismisses the idea, saying that his old friend looks entirely wrong for the part. Since we have seen Angel/Ignacio (or Bernal, at least) in drag, playing Ignacio/Zahara in the first half, perhaps those scenes *weren't* Enrique's visualizations, but rather those of the actor/writer.

Angel/Ignacio storms out, and the project seems dead. But Enrique senses something beneath the surface, that A/I has been deceiving him in some way, and soon discovers that the real story of Ignacio's adult life is quite different. When A/I returns to apologize, Enrique doesn't let on that he knows the truth (or some of it), instead dangerously taking the liar as his lover *and* giving him the lead in *The Visit* after all. Enrique compares himself to a character in one of his news clippings—a woman who leapt into a crocodile pit and embraced one of the reptiles as it devoured her.

This just scratches the surface of *Bad Education's* twists and folds, and the intricate way characters and events are doubled and tripled and reversed and skewed in a manner that evokes both *Vertigo* and *Adaptation*. Different actors play the same characters on different narrative levels . . . or maybe not.

Almodóvar himself describes *Bad Education* as a film noir, which seems fair. He has given Bernal what traditionally would have been the part of the femme fatale—Barbara Stanwyck in *The Strange Love of Martha Ivers* (1946) and *Double Indemnity* (1944), Jane Greer in *Out of the Past* (1947), Gene Tierney in *Leave Her to Heaven* (1945)—so grasping, ambitious, and ruthless that she inevitably sows the seeds of her own destruction. Near the end, as two characters are seen leaving "Film Noir Week" at a local theater, one of them says, oh-so-truthfully, "It's as if all the films are talking about us."

As Enrique, Martínez seems blander than he did in Julio Medem's brilliant *Lovers of the Arctic Circle* (1998)—perhaps by design. Although he is our eyes and ears, it is Bernal's Angel/Ignacio/Zahara who is the center of the story; Martínez is playing Nick to Bernal's Gatsby.

Or maybe it is simply that Bernal is so intense that he completely dominates the screen (except during a few moments of comic relief shared with the innately funny Javier Cámara, who played the obsessed male nurse in *Talk to Her*). Bernal smolders even when he's standing there doing nothing. And, crucial to the film's design, he is the only one of the drag characters who hasn't a whiff of either grotesquerie or genial camp. As a woman, he is— what can one say?—simply a knockout, likelier to turn the heads of straight guys than of anyone else.

Baise-moi
Paris when it sizzles

Directed by Virginie Despentes and Coralie Trinh Thi,
starring Karen Bach, Raffaëla Anderson (2000)

by Gerald Peary

FOR THOSE WHO GAG ON THE WHITE-SUGAR, SMILE-BUTTON
Paris foisted on us in 2001 by *Amélie*—streets sanitized of multicultural-
ism!—*Baise-moi*, made a bit earlier, offered a fabulous blast of fetid air. A
trashy, mongrel France was back in tow: rabid and randy, incisors bared,
dangerously off the leash.

Two pit bulls in heat, hardened and street-wise—Nadine (Karen Bach)
and Manu (Raffaëla Anderson)—are weary of being pushed around by the
neighborhood roughnecks (underemployed North Africans, strung-out losers, hard-muscled punks). To bring some entertainment into their humdrum
lives, they go on a giddy shooting spree across France, killing some people
for spite, others at random. "I feel really great!" one gal says after a gruesome
offing. "So great I feel like doing it again!"

When they aren't murdering, Nadine and Manu take screwing breaks
with various big-meat pickups. Additional philosophy: "The more you fuck,
the less you think, the better you sleep." Some of the guys they seduce, they
let get away. Others are shot dead postfornication, or run over. The killings
are graphic, bloody, and ugly. The sex is the real thing: blow jobs, hand
jobs, more. *Rolling Stone*'s Peter Travers called it *"Thelma and Louise* with actual penetration."

I'm a fan of *Baise-moi*, a first-film directorial collaboration of Virginie Despentes and Coralie Trinh Thi, who met while working on a safe-sex promo for French TV. But how can I defend a movie whose title translates as *Rape Me* (and by which it has become known for English-speaking audiences) without coming off as worthless scum?

I'll start by talking about the movie's undeniable energy and rah-rah pacing and editing, and by praising the on-camera ease of the two ex-porn actress leads: Bach, a Dietrich-cold Nadine, and Anderson, alternately funny and madly sadistic as the Jeanne Moreau–petite Manu. Also, the filmmakers are brilliant at capturing the ambience of a marginal, shit-kicker France of seedy poolhalls and street brawls.

As for my endorsing the sex and violence, it might be judicious to argue that the hard-core scenes aim for the beautiful, the artistic, the subtly erotic. But that's just not true: What we get is the primal jabbing of the most animalistic porn movies. *Baise-moi*'s balling is heartless, all below the belt.

How about rationalizing the violence as being motivated by a desire of women to get back at piggy men, including the pack of slobs who rape Manu? Isn't it an over-the-top feminist revenge movie in the Roger Corman tradition? Wrong again! Nadine and Manu kill men *and* women, anyone who happens to be standing by when the two get in a homicidal mood.

Baise-moi defies traditional justification. It's all unbridled rage, an unfocused mix of misogyny and misanthropy, terrorism undiluted on the screen. It was the great mad Frenchman Antonin Artaud who argued in *The Theatre and Its Double* that art must be like the plague, descending on an audience and gutting everything the polite crowd stands for. The bourgeois-friendly *Amélie* was France's Foreign Film nomination to the Oscars, while *Baise-moi*—anthrax unleashed!—was banned in its native country.

What kind of human beings could have made such a movie? Well, they weren't film-school types, though they shared a friendship with filmmaker Gaspar Noé (*Irréversible*); and Despentes, who wrote the 1995 best-selling novel on which *Baise-moi* is based, is a fan of the rigorous, sexually charged cinema of Maurice Pialat. Despentes grew up in a small French town and sang in a punk rock band. "I got into prostitution, occasionally, for a few years," she's explained, "and then I wrote the novel." In the book and movie, the crimes are irrational and impulsive. Despentes: "We wanted them to kill everybody. People in the wrong place at the wrong time. Some people are lucky and live. Some people aren't."

Trinh Thi hails from Paris, where she was a literature major. But university was too easy, so at eighteen, she quit to appear in porn films, which was even easier. Soon she was an X-rated star. As an adult, she turned to film directing, making, with *Baise-moi*, the kind of cinema she and Despentes wished they'd had available as teenagers.

Their two leads, Anderson and Bach, were discovered in a half-documentary, half-fiction film, *Exhibition 99*, in which ten porno actresses were interviewed as themselves between sexual interludes. They thought that Raffaëla Anderson, the little one, was hilarious, and that Karen Bach, the larger one, was intimidating, could beat someone up and down. Naïvely, the cofilmmakers were surprised when many male viewers said they felt threatened by the movie. But they enjoyed that the men were frustrated by being cockteased: The women dance together in their undies, but there's no payoff lipstick lesbianism.

In interviews, both directors have described themselves as feminists. Despentes has thanked the women's movement for contraceptives and a chance for her to work, earn money, have power. Trinh Thi's conversion to feminism was precipitated by her realization that women still didn't have the right to control sex, or to be as violent as men. Until *Baise-moi*. "We've seen movies forever with women badly treated, or not even in the story," Despentes told me. "Our movie is just a balance."

Basic Instinct

A geyser of pathology

Directed by Paul Verhoeven; starring Sharon Stone, Michael Douglas (1992)

by J. Hoberman

THE MIRRORED CEILING IS STANDARD BOUDOIR ISSUE IN PAUL Verhoeven's *Basic Instinct*, a movie that's been refracted through the media so often it seems to get off on watching itself. The camera somersaults out of the looking glass in the very first shot to glom onto a naked couple grinding loins on silken sheets. She straddles him, ties him to the bedpost, arches her back and rebounds with an ice pick. Clearly, Verhoeven wants to give new meaning to "over the top."

More inadvertently self-revealing than malign, *Basic Instinct* posits a sinister conspiracy of rich, beautiful, man-slashing crypto-lesbians amid goofball preening and ham-fisted dialogue. A forensic psychologist offers crime-scene cops an instant diagnosis of the ice pick killer: "a devious, diabolical mind . . . a deep-seated obsessional hatred . . . someone very dangerous and very ill." Yeah, like the murderer and who else?

Reaping a whirlwind of publicity (and violently mixed notices), *Basic Instinct* grossed $15 million over its opening weekend. In New York, where it was released the same day as Derek Jarman's *Edward II* and a report on the rise in gay-bias attacks, *Basic Instinct* was protested by a coalition of gay and lesbian groups, as it had been during production. Still, the movie's basic instinct is not simply homophobia. From its expulsive opening it becomes a veritable geyser of pathology.

Basic Instinct is nominally set in San Francisco (and thus an anthology of allusions to *Vertigo*, *Bullitt*, and *Dirty Harry*) but actually unfolds in the realm of unfettered desire. The atmosphere of super-consumption—cops in burnished-wood suites, interrogating suspects in a junior version of the Pentagon war room—is reinforced by ostentatious dolly and crane shots, carefully dappled light, casually superfluous helicopter overheads. (The budget has been put at $49 million.)

As with *Robocop* and *Total Recall*, Verhoeven places a Hollywood genre between quotation marks. It's as if he gave a routine *policier* the same madcap treatment he accorded middle-period Ingmar Bergman in *The Fourth Man*; as a thriller, *Basic Instinct* is more baroquely twisted than suspenseful, closer to De Palma than to Hitchcock. The biggest tension builder is the shot-countershot montage before cop Michael Douglas goes down on suspect Sharon Stone in one of the film's hypertheatrical, hot-and-slurpy sex scenes.

A hard-boiled wise guy who leads with his putz, Douglas here synthesizes previous roles from *Fatal Attraction* and *The War of the Roses* to *Black Rain* and TV's *The Streets of San Francisco*. He's a superego tied into a pretzel, a cop with an addictive personality who consistently does the wrong thing—most spectacularly, we gather, when two tourists wandered into his line of fire. (It's also suggested that he drove his wife to suicide.) As a result, *Basic Instinct* opens with Douglas in a heightened state of deprivation, having temporarily given up cigarettes, sex, booze, and cocaine.

American movies, at least those directed by Howard Hawks, made a fetish of professionalism. *Basic Instinct* is almost delirious in celebrating the absence of ethics. Or maybe it's a form of social criticism. The movie is so opportunistic it could be taking place in the brain of Donald Trump—this fantasyland is sprinkled with sleaze instead of Disney dust. Sentenced to psychiatric care after the tourist incident, Douglas sleeps with the police psychologist (Jeanne Tripplehorn) assigned to his case while she, in turn, circulates his confidential file—ultimately sold off to Stone's mystery novelist–cum–murder suspect, who explains that writers are amoral by nature.

This blithe lack of scruples has been recapitulated after a fashion both by Verhoeven's bland assertion that the crypto-lesbians are the movie's most positive characters and by screenwriter Joe Eszterhas's campaign to distance himself from a script for which, despite its being a virtual retread of his *Jagged Edge*, he received $3 million. The scenario also evokes the paranoid domestic mindfuck of Verhoeven's *Total Recall*, and chief among the movie's cartoonish pleasures is the spectacle of Stone playing a 90s-era Madonna to Douglas's diminished Arnold. With her repertoire of Lilith wiles and vampire smiles, Stone gives the snakiest performance since Amanda Donohoe in *The Lair of the White Worm*.

It's interesting that men (straight and gay) tend to be more disapproving of the film than women. Stone here is the ultimate bad girl, flaunting her transgressive power at every turn. Questioned by the police, she brazenly smokes in a no-smoking zone and confounds six seasoned cops (their faces pouring sweat) with frank sex talk, and further reveals that she's *sans* knickers. Whether or not that scene sells the movie, it's enough to send Douglas pirouetting off the wagon into a rough-sex *pas de deux*: "You've never been like that before," Tripplehorn observes after he slams her against a wall, rips her underwear, and pushes her face-down onto a chair to take her from behind.

From the Douglas perspective, *Basic Instinct* is one long, confusing come-hither look. (To reinforce the point, Dorothy Malone periodically traipses out of the woodwork to reprise her '50s impersonation of nympho excitement—rubbing her back against the wall, sucking in her cheeks, batting her bedroom eyes.) Stone pals around with female multiple-murderers—as opposed to killers of multiple females—and, perhaps, lives out her bestsellers. She explains her relentless interest in Douglas in terms of a work-in-progress about a detective who "falls for the wrong woman" and gets himself killed. It's the boudoir-mirror principle, life imitating art imitating life. Ultimately, Douglas will propose an alternative ending to Stone's scenario: "How about we fuck like minks, raise rug rats, and live happily ever after." Too bad for him, the completed manuscript is already spewing out of her printer.

"My wife says it comes out of all my sexual fantasies" has been Eszterhas's convoluted explanation for *Basic Instinct*. The former Mrs. E. notwithstanding, the women here are all infinitely manipulative, with two duplicitous shrinks (Stone's character has a Berkeley degree in literature and psychology) and each female being a potential killer, lesbian, or both. The running joke is that each can be awed, at least temporarily, by the power of Douglas's wand. The most comic demonstration of this feat is when Stone's leather-clad consort (Leilani Sarelle) menacingly materializes in the bathroom after spying on the action and Douglas out-machos her, bare ass to the viewer.

As this coy camera placement suggests, it is Douglas who is the movie's real love object; his reported $14 million paycheck dwarfs that of Eszterhas.

(It was also Douglas who was pressed into service to give *Basic Instinct* a "progressive"—or at least "libertarian"—reading.) So, is the movie homophobic or naturalistic when it gives Douglas's lumberingly faithful partner (George Dzundza) an unrequited crush? Dzundza is as jealous as Sarelle: "Goddamn sonofabitch, you fucked her. How could you fuck her!" That this tantrum was shot at a gay-and-lesbian country-western bar called Rawhide II suggests that Verhoeven, at least, understood the implications.

Less homophobic than misogynist, more ridiculous than not, *Basic Instinct* is full of fantastic projections, with all manner of doubling, evil twins, and shadow selves. (There's even a character named Hoberman, although I consider that less an acknowledgment of my panning Eszterhas's *Music Box* than a reference to former Touchstone president David Hoberman, no relation.) If half the murders go absurdly unsolved, well, Freud would understand that too. Just what do these women want? The lesbian activity, such as it is, is a surplus of sexual heat, a factor of an overall female uncanniness, the manifestation of a male's fear he might be expendable.

Basic Instinct is undoubtedly exploitative, but it's also unsettling. It's as if the female sex-toys in a garden-variety porn flick suddenly developed an unpredictable, vengeful autonomy. "Funny how the subconscious works," somebody muses late in the film. I dare say it's a riot. One man's basic instinct is another's high anxiety.

Behind the Green Door
Deconstructing Gloria

Directed by Artie and James Mitchell;
starring Marilyn Chambers (1972)

by Carrie Rickey

I WAS NINETEEN WHEN I SAW **BEHIND THE GREEN DOOR** IN
1972, the same age as Marilyn Chambers, a Meg Ryan type who played Gloria, the innocent babe abducted and whisked off to a private sex club where
onstage she is stripped, caressed by tender women in black cassocks, suck-
led by a coven of hippies, and penetrated by male trapeze artists in crotch-
less tights. Thus pleasured, Gloria becomes an avid pleasuregiver, fellating
one trapeze artist as she milks the other two, and whipping partners, club
patrons, and movie audiences into Chantilly cream.

Was my face red! Then, as now, I couldn't say whether it was from embarrassment, excitement, or some combination thereof. When the lights
came up, I recall lacing my boyfriend's fingers into mine and joking, "Now
that's process art."

Thirty-three years later, I'm amused that I felt compelled to intellectualize
the experience. (For the uninitiated, *process art,* uncle of deconstruction, applies to work that bares the means of its making.)

I'm also amazed that I got why the Mitchell Brothers' *Behind the Green
Door* was so passionately received by the academics, undergrads, and town-
ies who thronged the auditorium at the University of California, San Diego,
that night. The orgasmathon distilled the incense-and-peppermint scent of
1972, the different-strokes tolerance, the psychedelic-shack imagery. (A

prancing-fluids sequence employs the kaleidoscopic color-negative effect used by Richard Avedon in his famous 1967 shots of The Beatles.)

Because Jim and Artie Mitchell embedded Gloria's sexual initiation in a narrative (two truckers at a diner recount Gloria's story to the cook), my lit professor could compare it to Boccaccio's *Decameron* and Joe Sixpack could think it was an urban legend. And because the Mitchells framed Gloria's erotic immersion as a performance, my art professor could talk about it as performance art (not unlike Vito Acconci's onanistic conceptual short *Seedbed*), while the panting freshman boys and some marines from Camp Pendleton nearby related to it as live-action *Penthouse* pictorial. I'm sure some UCSD sociology professor cited the multi-culti demographic of the sex-club audience, and I know that my gay pals Melvyn and Jeff noticed the transvestites and homosexual members there.

And, heaven help us, I know that the teaching assistants in Manny Farber's film history class (my boyfriend and I included) actually made claims that the film's "money shot" in transfigured time owed much to cinema vanguardists Maya Deren and Stan Brakhage.

Behind the Green Door had something for everyone, even for the feminists who debated whether it objectified women or liberated them.

For a nascent feminist of limited sexual experience who had never seen an uncircumcised penis, it was . . . an eye-opener. Unlike the one other porn film I had endured, this wasn't an extreme-close-up montage of disembodied sex organs being Hoovered. The organs here were connected to real bodies and real faces, and the action seemed to take place in real time. What I remembered about the other porn film was that it was all about cascading, fountaining, erupting climaxes. What I remembered about *Door* was the foreplay. Yeah, I know, I'm such a girl.

In *Behind the Green Door,* Marilyn Chambers has honey-colored hair, flawless tawny skin, upturned nose, downturned mouth—the "99-44/100 percent pure" features that got her hired as the face on the Ivory Snow box. It was that 56/100th of impure lust that made all the difference, losing Chambers her lucrative contract with Procter & Gamble and bringing untold pleasure to ticket buyers responsible for making the $60,000 skin flick return grosses of nearly $30 million. Only the IRS knows how much it's made on video (or do they?), but it's still hugely popular and such a cultural force that Stanley Kubrick paid perverse tribute to it in the sex-club scene in *Eyes Wide Shut.*

After watching *Door* for the first time in more than thirty years, I am still captivated by Chambers, who is so in the moment that she puts Method actors to shame. Almost any woman can feign pleasure better than the women in the average skin flick, but Chambers is that rare actress in a porn movie whose body language doesn't have quotes around it. I'd never make the claim that you should see *Door* for the acting; still, I'd rank Chambers up there with Jeanne Moreau in *The Lovers* and Holly Hunter in *The Piano,* actresses who make eros onscreen seem as transcendent as it does in life.

Annabel Chong: Casting the First Pebble

by Gerald Peary

Back in my freelancing days, I went undercover on a triple-X film shoot as the "unit photographer." I was the one who, between takes, shot (shaky!) still pictures of the naked, upside-down cast. Which is to say I'm not the critic to toss pebbles at *Sex: The Annabel Chong Story,* Gough Lewis's documentary chronicle of a porn queen.

Others do it for me. "A picture like this makes me want to throw up," a friend told me, shuddering as she remembered the sweaty men trying to shove into the world premiere at the 1999 Sundance Festival. My friend figured she didn't need to see this Annabel Chong, a self-styled feminist who fucks 251 guys in ten hours to set the world's gang-bang record.

What can I reply? That I mostly liked this film, and that I have a kind of dumb admiration for the protagonist's brash and irrational wildness—even as, not good at all, she puts herself and others at risk for disease.

I'm influenced by having sat next to the star at a Stockholm Film Festival dinner. Call me a sucker, but I thought her smart and articulate. A gender-studies graduate from the University of Southern California, she spoke eloquently—even academically—about sexuality. Her real name is Grace Quek, and she grew up middle-class in one of the most puritanical developed countries in the world, Singapore. In a passionate, transgressive revolt, Quek left Singapore strictures behind to screw and suck on the American screen. As she says in the movie, "To do pornography is to be against the collective agreement of what it means to be a Singaporean. . . . Fuck them, they can lick my ass."

I have problems with the manipulative editing that gives Quek's life a downsliding trajectory: poor little porno girl! She abandons porn and confesses all to her mother in Singapore, but a gloomy finale finds Quek sashaying back into the sleazy embrace of her greaseball ex-employers.

My guess is that many people shook their heads over Quek's contradictions and self-deceptions. Granted, her final act is a dumb "feminist" decision, but hey, she's not Nixon, not Kissinger. Grace Quek hasn't started wars or backed dubious coups d'etats. She's only resolved to make fuck movies.

Reviewing *The Annabel Chong Story* afforded me the thin excuse to check out some of her actual porn. My video store had fourteen of her titles; I picked four (should I sample *Anal Queen?*) and fast-forwarded, searching for . . . I don't know what.

Quek has admitted she's not much of an actress. She's not an especially charismatic sex performer either, despite the promise of *Depraved Fantasies 3*. Instead, she has distinguished herself from the X-pack with her college-girl bio and special gymnastics. In several movies, she's made impossible room for simultaneous penetrations, with porn veteran Ron Jeremy cast inevitably as The Third Man. Then there's *The World's Biggest Gang Bang*, a 90-minute celebration of that record-smashing day, which is not at all about eros but everything about sexual athletics. Watching all those bodies going in and out of Grace, making Annabel Chong world-infamous, gave me a pounding headache. ■

Belle de jour
Love's labours' cost

Directed by Luis Buñuel; starring Catherine Deneuve,
Michel Piccoli (1967)

by Michael Wilmington

BEAUTY AND EVIL, MADNESS AND LIBERATION, THE SINS AND
indiscretions of the bourgeoisie: These are among the themes of Luis Buñuel's
great, gorgeous *Belle de jour*. Rereleased by Miramax in 1995 after it was withheld from theaters and video shelves for nearly three decades, this 1967
landmark—with Catherine Deneuve as a physician's wife trapped by sexual
obsession—remains one of the cinema's inarguable masterpieces and most
audacious turn-ons.

Belle de jour is still shocking and enrapturing, both a scandal and a classic,
even if the context has changed over time. It was made in the late '60s, when
movies were rampaging through a period of erotic liberation. Its once forbidden subject is taken from Joseph Kessel's 1928 novel about lovely but
frigid Séverine Serizy (Deneuve), whose desires are unlocked when she begins a covert double life as an elegant Parisian prostitute working for
Madame Anais (Geneviève Page) in an expensive brothel.

Belle de jour is a movie about the ecstasy and danger of turning fantasy
into reality. Images or moments can stay with you for years: the opening
ground-level shots of a horse and carriage, bells jangling ominously, rolling
through a tranquil yet sinister woods; the now legendary little box with its
mysterious buzz, carried by a plump Japanese client.

And the characters. How can you forget Page's chic lesbian madam? Or Françoise Fabian (later the Maud of Eric Rohmer's *My Night at Maud's*) as the gusty whore Charlotte? Or the urbane creepiness of Michel Piccoli as that discreet libertine and brothel aficionado Henri Husson? Or the black-leather dandyism of Pierre Clémenti as psychopathic hood Marcel, Séverine's obsessive lover? Or sly Francisco Rabal (Buñuel's "Nazarin") as Marcel's flamenco-singing crook/mentor Hyppolite?

More than anything, how can you forget the searingly lovely Catherine Deneuve?

Belle de jour was a showcase for the supreme artistry of its Spanish director Buñuel and for the photogenic glory of Deneuve. For Buñuel, it was the biggest commercial hit of a triumphant but bizarrely varied half-century career. For Deneuve at twenty-three, it was a coronation as Greta Garbo's screen successor, "the world's most beautiful woman."

Was she? In sheer movie terms, perhaps she was. (She'd get my vote.)

There's something hypnotically seductive about *Belle de jour,* and a large part of that is tied to Deneuve's image—the strangely impassive face, the impeccably tousled (and dyed) blonde mane, those bemused, ironic eyes. In *Belle de jour,* the whole gem-brilliant persona turns deeper, scarier. At once childish and adult, sluttish and chaste, timid and adventurous, Séverine is an exquisite enigma. Without Deneuve, would *Belle de jour* chill us as much?

Before *Belle,* Deneuve's most famous roles had been the heartbreaking ingenue of 1964's *The Umbrellas of Cherbourg* and the nightmare-ridden killer of 1965's *Repulsion.* In *Belle de jour,* the cool perfection of her beauty—so different from the impish sexiness of her ravishing older sister, Françoise Dorléac (who died in a car crash the year *Belle* was released)—becomes the icy core of a chain of cruel fantasies. What is Séverine thinking? Feeling? Unlike Joseph Kessel, Buñuel—and his scenarist, Jean-Claude Carrière—dig into Séverine's dreams: the sadomasochistic scenarios that enliven her safe married life with Jean Sorel's sweet Pierre. No one makes dream sequences quite like Buñuel—not even Alfred Hitchcock, who admired to distraction both *Belle de jour* and the other great Deneuve-Buñuel collaboration, 1970's *Tristana. Belle de jour*'s fantasies rival Buñuel and Salvador Dali's ferocious 1928 surrealist-dream short, *Un chien Andalou.*

Unusually, Buñuel's movie has no musical score. Yet it's full of reveries—Séverine's and perhaps Buñuel's—realized with such hard-edged clarity that they are inseparable from the film's life. (*Belle de jour*'s English subtitlers tried to ease the audience's way through this maze of illusion by putting the titles for the dream sequences in italics, but Buñuel himself insisted that the slightly censored "fantasy" sequence with Georges Marchal's necrophiliac Duke is real.)

In the end, there's nothing tawdry, misogynistic, or exploitative—or simplistic—about this nonpareil picture. Buñuel's style, which Jean-Luc Godard once compared to Bach, has a serene mastery, a cool intelligence and sympathy, that aborts any prurience. And though *Belle de jour* wasn't a project Buñuel initiated, or even a novel he much liked, he found in it the classic "Buñuelian" elements: dark comedy, *l'amour fou*, unsparing social criticism, and intoxicating, terrifying dreams. Sixty-seven when he made *Belle de jour*, Buñuel had already progressed through surrealism, rebellion, exile, and reemergence in the marginal postwar Mexican film industry (where, with the peerless cinematographer Gabriel Figueroa, he made classics like *Los Olvidados*, *El*, *Nazarin*, and *The Exterminating Angel*). Then came his incendiary return to Francisco Franco's Spain (where he shot the banned and hailed 1961 *Viridiana*) and his final lionization throughout Europe and the world. He seemed, still, the oldest surrealist and rebel when the Egyptian-French Hakim Brothers—producers who, like Miramax, preferred sexy films from star cineastes—gave him *Belle de jour* and made him a lord of the art film. (It was also Robert Hakim and his heirs who put *Belle de jour* in its long limbo.)

Is beauty simply in the eye of the beholder? Is perfection an illusory goal? Maybe. But, nearly four decades after it first stunned and infuriated moviegoers, Buñuel's *Belle de jour* still matchlessly evokes both improbable artistic perfection and dazzling, extraordinary beauty. It seduces us without blinding us; we see, too, with a humor dark and deep, the corruption beneath the façade. For the Duke de La Rochefoucauld, hypocrisy may have been "the debt that vice pays to virtue." But the great Luis Buñuel, artist and rebel, was another breed: the genius who always settled accounts.

Beyond the Valley of the Dolls
"Quality only Russ Meyer could approve!"

Directed by Russ Meyer; starring Kelly McNamara,
Casey Anderson, Petronella Danforth (1970)

by Roger Ebert

RUSS MEYER THOUGHT WRITING AND TYPING WERE PRETTY much the same thing. He liked to be within earshot when I was working on one of his screenplays, and if the typewriter fell silent he would call out, "What's the trouble?" This work ethic was, oddly enough, helpful. It eliminated all pauses for inspiration, and freed heedless flights of fancy.

At 20th Century–Fox, where Meyer had a three-picture deal, we had connecting offices, so he could listen for the typewriter. One day, well into the screenplay for *Beyond the Valley of the Dolls,* I laughed aloud at the keyboard.

"What's so funny?" Russ shouted from his office.

"Z-Man's a woman!" I shouted back.

Russ appeared in my office door. "How can he be a woman?" he said. "He's named Z-Man."

"I don't know," I said. "But he takes off his shirt and Lance Rocke shouts, 'My God, Ronnie! You've got tits! You've been a woman the whole time!'"

Russ thought about that for a moment. "I like it. You can never have too many tits in a movie."

After starting with a broad general premise inspired by *Valley of the Dolls* (three sexy women come to Hollywood, find fame, and are challenged by sex, drugs, and rock 'n' roll), we made up the story as we went along, usually during enormous meals at Musso & Frank. My first day on the job I told

Russ I planned to lose some weight, and he forbade me: "Beef, every night, trencherman-platter style. You need your strength."

Russ really did use phrases like "trencherman-platter style." His prose was rich in phrases that seemed lifted from the press releases of an alternate universe. Here is his description of *Beneath the Valley of the Ultra-Vixens,* another of my screenplays: "An end-around attack against women's lib . . . blasting through the male machismo syndrome . . . kicking the crap out of convictions, hang-ups, obsessions . . . the whole bag . . . sexually aggressive females, willing klutzy men, petroleum jelly, gingham and gossamer, tax-sheltered religion, black socks, bedroom prowess, bunko artists, big-breast fixation, rear window rednecks, therapeutic cuckolding, the 60-mile-an-hour zinger, born-again immersion, unfaithful girlfriends, limp-wristed dentistry, and virile garbage men."

Russ was famous as a tit man, but he liked work almost as much as he liked breasts. After inventing the skin flick with *The Immoral Mr. Teas* (1959), he took infinite pains in a genre where very few pains are required. "He is not the primitive or untutored artist he sometimes likes to appear to be," I wrote for *Film Comment* in 1973. "His method of work on a picture is all business, he is a consummate technical craftsman, he is obsessed by budgets and schedules, and his actors do not remember how 'turned on' a scene was, but how many times it was reshot. In a genre overrun by sleazo cheapies, he is the best technician and the only artist."

He was also a man of Rabelaisian appetites, fiercely loyal friendships, and great good humor. Women liked him—not only my wife, for example, but even my mother. The film critic B. Ruby Rich, who coined the phrase "Queer Cinema," famously called him America's first male feminist director, observing that in his films the men were the mindless sex objects. Most of the women who appear in sex films never want to see the filmmakers again, but at Meyer's funeral in September 2004, I counted the supervixens June Wilkinson, Erica Gavin, Kitten Natividad, Tura Satana, Sue Bernard, Raven de la Croix, Lavelle Roby, Cynthia Myers, and Haji. Ushi Digard wanted to come but was ill. At the wake and after the burial, they told fond, nostalgic stories of being made to carry film cans up mountainsides, of cooking meals on remote locations, of Russ nailing shut their motel room windows to enforce celibacy during the shoot.

The 2005 release of nineteen Meyer DVDs begins with *Vixen!,* the film that brought him fame and a front-page profile as "King Leer" in the *Wall*

Street Journal, and includes *Faster, Pussycat! Kill! Kill!,* which with *Beyond the Valley of the Dolls* is generally considered his best work. In *Up!,* the Kitten Natividad character paraphrases poetry by H. D. (Hilda Doolittle). Why? Why not? Meyer looked at his rough cut, thought the movie needed more breasts, and decided to add a nude Kitten "as the Greek chorus," filming her in the desert and up trees, while she provided a running commentary, "but not one that makes sense, because that would be a distraction." I pulled the poems of H. D. from my shelf. At the funeral Kitten told me, "It drove me crazy, trying to memorize that dialogue! What did it mean?"

Although Meyer came out of the American sexual revolution of the 1950s and shot eight of *Playboy's* first twelve centerfolds, his ideology had less in common with Hugh Hefner than with the surrealists. Implausibility was no barrier, continuity no requirement. He was in love with irrelevant voice-over narration; in *Beneath the Valley of the Ultra-Vixens* you can hear: "Small Town, U.S.A.! Pounding Pontiacs into Polarises! Knock on any door, and who will you meet? Your neighbor!" While writing *Ultra-Vixens* I asked him why, when the hero Homer leaves home and goes to the strip club, he doesn't realize his own wife is the stripper. "Explain it with a voice-over," Meyer said.

Ultra-Vixens (1979) turned out to be Russ's final film; he often spoke of making another screenplay of mine, *The Bra of God,* but it never happened. From 1980 to the mid–1990s he labored on a three-volume autobiography named *A Clean Breast.* Printed to his specifications on paper guaranteed to last 500 years, it is a massive work, described somewhat enigmatically on his website as "Quality only Russ Meyer could approve!" From his blurb: "Feast on a carnal adventure as the lensman describes in detail a Tinsel Town debauch replete with classic films and the most cantilevered women ever to undulate over the Earth's surface."

When *Beyond the Valley of the Dolls* was going into production, the skin-flick era was ending and hard-core pornography was appearing on American screens. Russ and I went to see *I Am Curious (Yellow)* on Hollywood Boulevard, and he emerged shaking his head. "I'll never do hard-core," he said. "First, I don't want to share my grosses with the Mob. Second, I've never been that interested in what goes on below the waist."

He and the studio were aiming for an R, but Meyer believed the ratings board had felt obligated to give the "King of the Nudies" an X rating. It was a very mild X, and Meyer wanted to reedit certain scenes in order to include more nudity (he shot many scenes in both X and R versions). But the studio, still in the middle of a cash-flow crisis, wanted to rush the film into release.

In all of Meyer's films, there are only two scenes that, for me at least, are erotic. Those are the lesbian scenes in *Vixen!* and *Beyond the Valley of the Dolls.* Meyer often told me his films were not really about sex: "They're Looney Tunes—cartoons. The big bosoms make them sell." It's notable that the DVD release of his work comes at a time when other skin flicks of the period are completely forgotten. "The films have a life of their own!" he marveled. "The sons of bitches just keep on playing!"

Although he may not have been much concerned about eroticism in his films, there is no doubt he was sincerely obsessed with breasts. There is a story I hope he would not mind my telling, even though it takes place toward the end, when he was lost to Alzheimer's. My wife and I went to visit him at home in the Hollywood Hills. He didn't know who we were. A caregiver came in with a bottle of water. As she left, he looked after her disapprovingly and said, "No tits."

Black Sunday
Losing my religion

Directed by Mario Bava; starring Barbara Steele (1960)

by James Verniere

FOR A CATHOLIC BOY IN THE EARLY 1960S, THE NEIGHBORHOOD movie theater was more than a cinema. It was an alternate house of worship, a place to experience what the Jesuits dubbed "pubescent tumescence" and adore the aptly named goddesses of the big screen. The movies made idolators of us all.

The synchronization of my preadolescence with the golden age of Britain's Hammer Films studio and its continental imitators was providential, and Mario Bava's gothic thriller *La maschera del demonio* (*The Mask of the Demon*), retitled *Black Sunday* by its U.S. distributor American International Pictures (and not to be confused with John Frankenheimer's 1977 terrorist movie of the same name), was a particularly memorable rite of passage. How apt to learn more than forty years later that *Black Sunday* is Tim Burton's favorite horror film.

Bava's solo debut is loosely based on "The Viy" by Nikolai Gogol, a story Vladimir Nabokov described in a 1944 monograph as "a gooseflesh tale; not particularly effective." *Black Sunday* tells of Princess Asa (Barbara Steele), a vampiric witch, who in the opening scenes is grotesquely mutilated—a spiked, demonic mask is hammered to her face—and put to death.

Two hundred years later in nineteenth-century Moldavia, Asa and her similarly disfigured and executed companion (Arturo Dominici)—possibly, in the spirit of the movie's hints of incest, Asa's brother—rise from the dead to wreak revenge on the descendants of their tormentors. Complicating matters, Asa is a dead ringer for one of her own lineage, the radiantly sexy Princess Katia (also Steele), whose body Asa yearns to possess.

Bava's *Black Sunday* is a gothic-erotic fever dream, a kinky, strangely Russo-Italo mix of violence, cleavage, bondage, and vampirism, featuring the exotic and beautifully photographed Steele in a tour de force—a dual good-girl/bad-girl role.

Exploiting the link between fear and arousal, the film's shrieking tagline was: "The Undead Demons of Hell Terrorize the World in an Orgy of Stark Horror!" What boy could pass this up?

Trailers for *Black Sunday* pitched the sex, horror, gore, and heaving breasts with gusto (as did the lurid and still sought-after posters for the film by Giuliano Nistri). In one nightmarish shot, a black-garbed, cobweb-encrusted Dominici rises wetly from a grave wearing the unforgettable mask with its Iron Maiden overtones, reportedly designed by Bava's filmmaker father, Eugenio (son Lamberto also became a director of Italian horror films).

In a justly notorious sequence, the hideously scarred, corpselike Asa hypnotizes a victim, forcing him to deeply kiss her proffered lips. In another shot, a hand rips away a piece of the unconscious Katia's clothing, triggering paroxysms of lust in at least one Catholic boy. The set design by the great Giorgio Giovannini (*La Dolce Vita, Fellini Satyricon*, et al.) includes a full-length nude (!) portrait of Asa-Steele.

Banned for eight years in Britain, the film was shot at Italy's Titanus Studios and was described by Samuel Z. Arkoff in his amiable 1992 autobiography *Flying Through Hollywood By the Seat of My Pants* as "one of the best horror films I had ever seen." (AIP heads Arkoff and partner James H. Nicholson routinely went to Italy to pick up films for the American market. AIP was also, of course, the distributor of *I Was a Teenage Werewolf* [1957], a B-movie horror film that arguably speaks more urgently about adolescent rage and desire than *Rebel Without a Cause*).

In Carlos Clarens's 1967 study *An Illustrated History of the Horror Film*, he describes *Black Sunday* as a "relentless nightmare," boasting "the best black-and-white photography to enhance a horror movie in the past two decades."

Despite a modest budget, the film is densely atmospheric. Like Val Lewton, whose trademark chiaroscuro was as evocative as it was cost-free, Bava uses twisted branches, cobwebs, and gnarled roots in the foreground to give his scenes depth and what Edgar Allan Poe might have described as a touch of the grotesque and the arabesque. Making her entrance leading a pair of mastiffs on leashes, Steele's Katia is breathtakingly radiant, a gothic fairy queen. A later scene in which the empty eye sockets of the witch's ravaged face fill up with fluid is one of the most memorably creepy moments in horror films, even though it may have been achieved with sodium bicarbonate or even poached eggs.

Black Sunday has roots in German Expressionism and in Universal's 1930s horror classics. But Bava adds the sex and violence popularized by Hammer's Technicolor films and Italy's peplum genre. If Bava is no Murnau, his ingenious effects (See a sarcophagus explode!) and flair for frightening and titillating viewers contribute immeasurably to the film's power.

Scenes involving a haunted road and a spectral coach will remind many of Murnau's *Nosferatu* (1922). Other scenes echo Terence Fisher's 1958 Hammer hit *Dracula* (U.S. title *Horror of Dracula*). That *Black Sunday* is Italian in origin, although set in the Ukraine, made it stranger to me than any Hammer film and more resonantly weird. Bava would come close to repeating his *Black Sunday* achievement only once, in the similarly Russian-set "Wurdulak" episode of his follow-up film *Black Sabbath* (1963), featuring the great Boris Karloff.

According to Tim Lucas, author of the *Black Sunday* DVD liner notes, Steele, who is British, had walked off the Elvis Presley vehicle *Flaming Star* (1960) before being cast in the film. With her impossibly large, otherworldly eyes and swollen lips, she had what Bava described as "the perfect face" for his purposes. That perfect face would appear later in films by Federico Fellini, Louis Malle, and David Cronenberg.

After being introduced to Steele through the movies, I stalked her on late-night TV, where 1960s European horror films (although in disappointingly edited form) were an after-midnight staple. It's hard to describe what makes the twenty-three-year-old's work so unforgettable, especially since the film was dubbed for its U.S. release and the voice used is not Steele's. Much of it had to do, obviously, with how impressionable I was at the time and how Bava captures her sexiness in both roles. Steele's Katia is wildly desirable, yet even the evil and repugnant Asa is sexy—Death and the Maiden wrapped up in the same hideously seductive package. By conflating sexual desire and feminine charms with death, sadism, and devil worship, Bava casts a spell that is both rapturously erotic and blasphemous.

To a Catholic boy about to lose his faith and dreaming of losing his virginity, the combination was irresistible.

Blue Velvet

In one ear and out another

Directed by David Lynch; starring Isabella Rossellini, Dennis Hopper, Kyle MacLachlan (1986)

by Andy Klein

THE OPENING CREDITS OF DAVID LYNCH'S **BLUE VELVET** ARE superimposed over a widescreen curtain of—what else?—undulating velvet, bluer than blue, accompanied by Angelo Badalamenti's dark main theme sounding ever so slightly out of kilter, like an off-center record. As the credits end, the music gives way to the eponymous Bobby Vinton oldie, and the camera tilts from a clear sky to a white picket fence setting off impossibly red flowers. Thanks to some trick of cinematography or production design, that shade of red is beyond reality, both beautiful and unsettling; later, in the film's dense interweaving of images, the same red will be associated with lipstick and blood. Both the sadistic villain (Dennis Hopper) and the sensuous lady-in-distress (Isabella Rossellini) will smear the hero's left cheek with red. But, in Lynch's perverse world, the lipstick will come from Hopper's kiss, the blood from Rossellini's knife.

The flowers are the first image in a montage of idyllic small-town life, but everything is a bit off: Shots stay on screen too long or are cut off in midmotion, regular speed is intercut with slow motion. We feel like ghosts trespassing in someone else's dream. A man waters his suburban lawn; a close-up shows the hose badly attached to the faucet, jiggling ominously. The hose becomes entangled with a bush. The man tugs to free it. The sequence drips with foreboding, as though—heaven forbid—the hose might come undone. Suddenly, the man grabs at his neck and collapses, convulsing—a seizure? a stroke?—we never find out exactly. Whatever ails him can have no direct connection to the hose, yet an indirect link is made: The hose ends up near the stricken man's groin, continuing to spray white foam in symbolism so obvious it's comic. The town is bursting with nearly out-of-control sexual tension.

As the man lies there in mock orgasm, there is a final anti-*Saturday Evening Post* joke. A toddler and a cute mutt wander into frame. The toddler looks dispassionately at the body while the mutt laps at the water spouting from the hose. Just another story about a boy and his dog.

The camera then tracks along the ground, revealing that the green suburban lawn hides hideous crawling bugs.

Thus are the film's major themes suggested in little more than two minutes, even before the arrival of our hero, Jeffrey Beaumont (Kyle MacLachlan), the college-age son of the man with the hose. On his way back from visiting Dad in the hospital, Jeffrey discovers a human ear, more or less in his own backyard. Impatient with the official investigation, he pokes around with some help from the police detective's daughter (Laura Dern), which quickly leads to intrigues involving a nightclub chanteuse (Rossellini), her gangster lover (Hopper), and the entire seamy subculture beneath the town's placid surface.

The opening, with its overly rich colors and sappy (but effective) pop song, invokes the Technicolor soap operas of Douglas Sirk, particularly *Written on the Wind* (1957), which managed—within the restrictions of '50s commercial cinema—to deal with impotence, infidelity, and "nymphomania" ('50s lingo for any aggressive female sexual behavior). The passage of nearly thirty culturally eventful years means that for better or worse, Lynch can be considerably more explicit. Where Sirk only hinted, Lynch shouts.

Nonetheless, many were shocked by *Blue Velvet*, dismissing it as tasteless or smutty. Certainly part of that is due to the horrifying (almost to the point of comical) scene in which Hopper's Frank Booth—eyes and veins bulging, sucking on some kind of unnamed gas—humiliates, violates, and generally brutalizes Rossellini's Dorothy Valens, all while calling her "Mommy."

The film shocks and upsets in a way that goes beyond its scenes of sadism and sexual decay. It implicates even its relatively innocent hero in the sickness of its villain. The repetition of images and the distinctive visual style suggest meanings that are all the more powerful for registering subconsciously, and the movie gets to us because it invokes our own connection to Frank.

After all, what is Frank but the ultimate party animal? There is a scene where, high on something or other, heading out to a joyride, he shrieks, "Let's fuck! I'll . . . fuck . . . anything . . . that *moves!*" It's a funny moment, but also scary, like John Belushi's Bluto screaming "Let's party!" but taken to the ugliest—if not entirely illogical—extreme.

If Frank is the most grotesque villain in American cinema, he gets real competition from Dean Stockwell's Ben. The former child star—in a role rather different from *The Boy with Green Hair* (1948)—is only onscreen for a few minutes, playing the proprietor of what Frank calls "pussy heaven." (In describing the character for Stockwell, Lynch reportedly said, "He's the guy *Frank* looks up to.") The framing at one point presents Ben as a mirror image of Jeffrey, suggesting that Ben is the Portrait to the boy's Dorian Grey, the decayed version of a hero corrupted by association with Hopper's id-monster.

Early on, the camera tracks into the canal of the severed ear that instigates the plot. The ear (a left ear, for the record) is rotting and filthy; Jeffrey's left ear is itself not whole, having been pierced. A few minutes from the end, the camera pulls back from Jeffrey's right ear and finds him in a cheerier, sunnier world. He opens his eyes. This apparent awakening doesn't blatantly demand that everything between be taken as a dream. We have, however, gone in one ear and out another, traversing Jeffrey's brain on a tour of the jumbled, surreal dreams of young male sexuality: a world of spiritually pure virgins, threatening homoeroticism, and sex with Oedipal overtones. Like *Star Wars*, *Blue Velvet* makes real the fantasies of adolescence; the difference is that Lynch admits to fantasies that George Lucas would never cop to.

Body Heat

Tease me, please me

Directed by Lawrence Kasdan; starring Kathleen Turner,
William Hurt, Mickey Rourke (1981)

by Peter Travers

A **TEASE: WEBSTER'S** DEFINES IT AS "THE ACT OF TANTALIZING,
especially by arousing desire without intending to satisfy it." I call it *Body
Heat*.

With this gorgeously lurid take on 1940s film noir, screenwriter Lawrence
Kasdan (*Raiders of the Lost Ark*) made his striking debut as a director, and put
newcomer Kathleen Turner, then twenty-seven, to the task of teasing men to
mad distraction. It worked, at least on me. And it worked on Ned Racine, the
sleazy, sleaparound lawyer played by William Hurt, for once without his
dull, insular glaze.

The *boing* factor kicks in immediately when Matty Walker, Turner's leggy,
luscious sexpot, struts past in high heels. Admittedly, that strut doesn't always work on women. In the *New York Times*, Janet Maslin found life in the
movie, but only in "those parts that don't involve Miss Turner, who keeps her
chin high in the air, speaks in a perfect monotone, and never seems to move
from the position in which Mr. Kasdan has left her. Yet her allure is supposed
to be the magnet that leads Ned away from the straight and narrow." Ouch.
I feel like a fool for getting hooked. But isn't that the point of *Body Heat* (and
all femme fatales)—to make fools of men?

Ned is the perfect patsy for Matty. She needs someone to help kill her
rich husband, Edmund, played with shady menace by Richard Crenna.

Who better than Ned, a guy who thinks with his dick? Her seduction of him, as choreographed by Kasdan, is a doozy.

It's a hot, sultry night in Miranda Beach (it's always hot and sultry in this movie) when Ned spots Matty strolling near a pier in a clingy, white dress. She lights a cigarette and turns to the ocean, hoping for a breeze. From be- hind—and it's far sexier this way—she lifts her hair, exposing the damp nape of her neck. Ned hits on her, awkwardly: "You can stand here with me if you want, but you'll have to agree not to talk about the heat." She peers at him: "You're not too smart, are you?" Ned concurs. "I like that in a man," she says in a throaty voice Lauren Bacall would envy.

"What else you like—Ugly? Lazy? Horny? I got 'em all." Her retort? "You don't look lazy."

Ned learns that Matty is from the posh enclave of Pinehaven. "You look like Pinehaven," he tells her. "Well tended."

Matty sinks her hooks in when Ned buys her a cherry snow cone and she spills it on her dress right over her breast, some would say her heart. Matty informs Ned that her temperature tends to run a few degrees high. "Around 100 all the time, it's the engine or something." Ned suggests a tune-up. "Don't tell me," she sasses, "you have just the right tool."

Later, when her husband is out of town, Matty invites Ned over to hear her wind chimes, but sends him off with a chaste kiss and a cool "now please go." Huh? What? But wait. As Ned heads for his car, he turns back to see Matty framed through a window. Ned tries the doors and windows—all locked. Here's the thing: She doesn't move, she just stands there and smol- ders. I mean, she's smoking. There's enough come-on carnality to singe the screen. Ned stares back until he can't take it anymore. Forget about knock- ing on the door; he smashes a window with a patio rocker to get at her faster. The two go at it on the floor. Ned buries his face in her hair, inhaling her. As sexual teases go, this baby belongs in the time capsule.

That's when Matty executes the *coup de grâce*. She describes her husband as "small and mean and weak," whereas Ned's got the right stuff. What's a guy to do? The steamy sex has him rolling off Matty's bed onto the floor, cry- ing "Enough!" Sex has dulled his other senses. The murder is committed— no fair telling how. Ned disposes of the body in an abandoned beach club. The club is torched, not just to keep the heat and flame motif going but to implicate Edmund's business partners. Mickey Rourke makes a strong impression as Hurt's arsonist pal, as does Ted Danson as an assistant DA who begins to suspect his friend Ned of the murder.

There's no denying that Kasdan is reworking classic crime territory, most notably Billy Wilder's 1944 *Double Indemnity*, in which Barbara Stanwyck wrapped poor Fred MacMurray around her sexy anklet, and Tay Garnett's 1946 *The Postman Always Rings Twice*, in which John Garfield was a willing patsy for Lana Turner, who did wonders with her bare midriff. Kasdan's incantatory style, with its you-put-a-spell-on-me vibe, suits the material perfectly. The snappy dialogue he wrote is burnished with the pulp-fiction memory of James M. Cain and Raymond Chandler. When the jealous Ned tells Matty not to wear provocative clothes and she points out that she's only guilty of a blouse and a skirt, he comes back at her with the right snap: "You shouldn't wear that body."

Maybe it's appropriate that such an enticing setup should let us down when it comes time to connect the plot dots. But even then, Matty keeps things tantalizingly ambiguous. "I really do love you," she says in a farewell line to Ned that contradicts everything that has come before. Or does it? Remember this about *Body Heat*: It's a tease.

Butch Cassidy and
the Sundance Kid
Who are those guys? Mine . . .

Directed by George Roy Hill; starring Paul Newman,
Robert Redford, Katharine Ross (1969)

by Lisa Schwarzbaum

MOST OF WHAT FOLLOWS IS TRUE.

The first time I saw *Butch Cassidy and the Sundance Kid*, in the autumn of
1969, I was a teenager, and I developed an acute fever, and I didn't know
why except that I knew I urgently needed to see *Butch Cassidy and the Sundance Kid* again as a remedy. The second time I saw it, a week later, my illness had localized into a flush, an itch, a *need* to watch again as Butch said,
"I got vision and the rest of the world wears bifocals," and Sundance said,
"I'm better when I move," and Butch said, "Who *are* those guys?" and Sundance confessed: "*I can't swim!*"

The third time, a week later still, I had committed William Goldman's
screenplay to memory. I had drenched myself in the plinky-plink pleasures
of Burt Bacharach's "Raindrops Keep Fallin' on My Head." And I had em-
barked on what would become a lifelong reverie on a theme of whether I'd
prefer to be with Butch (cooler) or Sundance (hotter). What about a *ménage
à trois*? Come to think of it, did I want to be their squeeze, or a train-stop-
ping, bank-robbing member of their Hole in the Wall Gang?

I was a teenaged girl hypnotized by the blue of Paul Newman's eyes, the
yellow of Robert Redford's hair, and the way the whole movie, with its palette

of afternoon-sun tones, showed off the movie stars to such fine advantage: Even caked with blood and streaked with dirt, they looked natty. I was a teenaged girl, and I imagined that I took the place of Etta Place, with Sundance directing *me* at gunpoint to "Keep going, teacher lady" as I disrobed. (After a night of—what? the movie was too demure to linger on the particulars of Sundance in the sack—I'd take a nice ride on Butch's bicycle the next morning.)

I was a sucker for six-shooters and horses and witty, urbane banter out of the mouths of Wild West outlaws who were more fun and less unlawful than any other outlaws I was used to seeing in the movies, and certainly suaver than any gawky boys I knew at the time. These guys were criminals and fugitives, but they were also gallant gentlemen, and I hoped one day to meet men who might banter half so amusingly or look half so beautiful.

In the many years since those days of adolescent arousal, I've probably watched *Butch Cassidy and the Sundance Kid* two dozen times, and the years have not dimmed my delight in the tinkling charms of Goldman's cocktail-cowboy script or in George Roy Hill's ingratiating production. Older now, I am aware of the ways in which the movie doesn't meet the kind of rigorous standards set by the kind of serious, bantering men I have in fact come to love: It is, my brooding men say, a manicured *faux* Western for people who don't understand Westerns. It's a thing of middlebrow surface shine and commercial appeal, apolitical and shadowless. It's the anti–*Bonnie and Clyde*, and that ain't good. It is, they all but say, too easy, and therefore too easy to love.

Older now, I also realize it's that very ease that gives *Butch Cassidy* its erotic power. And I'm the more grateful for the lightness with which the whole enterprise is tethered to consequence.

WHO *ARE* THOSE GUYS?

It's the dangdest thing: My own adulthood has allowed me to love the movie all over again, with an affectionate appreciation I couldn't have untangled from my own awakening sexual desires when younger. Back then, all I knew was that the Sundance Kid—which is to say, Robert Redford at the peak of his model-suitable-for-Sundance-mail-order-catalog loveliness—turned me on with his physicality (that disco mustache!), while Butch—

which is to say, Paul Newman at the zenith of his manly impishness—
turned me on with his personality, his good cheer. The real love story in any
buddy picture is between guy friend and guy friend, of course. But these
days, with the perspective of experience and a critic's reference shelf of essays about subtext, I know that much of what is marvelous in *Butch Cassidy*
lies in the movie's blithe, unthreatening pansexuality: Butch and Sundance
are a couple (metrosexuals before their time? feminists with the girlfriendly
intimacy of Thelma and Louise?). Sundance and Etta are a couple, Etta and
Butch are a couple, Sundance and Etta and Butch are a trio. And there's always room for me.

They come to no good, of course, those *banditos yanquis* stranded in backwater Bolivia. Their luck depleted, their crimes outweighing their charisma
(especially after they kill men in the course of ironically honest employment
as payroll guards), the two are due for punishment. And we all know they
get it, in a spray of bullets, in the movie's famous last scene. But even at the
climactic moment of death, something about the pair defies desecration, or a
marring of their pulchritude. These are not characters we want to see bleed
and convulse, destroyed by the world's real violence, like Faye Dunaway and
Warren Beatty in *Bonnie and Clyde*. These are men we want to keep whole
and unscarred, the better to dream about.

Frozen forever in mid-blaze as they leap and shoot their last, then en-
shrined in sepia for safekeeping, Butch and Sundance—the characters, the
men—are as precious to me, and as uncontaminated by reality, as the memory of a high school crush. The movie, on the other hand, rubs pleasurably
up against the reality of my own life (changing as it has over the years) each
time I rewatch. Always, I get a bang out of it.

Bye Bye Birdie
One girl, one special girl

Directed by George Sidney; starring Ann-Margret, Dick Van Dyke, Janet
Leigh, Bobby Rydell (1963)

by Jami Bernard

I SO WANTED TO BE ANN-MARGRET. EVEN NOW, I GET A CONTACT
runner's high watching her pant breathlessly toward me on an invisible
treadmill against a bluescreen background, her hair blown wild by an off-
screen fan, as she sings her heart out about the Elvis-like rock star who has
been drafted into the army before she can fulfill her sexual destiny in his
arms. "No more sighing / Each time you move your lips / No more crying /
When you twist those hips!" She hugs herself, bunches the sides of her skirt
like an overstimulated child who can't contain herself on Christmas morning, practically explodes from a propulsion of sexual energy. This, she
seemed to promise, is what losing your virginity is all about; how lovely to
be a woman.

   Directed by George Sidney and adapted from the Broadway show, with a
score by Charles Strouse and lyrics by Lee Adams, *Bye Bye Birdie* used the
model of mass rock-star worship to describe infectious sexual fever in the
American heartland. The catalyst for this eruption of hormones is the arrival
in Sweetapple, Ohio, of Conrad Birdie (Jesse Pearson), there to tape a
farewell segment of *The Ed Sullivan Show* before his military conscription,
and to kiss one lucky, randomly chosen teenage girl in a gesture to all the
other girls in the land who want it too. (Ann-Margret would practically live
out the story's promise by falling in love with the real Elvis when she

costarred with him the following year in *Viva Las Vegas*.) In the brilliant "Honestly Sincere" number, Birdie bemusedly accepts a ceremonial key from the mayor—it's really the key to the chastity belts of the ladies of Sweetapple—then straps on his guitar and effortlessly lays claim to every one of these ladies for miles ("Oh, baby! Oh, honey! Hug me! Suffer!"). Simply by making eye contact, strumming a single chord, or jutting his pelvis their way, Birdie and his implicit sexual promise make the women faint dead away, singly and in comically choreographed batches; the fusty mayor's wife can't keep her knees together. When Birdie finishes his song and seems satisfied with the head count, the camera (mounted on what was then the largest mobile boom ever built for a movie) pulls back to reveal a town laid to waste, with fallen females and failed hearts as far as the eye can see. This comic punch line, based on the battlefield-triage shot in *Gone With the Wind*, shows the revenge of the nascent urban pop culture on the mores and values of middle America.

Arriving as it did in 1963, *Bye Bye Birdie* provides a middle ground between the chaste Doris Day school of 1950s movie courtship and the sexual frenzy—in real life as on film—that was in the works. The movie seems family-friendly, yet it heaves with sexual subtext. *Film Quarterly* called it "more startling and obscene than anything you will find in the ripest of art films," although that's giving perhaps too much credit; except for one unfortunate number, a musically implied gang-rape at a Shriners' convention, the numbers are coy or exuberant, never nasty. Each number relishes its sexual irony: the young lovers pledging old-fashioned values in "One Boy" ("One boy, one special boy, one boy to laugh with and joke with, have Coke with") when they are barely moments away from inflaming each other with sexual one-upmanship; the gorgeous tableau (ending in a Crayola meltdown) in "The Telephone Song" of teenage gossip that spreads lubricity through the town's sizzling wires; the supremely self-involved Birdie feigning sincerity in "Honestly Sincere"; Ann-Margret extolling the virtues of maturity in "How Lovely to Be a Woman" while stripping down, nearly in one take, from feminine wear to tomboy gear; and, of course, the amazing "A Lot of Livin' to Do," in which sexual need seems to burst through Ann-Margret's midriff like the voracious *vagina dentata* in *Alien*.

In 1963, there was nothing to equal Ann-Margret's midriff—at least not for young girls who desperately wanted to wear those capri pants and ditch the safety of "going steady for good" in order to ride off with the bad boy on the motorcycle. Once Ann-Margret's Kim McAfee sees how "lovely" it is to "change from boys to men," down comes the hair! Out comes the midriff! She's gotta lotta livin' to do! Scratch many women today and you'll find a kitten with a whip.

Swedish showgirl Ann-Margret Olsson was twenty-two when she made *Bye Bye Birdie*. She was young enough to play Kim, the quintessential teenager chosen at random to receive Conrad Birdie's televised farewell kiss, and she was old enough to bring real sexual danger to the scene where she threatens to "drink champagne as though it were water!"

The movie follows the push-pull of two couples as they get up the nerve to go all the way. There's the going-steady teenagers Kim (Ann-Margret) and Hugo (Bobby Rydell), and the middle-aged songwriter Albert (Dick Van Dyke) and his forever fiancée Rosie (Janet Leigh). It's the females of these two couples who are itching to get it on, and when their guys won't satisfy them, they temporarily look elsewhere. Albert and Rosie finally consummate their endless engagement—we see them the next morning on a terrace, asking each other if they are "disappointed," presumably about how they look in their pajamas but really about the previous night's performance. Sex relieves Rosie's tension and severs the apron strings that tied Albert to his domineering mother.

I was never much interested in that pair. For me, it was all about Ann-Margret. Conrad Birdie is a MacGuffin; the movie's heart, soul, and midriff belong to Kim McAfee as she makes that delicate transition from Daddy's little girl to sex kitten. "Daddy dear, you won't know your daughter!" she sings as she discovers, over the course of the lotta-livin' number, her full sexual potency. She doesn't even know where to begin. "There are men just ripe for some kissing / And I mean to kiss me a few / Oh those men don't know what they're missing / I got a lot of livin' to do!" As Kim slowly, deliberately paces the nightclub, the music holding its breath while the patrons keep time by slapping their thighs suggestively, all the teen boys silently fall into line behind her. At the front of the club, Conrad Birdie in his tight leather and insolent smile flings wide the doors to the night air and the rev of the motorcycle. Kim McAfee sees her future, and it's delicious.

Carmen Jones
Dat's love

Directed by Otto Preminger; starring Dorothy Dandridge,
Harry Belafonte, Pearl Bailey (1954)

by Jami Bernard

I'M GOING TO FUCK YOU, FUCK WITH YOU, FUCK YOU OVER, AND
you're gonna love it, and we'll all go down in flames, sings Dorothy Dandridge in *Carmen Jones*.

Oscar Hammerstein II put it more decorously when he rewrote the lyrics
to Bizet's opera *Carmen* in 1943 for an updated Broadway musical version
with an all-black cast. Nevertheless, that's the blunt message of producer-director Otto Preminger's 1954 movie adaptation, and the message would have
come through even if the lyrics had stayed in French (which I wish they had;
the Hammerstein lyrics are clunky, often tin-eared, defying the glory and
fever of the Bizet score).

Frankly, the message would have been clear without words at all. It's written all over the bodies and faces of Dorothy Dandridge and Harry Belafonte
as they negotiated that Hollywood tightrope between the stereotype of the
carnal African American and the novelty and daring of portraying adult
themes and sexuality in an all-black movie milieu.

Preminger, for all his bullying, truly believed in the project (he reveled in
making provocative fare like *The Man with the Golden Arm* and in confronting
censorship boards) and pushed it along when studios weren't interested. It
was the first all-black film musical since 1943's *Stormy Weather* and *Cabin in
the Sky*. Preminger clearly believed in his leading lady too; although he resis-

ted her at first while testing every black actress and singer out there (including nervous newcomer Diahann Carroll, who snagged a bit part), Preminger became Dandridge's lover and mentor after finally seeing the Carmen in her—a parallel to the Bizet material right down to the relationship's obsessive overtones.

Carmen Jones is *hot*, made hotter by our knowing it will all end badly—foreshadowed right up front by Dandridge's show-stopping "Dat's Love" while Carmen loads her lunch tray in a Southern military-base cafeteria. It's a deceptively simple scene—note the elaborate blocking—as this one song pretty much tells the whole *Carmen Jones* story right to its tragic but inevitable conclusion.

Everyone in the cafeteria is dressed in military-drab fatigues for the men and factory garb for Carmen's sister parachute workers—except Carmen, who enters late, regally, wearing a blood-red skirt, the color of the rose she will fling like a gauntlet at Belafonte's WWII serviceman Joe at the end of her number. She's a rogue spirit, set apart by her sexuality, certainty, and independence, and also by her fatal belief in superstition—the clock is always ticking for her. She sings. (Both Dandridge and Belafonte were dubbed, unfortunately, to get a more operatic effect—Dandridge by Marilynn Horne and Belafonte by Le Vern Hutcherson—but Dandridge's performance is one of the great lip-synchs of all time.) Carmen leisurely contemplates both lunch and romantic possibilities, joking, flirting, choosing, and zeroing in on Joe, an officer who, oblivious, lunches with his fiancée. It's his obliviousness Carmen likes as much as his mighty chest and good looks; as the other men make clear, she can have them all, but she's not in it for sex, she wants something deeper (and, yes, creepier). The lyrics enumerate Carmen's moods: conquest ("You go for me, and I'm taboo, but if you're hard to get I go for you"); power ("Boy, my baby, dat's de end of you"); masochism ("One man treat me like I was mud, and what I got that man can get"); and, of course, fate ("Dat's love," the song's title and oft-repeated refrain).

Joe is ordered to transport Carmen to a holding cell after a catfight with her coworkers, and it doesn't take long for him to succumb. Not without a struggle, though. The upright Joe, who was about to marry that hometown drip Cindy Lou (Olga James), ignores Carmen's come-ons, literally swatting her away. He tussles with her in the dirt, binds her hand and foot, slings her over his shoulder—all just adding to the thrill, his and ours. He was only recently discussing his sainted mother with his virginal fiancée, but the physicality of these interactions with his prisoner stir the beast in him.

What saves the movie from exploiting racial stereotypes is that the Bizet scenario—so familiar in any case—fits comfortably with just about any ethnicity. Black, white, or nineteenth-century Spanish soldiers and toreadors—most cultures have a soft spot for endless love. *Carmen Jones* is lustful but it isn't about lust, it's about people undone by obsession, pride, fate, human nature. Joe is doomed the moment he succumbs to Carmen, and not because he can't go back to Cindy Lou (she shows up near the end to drag him home to Mama, but by then he's got dark circles under his eyes, always a warning sign in movies). Joe's a goner, and the obsession eats away at him until, on the run, he is reduced as much by his inner environment as his outer one—he paces a one-room Chicago tenement like an animal, waiting for Carmen's return, totally dependent on her emotionally and financially, consumed by jealousy and rage.

Carmen could have easily seemed a fickle good-time girl who throws Joe over when something better comes along (the prizefighter Husky Miller, a vernacular of Escamillo, the opera's toreador). Amazingly, Dandridge turns it into a kindness to leave Joe, an act of love and pity. She takes up with the fighter mostly to make the rent and food money for Joe, now a wanted man who can't leave the love nest no matter how fetid it has become. The last time she leaves the apartment, she knows it's for good, and Joe senses it too; Carmen knows Joe's fate will be worse if she sticks with him. We can see this only in the distressed, haunted way Dandridge has Carmen regard her lover as she sets down the groceries she has probably paid too high a price for. (That she now wears a more subdued coral also signifies she's no longer on the make; at least, not in her heart.)

Before Joe falls for her, all is electric, erotic tension, and after it goes sour, there is the sad release of the mercy fuck. In between, there is a wealth of sexy tenderness: She polishes his shoes, he polishes her toes and blows on them to dry. These scenes between Belafonte and Dandridge are intimate and loving, quite unlike anything African-American actors were allowed to do on film until relatively recently. As the film historian Donald Bogle describes in his *Dorothy Dandridge: A Biography*, Dandridge was at a point in her career where she was being touted for her body—"the new-style sex goddess of the Eisenhower era"—and it offended her sense of dignity and professionalism. Yet she desperately wanted the career-making role of Carmen, which required that she ooze desire and availability, just as promised in that hated publicity. Dandridge reconciled her conflict, more or less, by tackling the role with fierce, perhaps obsessive, concentration and thoroughness. As with her affair with Preminger, her life for a time paralleled the movie's story line. What we see onscreen is not sex, but the sexiness inherent in command, control, and determination. Carmen has a lot at stake; Dandridge, too.

She was nominated for an Oscar and was crushed when she didn't win.

One final note about Pearl Bailey, who plays Carmen's friend Frankie. Bailey has the movie's second sexiest number after "Dat's Love" when the music drives her into a passionate, joyful frenzy at Billy Pastor's bar. According to Bogle, Bailey keenly wanted the lead and resented Dandridge all through the shoot. (Bailey had the voice, guts, and presence for Carmen, but not the right looks.) She must have known that in this second-banana role, her only shot was the "Beat Out Dat Rhythm on a Drum" scene, and she grabs it by the throat. Like the other actors, Bailey is hampered by the "modernized" Hammerstein lyrics that come dangerously close to stereotyping (is Frankie responding to the call of the African tom-toms?), yet she brushes all that aside and, with jaw-dropping authority (and her own, undubbed voice), turns the number into something approaching ecstasy—the very opposite of the movie's fatalism. Carmen can have any man she wants, she seems to be saying, but look who can steal a song.

Contempt
The real thing

Directed by Jean-Luc Godard; starring Brigitte Bardot, Jack Palance, Michel Piccoli (1963)

by Desson Thomson

THE TALK IN JEAN-LUC GODARD'S DREAMLIKE, STRANGELY wonderful *Contempt* is of gods, Greek gods specifically, and of such classical figures as Odysseus and Penelope. The people doing the talking are three very different men: crass Hollywood producer Prokosch (Jack Palance, in transcendently boorish form), a crime novelist–turned-screenwriter named Paul Javal (Michel Piccoli), and Fritz Lang, the German director who plays himself. All three are involved in a movie project that aims to retell *The Odyssey*.

But they are at cross purposes. Lang wants the film to be an artistically profound treatise on classicism and other subjects. The producer, Prokosch, wants to make a movie along the lines of a Joseph E. Levine–style *Hercules* picture. He wants girls and action. And he has hired Paul to do the rewrite.

For all this chatter, there's one thing that really commands our attention: the sultry blonde fussing and fretting in the background. She's Camille, Paul's wife, a former typist who is frankly bored with all this movie palaver. She'd rather be spending time with her husband, and remembers the days when he was just a two-bit playwright, not caught up in the Hollywood game.

She may be Camille, but we don't think of her as anyone but the actress playing her: Brigitte Bardot, the smoldering sex symbol of the 1960s, whose very presence in this highbrow picture is a perpetual exclamation point.

(Bardot crashes the set of a Godard picture!) With a physique that would launch a thousand sculptors, she's all curved limbs and lips, with a lustrous, tousled mane (she combed her hair with her fingers, I remember reading once) and a feline, mascara-eyed scowl. Her every movement, whether a petulant glance or an arching of her back, is a monumental upstaging of anyone else who dares appear in the same CinemaScope frame.

In the movie's stunning opening scene (which owes almost as much to Georges Delerue's passionate score as to Bardot's voluptuousness), she lies next to Paul and asks him about her body.

"Can you see my feet in the mirror?"

"Yes," he replies.

"Do you think they're pretty?" He does.

She puts him through a barrage of similar questions about her ankles, knees, thighs, hair, face, breasts, and (as the coy English subtitle puts it) her "behind."

Yes indeed, he loves every detail.

"Then you love me totally?" she asks.

"I love you totally, tenderly, tragically," he replies. Too bad Paul doesn't appreciate the gift he has before him or anticipate how fast he's about to lose it.

Prokosch, bullishly attracted to Camille, invites the couple over for a drink. He pointedly asks Camille to accompany him in his red Alfa Romeo sports car, instructing Paul to follow them in a cab. Camille looks at her husband, fully expecting him to resist. But Paul, possibly feeling he has nothing to fear, and definitely in thrall to the man about to write him a big check, lets her go. Camille is outraged, convinced Paul is tacitly allowing Prokosch to make a pass at her. Over the next twenty-four hours, her contempt for her husband dismantles what's left of their love.

What is Paul's moral crime, exactly? It's self-absorption brought on by money and ambition. In that instant, he has failed to appreciate the harmonic convergence of Camille's love, youth, and beauty. He has let love go, and in what amounts to mythical tragedy, there is no way to retrieve it.

While Paul and Camille argue later in their Rome apartment, Godard makes explicit use of widescreen to show the gulf between them. The camera slowly pans from one face to the other but never shows them together in the same composition. They might as well be in different worlds. Godard, whose marriage to his regular screen muse Anna Karina would end two years later, charts this romantic dissolution in excruciatingly precise increments. It's as if this onscreen breakup is a harbinger of his own; it's all too prescient that Bardot at one point dons a black wig that makes her eerily reminiscent of Karina.

Contempt is about many things: the hemorrhaging of love, the tyranny of money, and the inexpressible differences between men and women. It pits art versus commerce, philistinism versus aesthetics. It finds juxtapositions between Hollywood and the Nazi propaganda machine. It openly mocks the American producer Levine, who partially funded the movie, and Carlo Ponti, the film's Italian producer, whose dubbing of *Contempt* and his alteration of Delerue's score was tantamount to sabotage.

It's also one of the great movies about movies, with its film-within-a-film and its striking widescreen images and formal compositions by the great cinematographer Raoul Coutard.

But in the end, the film is about Bardot as she reclines naked on various surfaces: a feathery white bed, a bluish sofa, and the roof of Prokosch's seaside villa. While the men joust verbally about how to remake *The Odyssey,* she's the real classic, an intriguing symbol of modern fame (at least she was in the year 1963) and timeless beauty. Warmed by the Mediterranean sun and framed against an awesomely blue sea, she lives in this moment forever, like the statues of Athens. She's a pop icon who remains beguilingly transcendental.

Crash
Cronenberg and sex drive

Directed by David Cronenberg; starring Deborah Kara Unger,
James Spader, Holly Hunter (1996)

by Jonathan Rosenbaum

THE LAST TWO PARAGRAPHS OF J. G. BALLARD'S INTRODUCTION
to his 1973 novel *Crash* point to a seeming paradox at the heart of David
Cronenberg's masterful film adaptation as well as of the original—that
pornography, by virtue of being political, can play a cautionary role rather
than, or in addition to, a prescriptive one:

> Throughout *Crash* I have used the car not only as a sexual image, but as a
> total metaphor for man's life in today's society. As such the novel has a po-
> litical role quite apart from its sexual content, but I would still like to think
> that *Crash* is the first pornographic novel based on technology. In a sense,
> pornography is the most political form of fiction, dealing with how we use
> and exploit each other in the most urgent and ruthless way.
>   Needless to say, the ultimate role of *Crash* is cautionary, a warning
> against that brutal, erotic, and overlit realm that beckons more and more
> persuasively to us from the margins of the technological landscape.

The novel and film are in English, but could be said to speak a foreign language. This is certainly true for me. After many tries I still haven't made it all
the way through Ballard's slim novel—in part because the writing, though perfectly pitched, remains at the same obsessional and ultimately monotonous

intensity throughout—and my initial response to the film was guarded disappointment. On second viewing, I'm inclined to think that respecting Ballard's radical content is a formally adventurous move. A lot depends on one's point of reference. Compared with the novel, the movie might seem predictable. But compared with other movies, it stands alone.

Almost as spare as late Bresson, Cronenberg's *Crash* focuses on half a dozen individuals who aren't so much characters as separate versions, aspects, or stages of the same character; all are car-crash veterans and most have sex with each other. We first meet Catherine and James Ballard (Deborah Kara Unger and James Spader), a married couple who recount their casual flings during sex with each other.

In the first crash we see James collide with another car on a freeway because he's looking at a set of storyboards while driving. Unlike the crashes we usually see in movies, but like all the crashes in this film, it's over in a flash, the makes of the cars are irrelevant, and there's no explosion—three early clues that this is an art movie. Cronenberg has his own way of making the event baroque: The other driver is thrown through his windshield and dies on the hood of James's car. His wife, Dr. Helen Remington (Holly Hunter), is kept in place by her seat belt; as she breaks free she exposes one breast, and it's not clear whether this is inadvertent. The moment represents a modulation in the way the film handles sex, an eerie and sustained key change.

James and Helen are shocked into seeing a new kind of erotic possibility, which is explored when Catherine visits James in the hospital, when he encounters Helen in the hospital and afterward, and when all three get acquainted with Vaughan (Elias Koteas), a survivor of multiple crashes. Vaughan introduces them to an entire cult built on the erotics of car crashes, including former racecar driver Colin Seagrave (Peter MacNeill) and Gabrielle (Rosanna Arquette), who wears leg braces and a full-body support suit like fetish wear. It all sounds like a joke, but the film rigorously, solemnly follows these characters as they compulsively replay and comment on a Swedish crash video, restage accidents, have sex in cars, photograph people having sex in cars and crash victims, or crash their cars into one another's as a kinky kind of love play.

According to Tom Shone's interview with Ballard in the *New Yorker*, the film opened in the United States only after a lengthy wrangle between the Ted Turner "who owns the film's distributor [Fine Line Features]" and the Ted Turner who thought the film might encourage people "to have sex in their cars while driving at high speed." It also should be noted that Cronenberg disagrees with the characterization of the novel given by Ballard. Speaking to Gavin Smith in *Film Comment*, he called Ballard's writing "antipornographic," registered his belief (which I share) that his film is more pornographic than the novel, and said he considered neither the novel nor the film a cautionary tale. (If movies can inspire violent deaths—and given that they're part of life, I'm sure they can—I'd wager that hundreds of other titles in the Turner vault are more likely than *Crash* to inspire such behavior.)

It's difficult to say just what *Crash* is. Ballard doesn't know, nor does Cronenberg. Neither Turner nor I can slap on a label like "pornographic" or "cautionary" and make it stick. It looks romantic but isn't, feels pornographic but isn't, appears to be set in the present but isn't. That's what makes it so interesting, even if it leaves us all in a critical quandary.

Crash begins with the credits floating toward the viewer like cars slicing through a night fog, with lights flickering past the letters. A similar conflation of cars and freeways with imagery suggesting outer space recurs frequently. Camera movements are like caresses, whether they're gliding around airplanes, cars, or human bodies. But for all the lyricism Cronenberg is able to glean from his unlikely subject, the overall emotional tone is melancholic rather than tragic, in contrast to *Naked Lunch*.

Much as that film was about the dark side of artistic creation, *Crash* is about the dark side of sex and passion. It's a minimalist work, and a perfectly realized one. Its art-movie ancestors are the bumper-car sequence in Bresson's *Mouchette*, the anonymous battles and tournament crowd in Bresson's *Lancelot du lac*, and the flirtatious "cruising" of the heroine in a car by the hero in a plane in Antonioni's *Zabriskie Point*. If it adds up to less than any of those pictures, and less than *Videodrome* or *Naked Lunch*, that is basically because a story that admits neither characters nor development in the ordinary sense depends on only a few poetic metaphors and nuggets of emotion. As prophecy, it's suggestive but limited.

Crimes of Passion
All aboard

Directed by Ken Russell; starring Kathleen Turner,
Anthony Perkins, John Laughlin (1984)

by Peter Travers

KINKY IS IN THE EYE OF THE BEHOLDER. BUT DAMNED IF KEN
Russell doesn't behold it with a wicked eye second to none. *Crimes of Passion*,
roundly trashed by critics when it debuted in the Orwellian year of 1984, is
the *Citizen Kane* of kink. Within its 101 chaotic minutes —plus six more hot-
stuff ones on the unrated DVD—this hellzapoppin' sex thriller conjures
thoughts of Joe Orton, Groucho Marx, Alfred Hitchcock, *Fatal Attraction,*
and those porn videos your cousin Herbie stashes in his locker.

The British prodigy Russell had won a directing nomination from the conservative Academy for his 1970 adaptation of D. H. Lawrence's *Women in
Love,* but by the time of *Crimes of Passion,* he had become the dirty old man
of cinema. "This is not the age of manners," Russell proclaimed. "This is the
age of kicking people in the crotch and telling them something and getting a
reaction. I want to shock people into awareness. I don't believe there is any
virtue in understatement."

Crimes of Passion, ostensibly about America's self-deluded approach to sex,
reveals Russell as a man of his word. Kathleen Turner—in an uninhibited
performance that she still hasn't topped for fierce courage and fiercer fun—
put her then-new Hollywood stardom at risk by letting Russell's camera
drool all over her naked body. In this movie, she does things to men that you
just don't expect from Michael Douglas's leading lady of *Romancing the Stone.*

I could mention her facility with a cop's phallic nightstick, but I'd be jumping ahead.

First, let me explain that Turner plays Joanna Crane, a prim sportswear designer so involved with her career that her husband splits. Nothing kinky there, until we learn that Joanna moonlights as China Blue, a $50 hooker in an uber-sleazy red-light district. "How low can you get?" asks one of her johns. "As low as you can afford," she sasses. It's not the money she needs, it's the human interaction she can't get from her career.

China gets a little too much of that human interaction with the Reverend Peter Shayne, a deranged street preacher played by Anthony Perkins in a manner that makes his *Psycho* character, Norman Bates, seem the very model of well-adjusted humanity. First seen ogling a stripper, he follows up by delivering an impassioned sermon on the evils of the flesh. His prayers for China Blue's lost soul are mixed with obscene comments about her all-too-available body. China tries to laugh him off: "The last reverend who tried to save me lived to regret it. I chased him all around the church until I caught him by the organ." The Rev believes "whores and metaphors don't mix"; he wants the truth. "This is a fantasy business, Reverend. You can have any truth you want," says China. To see Perkins sing "Shout 'hallelujah,' c'mon, get happy!" before stabbing a blow-up sex doll with a silver dildo is to find new meaning in the word *unpredictable*.

That goes as well for the unbridled script by Barry Sandler, which has China Blue dress as a stewardess and announce to a startled client: "This is Flight 69, so unbuckle your belt and let your big bird rise and rise. Please remember, while we may run out of Pan-Am coffee, we'll never run out of TWA-T."

China's dialogue allows Joanna to blow off her inhibitions, but there are times when anger pierces her cool. A wealthy couple picks up China in their limo; when the man sticks his tongue in her ear, his wife warns: "These people are dirty and disgusting." China bolts from the limo shouting curses, her armor pierced.

The film's emotional focus is Bobby Grady (John Laughlin), a private investigator (Joanna's boss thinks she's involved in industrial espionage) who gets more than he bargained for when he knocks on China's door. Bobby's wife, Amy (Annie Potts)—his childhood sweetheart—doesn't understand him, at least sexually. She's more concerned with material trappings. No laugh from her when Bobby ties basketballs to his feet and spits out milk in his best impression of a penis.

Bobby leaves his wife, and from the moment he enters China's lair, kinkiness runs amok, with China fulfilling his every sex fantasy. She removes his shoes and socks and sucks his toes as if they were aching hard-ons. For foot fetishists, this scene belongs in the pantheon. And she doesn't stop there. Wearing spiked heels and a lewd smile, she moves up to Bobby's crotch like an explorer who's spotted the holy grail. Laughlin's expressions as he's treated to a tongue bath his wife wouldn't have dreamed of administering have a transcendent goofiness, but his sexual awakening is also unexpectedly touching.

At first, China is put off when Bobby expresses feelings for her. "I'm a hooker. You're a trick. Why ruin a perfect relationship?" But as China starts to share his deeper passion—they're both bruised romantics at heart— Russell tries to take the movie to emotional levels it can't sustain.

The critic David Thomson has trashed Russell for being "oblivious to his own vulgarity." I wouldn't have it any other way. What gives *Crimes of Passion* a timeless X-factor is the way it rubs kinky sex in our faces to make us see how hopelessly hypocritical we still are on the subject, especially at a time when Janet Jackson's exposed nipple on television has stirred a new age of Bush-league Puritanism. Now more than ever, China Blue can help us find our inner Marquis de Sade.

Days of Heaven

How ya gonna keep 'em down on the farm?

Directed by Terrence Malick; starring Richard Gere,
Brooke Adams, Sam Shepard (1978)

by Eleanor Ringel Gillespie

DAYS OF HEAVEN IS A MOVIE YOU WANT TO HAVE SEX DURING.
Terrence Malick's 1978 magnum opus shimmers with the sensuality of a
languorous summer afternoon: undulating wheat fields, serene and ripe;
plush billowy clouds scudding across the sky; the lulling buzz of insects;
and, in the background, the simmering eroticism of a love triangle seething
with greed, desire, and deceit.

The movie's story line—as primal as it is starkly moralistic, almost Biblical—is about a paradise lost, dismantled by human corruption and weakness. Sin comes to this Garden of Eden in the Texas Panhandle and, in its
wake, plagues of locusts and hellfire destruction.

After accidentally killing a man in a fight at the Chicago steel mill where
he works, hot-tempered Bill (Richard Gere), his lover, Abby (Brooke Adams),
and his little sister, Linda (Linda Manz), take off for the wide open spaces of
Texas—still a frontier in the early twentieth century—where it's as easy to
hide from the law as to change your identity. Just like Abraham and Sara in
Egypt (as told in Genesis), Bill and Abby pose as brother and sister.

They find migrant work harvesting wheat for a rich, lonely farmer (Sam
Shepard). Isolation has made him awkward with people. So has a diagnosis
of a terminal illness. But he's attracted to Abby, something her "brother"

encourages. Bill sees the farmer's bad health as their good fortune: Abby will marry him and soon enough inherit his money and land. What Bill (and Abby) don't count on is that she develops feelings for her new husband, which churns up murderous jealousy in Bill. Like the workers dotting the limitless golden fields, Bill and Abby reap what they sow. Punishment is doled out with Old Testament fury and inevitability.

Malick is blissfully indifferent to the things Hollywood considers essential. Stuff like, oh, action, dialogue, character development, which to him are just a backdrop for the film's intense, lyrical images, indelibly lensed by cinematographer Nestor Almendros. A single grasshopper gnawing a stalk of wheat (which presages the disaster to come) gets a better close-up than most of the actors. This willful inversion just wasn't done in Hollywood movies. Even John Ford kept Monument Valley in the background and John Wayne up front. The result is an implicit emotional detachment that turns conventional notions of love, sex, and romance upside down.

A further distancing device is Malick's use of Manz as the film's narrator. She's like a color commentator at a sports event, talking about whatever catches her attention. Sometimes it's a salient observation; more likely, it's a child's scattered chatter. Of some strangers on a riverbank, she notes, "You couldn't tell what they were doin'. They were probably calling for help. Or burying somebody."

Malick used the device of the naïve girl narrator earlier in *Badlands* (see it), with Sissy Spacek's oblivious teenage baton twirler dispassionately commenting on the murderous crime spree she and boyfriend Martin Sheen pursue across the Dakota Badlands (based on a true incident in the '50s). Manz uses the same flat, affectless voice, the same randomness in which a corpse has no more weight than a puff of dust. At the end, she and her new best friend skitter off toward the horizon, into the vastness of a Promised Land still searching for its people.

Malick originally wanted John Travolta for *Days of Heaven,* but the actor was otherwise engaged. It turned out to be a fortunate swing-and-a-miss. Travolta was too well-known by then, and his celebrity would have unbalanced, even overwhelmed, the picture. Malick cast the little-known Gere instead, and it was a masterstroke. Early in his career, Gere was a recessive, pretty-boy blank. He didn't really find his footing until 1990's *Internal Affairs.* But that initial remoteness serves the movie perfectly, as does Shepard's patented flintiness, later showcased to perfection in *The Right Stuff.* (In fact,

Shepard scored with female audiences for a heretofore unrecognized snaggle-toothed sex appeal.)

Adams's Abby is something of a cipher (ah, the usual trouble with writing the part of The Girl), but there's something intriguing in the actress's restraint and in the sexy downturn of the corners of her mouth. The most pungent presence, however, is Manz, whose narration is so distinctive it was included on the original soundtrack album. Her "whatevah" attitude is still oddly contemporary.

Malick finished the film and went into Salingeresque reclusion. (He finally returned in 1998 with the WWII film *The Thin Red Line*.) His disappearance somehow echoes the grace, mystery, and remove of *Days of Heaven*, which takes us beyond narrative, beyond language, beyond emotional connection and into a place of pure sensation.

If someone you love—or maybe merely lust after—invites you over to watch the DVD, remember two things: safe sex and the pause button.

Deep Throat
Porno chic

Directed by Gerard Damiano;
starring Linda Lovelace (1972)

by Emanuel Levy

IT WAS MADE QUITE ROUTINELY FOR THE NICHE-MARKET PORN industry. But *Deep Throat,* surprisingly, became one of the decade's top-grossing films. When it opened on June 11, 1972, at Manhattan's World Theatre, no one anticipated that this or any hard-core movie could become such an "event." Word got around that *Deep Throat* was the first stag film you could see on a date, preferably at lunch time; thus was born porno chic, with respectable artists like Mike Nichols telling Truman Capote not to miss it.

Deep Throat became the first crossover adults-only film hit, titillating audiences previously biased against the genre. Its quick and effective move into the mainstream was a byproduct of extensive media coverage (particularly in the *New York Times*) and a steady stream of celeb ticket-buyers, such as Jackie Kennedy and Marlene Dietrich. Once the movie garnered national attention, it became a cultural phenomenon, with references, both serio and comic, on TV shows like Johnny Carson's.

Artistically speaking, *Deep Throat* doesn't live up to its reputation. However, it was superior to its competitors of that time. The technical quality was above the norm for such fare, including sharp color photography and a satirical score that spoofs, among other things, Coca-Cola's "It's the Real Thing" TV ad. Most reviewers did not bother to list the cast, reflecting the prevailing bias that porno performers were not really acting and thus didn't deserve credit for their efforts. Some of the anonymity was due to the actors themselves, who hid behind pseudonyms—including the film's star, Linda Lovelace (née Linda Marchiano).

Years later, Lovelace claimed in her memoir *Ordeal* that she was drugged and hypnotized into performing the sex acts. This is still at the center of much debate about pornography.

Writer-director Gerard Damiano (billed as Jerry Gerard) had made a number of stag films before casting (and renaming) his young actress. A suburban girl from Long Island who dreamed of becoming a flight attendant, Lovelace revealed "a close affinity for fellatio," the director said. It was an understatement, although he didn't discover the depths of her talent until the camera began rolling. Once Lovelace's "specialty" became apparent, Damiano decided to construct the whole movie around it.

The plot concerns a young woman named Linda Lovelace who's devastated because she fails to "hear bells," no matter how many partners—as many as fourteen—she has. A visit to her friendly and accommodating doctor reveals that nature has played a nasty trick on Miss Lovelace—her sweet spot is located in her throat, and so has not been receiving adequate stimulation. With therapy and practice, she finally experiences euphoria, along with the fireworks and bells she's been missing. In the film's happy ending, she hooks up with a man whose credentials rival her own.

If my count is accurate, *Deep Throat* offers seventeen scenes of explicit sex, a high ratio considering the running time of 62 minutes. Allowing for a sequence of Lovelace driving around Miami during the credits, plus scenes of a swimming pool, fireworks, and a rocket launch at Cape Kennedy, that amounts to a sex act roughly every three minutes. Just about every sex act imaginable is depicted in anatomical detail, including group sex, explicit penetration, fellatio, cunnilingus, female masturbation, and sodomy.

Even beyond its plot or oral gymnastics, *Deep Throat* made history for its tongue-in-cheek approach to hetero hard-core (humor had always been part of gay porno), proving that the genre needs comic relief as much as thrillers or actioners do.

To escape the cold winter, the production headed to Miami, where *Deep Throat* was shot over six days. Joining Lovelace onscreen was the production's assistant cameraman, Harry Reems (née Herbert Streicher), an actor with Shakespearean ambitions who had hoped to be signed by a major agent. There was a naïve belief among actors at the time that experience in the adult industry could lead to mainstream gigs. Reems ventured into porno "strictly for the money," and filled in as the doctor who locates the protagonist's errant clitoris only when the lead porno star failed to show up on the set. Later in his porn career, Reems descended into the drug-and-music culture, reaching a point where he was too drunk to get an erection on cue. Today, reformed, he sells real estate in Park City, Utah, home of the Sundance Film Festival.

The disproportionate ratio of the film's budget to its box-office gross is still striking. Made for the minuscule sum of $25,000, *Deep Throat* became a $600-million global phenomenon that's considered the most profitable film in history. Who got the money? Certainly not the vastly underpaid talent. Lovelace, who became an overnight celeb, was paid $1200, and Reems received only $250 and more than his share of trouble down the road.

Context is crucial. *Deep Throat* was released amid the nation's most significant social movements: sexual liberation, the Vietnam War backlash, the Black Panther movement, feminism, gay liberation, equal rights. It was the last decade in which political activism had such meaning and impact. Moreover, in 1972, the nascent porno industry was benefiting from the decline of the Hollywood studio system, and it would be at least a decade before the industry changed once again with the VCR revolution. It's doubtful that if *Deep Throat* were made today, it would have such an impact on American culture.

Shortly after its premiere, *Deep Throat* became the target of President Nixon's war on "the backwater of filth that had washed upon American shores." With the Nixon administration manipulating Congress and the media, legal action was instigated on city, state, and federal levels in attempts to clamp down on porn. Theater owners and distributors who handled *Deep Throat* were charged with a variety of offenses. In a blatant attempt at industrywide intimidation, federal prosecutors charged Reems with conspiracy to transport obscenity across state lines. Damiano and Lovelace were able to plea-bargain their way out of court; later, they testified against Reems, who was found guilty in 1976. Civil liberties groups, along with such Hollywood stars as Jack Nicholson and Warren Beatty, rallied to his side, and eventually the conviction was overturned.

Deep Throat benefited immensely from its counterculture milieu. Making pornography at that time was partly motivated by the belief that adult films were a natural offshoot of self-expression, liberation, and artistic experimentation. Yet there was a huge divide between the filmmakers' goals and the legacy they inadvertently left, one whose reverberations continue today.

Much of this is outlined in *Inside Deep Throat,* a documentary which premiered at Sundance in January 2005 with local realtor Harry Reems in attendance. Combining facts and personal recollections, *Inside Deep Throat* is a culturally significant work that, despite flaws, is a must-see for anyone who wants a close look at the cultural wars of the tumultuous 1970s.

Written and directed by Fenton Bailey and Randy Barbato, the documentary's sociopolitical dimensions—like those of *Deep Throat* itself—go beyond artistic merit, raising such hot-button issues as censorship, morality and sexuality, pornography and sexual politics, and the impact of cinema on pop culture. It boasts a parade of larger-than-life personalities, including director Damiano, production manager Ron Wertheim, and the assistant cameraman–turned–leading man Reems. It offers testimony from an array of intellectuals (Gore Vidal, Norman Mailer), *enfants terribles* (John Waters, whose *Pink Flamingos* was also released in 1972), and feminists (Gloria Steinem, Camille Paglia), plus law professor Alan Dershowitz, publisher Hugh Hefner, theater owners, distributors, opinion-makers, and FBI agents. *Deep Throat* was positioned "between crime and art," according to Mailer, and "opened a can of worms," according to Vidal. "Damiano made the film in order to get laid," claims the production manager. "The movie changed the sexual practices of Middle America," says sex specialist Dr. Ruth Westheimer. "People learned a lot about female anatomy and different kinds of orgasm," says one feminist. It "revolutionized the whole notion of female pleasure," declares Berkeley scholar Linda Williams.

Some of the most illuminating and hilarious recollections are from ordinary housewives, like the one who complains: "The government is not going to tell me if I can see a dirty picture." Indeed, after this watershed movie, many Americans began to think of sexual practices and sexual gratification in entirely new ways. As one witness says, "Fellatio was not new, but *Deep Throat* made it more widely acceptable."

While this aggregate of lively reflections is the documentary's most impressive attribute, it also makes the absence of key players more noticeable. Lovelace died in 2002 of injuries from a car accident, and though there are interviews with her sister and a high school classmate, there are only brief statements from Lovelace's daughter, and none from her son or the father of her children.

One of the ironies of *Deep Throat* is that Nixon, the porno industry's major foe, was forced to resign due to the scandal over Watergate, which had occurred in June 1972, the same month of the *Deep Throat* premiere. In *All the President's Men,* the key source for the incriminatory evidence that brought Nixon down was given the alias "Deep Throat," which stuck, famously, until the informant's true identity was recently disclosed.

The critical consensus now is that *Deep Throat* was more than a campy, comic romp. It became an emblem of repressive forces that tried to curtail individual expression and creativity. Going beyond artistic or personal values, *Deep Throat* represents a unique moment in American cultural history when buying a ticket to see a dirty movie was a political statement: movie-going as a revolutionary act.

Don't Look Now

The shock of the gloriously domestic

Directed by Nicolas Roeg; starring Julie Christie,
Donald Sutherland (1973)

by Sheila Benson

IT SEEMS IMPOSSIBLE NOW TO IMAGINE THE FUROR THAT
Don't Look Now kicked up in 1973 for its single sequence of a married couple making love. Not to sound disingenuous, but these weren't just any
naked lovers—Julie Christie was the screen's reigning goddess, Donald
Sutherland its ultimate Mr. Cool.

At the time, Christie had an Oscar (*Darling*), a blockbuster (*Dr. Zhivago*), a
certified masterpiece (*McCabe & Mrs. Miller*), and Warren Beatty under her
belt, while Sutherland had become indelible in two radically different pair-
ings: with Elliott Gould in *M*A*S*H** and Jane Fonda in *Klute*.

Don't Look Now would be something completely different. Still ranked in
the first 5 of the Top 100 Cult Films by the London *Times*, it's Nicolas Roeg's
time-bending film about grief, bereavement, and the inevitability of fate. Or,
possibly, about the uselessness of denying the mysterious gift of second sight.

Taken from a short story by Daphne du Maurier, "the mistress of unease,"
Allan Scott and Chris Bryant's adaptation heightened the story's immediacy.
But it was Roeg's eye, his flair for atmosphere, and his soul-shriving scenes
bookending the film that gave it an international buzz quite apart from the
fame of its stars. Oddly, what spoke to me then—and it speaks even more
strongly now—was that the eroticism came from long-married lovers.

Virtually the whole story is contained in the intricate opening sequence: seven minutes and 103 cuts containing images from the present and future—broken glass, water, a spreading red stain, a child in a red slicker. The Baxters are spending a lazy Sunday afternoon in their comfortable fortress of an English country house, architect John (Sutherland) scanning slides, wife Laura (Christie) reading, their children playing outside.

These moments lull us, bringing us unsuspectingly to the instant when the lives of John and Laura change into Before and After. Before their daughter, Christine, in her red slicker, loses her footing and falls into the pond. Before John, alerted by something he can't see or hear, rushes outside, plunges into the weedy muck to save her—and can't. Before Laura goes to the door to see about the noise—and screams. After is their life without a daughter.

The rest of the film is set some months later in Venice, early winter. The Baxters' son has been shipped off to boarding school (oh, the English). John, with the patronage of a most elegant bishop, is restoring an old church while he and Laura try to pull their lives together.

As they're lunching in a small restaurant, Laura is told by one of two older Scottish sisters touring Venice that Heather, the blind, psychic sister, has "seen" Christine sitting between them in a red slicker, laughing and happy. Laura faints from shock, although when she checks out of the hospital, she's radiantly happy for the first time since the drowning, and eager to find Heather again. To John, mediums, spiritualism, messages from the dead are "mumbo jumbo"; he is flatly unwilling to go down this path.

It's with this between them that John and Laura return to their ornate, shuttered hotel room to relax before dinner. Roeg gives the scene the most wonderfully offhand feeling; Laura puts on music and pins up her hair before her bath, John catches something in the paper he wants her to read. The back and forth between them carries the easy weight of a couple as comfortable with each other as with their own naked bodies. It's the most gloriously *domestic* sequence.

When they're lying together on the bed, reading the paper—she in a light robe, he naked from the shower (except for his watch)—she strokes his shoulders lightly with the backs of her fingers. He turns yearningly toward her. Under the beginning of this scene plays Pino Donaggio's simple piano tune from the movie's peaceful opening, thus uniting two Befores in our mind.

Roeg intercuts their passionate present with snippets of them dressing in the flushed aftermath of lovemaking. There is the sex—enormously tender, increasingly sensual—and then there is the memory of it. As Laura slips into her silver V-necked sweater, her skin still glows pink from the friction of their bodies; as John's hands gently pull Laura's robe from her naked hips, so we see her fingers smoothing a skirt over her hips when she dresses again. It gives the long, lyrical sequence a haunting sense of pensiveness and the passage of time, however brief; it's also the least exploitative erotic scene in cinema. Every moment has a reason: to make sense of a muted smile in the final frames.

Now dressed, Laura puts their sheets in a hamper, holding one back to press to her face for a second, catching its smell one more time—a moment so acute in my memory it makes tears well.

I'd always felt that the sequence marked the first time they'd made love since Christine drowned, but it was only a hunch until, at a film festival, Donald Sutherland said that was *exactly* the case. If that's so, given the short time frame of the Venice sojourn, the scene is crucial; without it the grisly finale would be crushing.

The menace that can be Venice is rampant: the fright of being lost in damp nighttime streets; a maze of bridges that seem to lead nowhere; stagnant canals; rats; and a scream most definitely not from a cat. There is also a knife-wielding murderer scuttling about these ancient alleyways.

Don't Look Now is actually *Don't Look Away*: Don't look away or you'll miss a piece of the mosaic. As John, ignoring every warning, hurtles toward his death (or his reunion with Christine), ultimately to lie in a final spasm of spurting blood, Roeg builds to a monumental closing. Past and present flash by—especially those first prophetic shots—like a riffling deck of cards, each with an image of John, living and loving, until death and its swelling aftermath turn into seven bravura minutes of epiphany and celebration.

Considering a scene of such carnage, the film isn't oppressive if you study Laura's faint look of peace on the funeral barge. As Roeg himself has said (in an interview with British Film Institute author Mark Sanderson), "Laura has survived, triumphant—death shall have no dominion over her—their happiness may be in the past, but it was real and it will always remain so."

Ecstasy

And the agony . . .

Directed by Gustav Machaty; starring Hedy Lamarr (1933)

by Kevin Thomas

IN 1933, TWENTY-YEAR-OLD HEDY KIESLER, A MAX REINHARDT discovery and daughter of a Viennese banker, starred in *Ecstasy* for eminent Czech director Gustav Machaty. It was the young actress' fifth movie, but a discreet skinny-dipping scene triggered a notoriety that would hound the renamed Hedy Lamarr almost until her death in obscurity at eighty-six. The scene stirred an international censorship controversy: Hitler banned the film, Pope Pius XII denounced it, and Kiesler's first husband, Austrian arms merchant Fritz Mandl, reputedly spent a fortune trying to buy up all the prints.

Ecstasy was then released in Europe and America in a censored version, which brought Hedy to the attention of MGM's Louis B. Mayer. He imported the movie's star attraction to Hollywood and changed her last name to Lamarr, perhaps in recollection of the silent era's Barbara La Marr, an even more ill-fated star who couldn't handle fame and died young. Mayer billed the raven-haired Hedy as "the most beautiful girl in the world" (Barbara La Marr had been "the girl who was too beautiful"). While many cinephiles agreed Lamarr was exceptionally lovely, Mayer's superlative would prove a curse to a capable actress thereafter confined largely to femme fatale roles. The moniker was also a hindrance to a woman far more intelligent than the public initially realized. Only in the 1990s was the reclusive star acknowledged for her role in inventing sophisticated radio technology that continues to have vast applications today.

Although technically a talkie, *Ecstasy* is essentially a silent film with dialogue so spare it could have been rendered in intertitles. That it is a talkie, however, underscores a visual medium's expressive power in the hands of an artist like Machaty, who fully grasped the magic interplay among imagery, camera movement, and editing. For this sophisticated European, sexuality was simply natural, and he expressed this with a blend of discretion and candor rarely found onscreen. The movie still seems daring in its honesty, especially when seen against today's puritanical backlash from the religious right.

This adroitly paced 89-minute movie values mood over plot, featuring fairly long sequences rich in visual detail. Still clad in her wedding gown, Lamarr's Eva is jauntily carried over the threshold of a sparely appointed, art deco apartment by her middle-aged groom, Emil (Zvonimir Rogoz). Emil's alacrity is misleading. Once home, he reverts to rigid routine, aligning the contents of his pockets atop his bureau with military precision. In contrast, Eva contentedly improvises a vase for her bridal bouquet by repurposing a tin pail in the kitchen. Our final glimpse of the ill-suited newlyweds is of the groom dozing in a chair.

In subsequent scenes, Emil is self-absorbed, perhaps because marriage has revealed that he is frozen into impotence. An increasingly unhappy Eva flees to her unsympathetic widowed father's baronial estate and files for divorce. Her spirits lifted by being close to nature again, she rides her horse through the forest, pausing for the now infamous dip in a stream.

While Eva bathes, her horse detects a nearby filly and runs off, along with her lounging pajamas. She chases after, only to discover that Adam (Aribert Mog), a handsome, husky engineer supervising a railroad construction, has intercepted the horse. In amusement, he tosses Eva the errant clothing.

Despite the potential awkwardness of the situation, there is mutual attraction between Adam and Eva in this veritable Garden of Eden. Later that hot summer evening, Eva, in her longing and frustration, seeks out Adam's cabin for a sexual awakening à la Lady Chatterley. It is this sequence that gives the film its title, and which suffuses Eva's features as she discovers the essence of sexual passion. It's also a remarkably expressive sequence, one that would better suffice as a lightning rod for controversy than those water-lily glimpses of chaste nudity.

The plot and mood now speed to a deeply ironic and wrenching culmination. In an astonishing coda reminiscent of Soviet films and King Vidor's

Our Daily Bread, a montage shows farm workers and laborers who are clearly happier in their rugged existence than are the educated classes—Adam, Eva, and especially the hopelessly clenched Emil—in theirs.

Ecstasy was preceded by such esteemed Machaty films as *The Kreutzer Sonata* (1928) and the visually striking *Erotikon* (1930), which attest to the director's worldliness. The former deals with an unhappy marriage where the wife is drawn to a handsome violinist, the latter with a chic, happily married woman who is yet dangerously drawn to the seducer who caused her past grief. As in *Ecstasy,* Machaty, who died in 1963 at sixty-two, was blunt about the power of sexual attraction.

As for Lamarr, her career virtually ended with Cecil B. DeMille's *Samson and Delilah* (1949), though it staggered on in the '50s. She was briefly dragged back into the spotlight courtesy of a 1966 shoplifting charge (for which she was subsequently acquitted), and again in 1992 in Florida on a similar charge, later dismissed. Along the way she married six times, bore two children, and retreated from the public eye. Then Boeing trotted out a glamour portrait of Lamarr in 2003 as part of its "Don't Let History Happen Without You" recruitment campaign, because of a long-ago patent she shared with a friend, the avant-garde composer George Antheil. Together they devised a torpedo guidance system predicated on randomly hopping radio frequencies. This technological achievement has lately inspired a slogan: "Think cell phone and thank Hedy Lamarr."

Lamarr learned about radio technology over dinners with her first husband's clients. (She left the marriage in 1937 when Mandl began selling weapons to Nazis.) Early in the war years, she articulated her invention as a way of protecting U.S. radio-guided torpedoes from enemy jamming. Antheil, who had composed music for fourteen simultaneous player pianos, suggested using piano rolls to hop the signals over various frequencies. Anyone trying to jam a signal would hear only the random noise of a spinning radio dial.

Lamarr and Antheil offered their 1942 patent to the government, which rejected it as cumbersome. Twenty years later, Sylvania built on the Lamarr-Antheil prototype, whose patent had expired, and this variation was installed on ships sent to blockade Cuba. It was eventually embedded in the U.S. nuclear command and control system, and today is the basis for "spread spectrum" cell phones. Aware of the irony, Lamarr's son Anthony Loder—his father was British actor John Loder—sells such devices in his Los Angeles electronics store.

Will the stigma of Hedy Lamarr's early nude scene ever fade? Perhaps it will now that *Ecstasy* is being reevaluated as a masterpiece, thus shifting the focus of the discussion. It also contains Lamarr's finest performance, indicating she was better suited to the miming of the silents than to the glossy MGM productions of the '30s and '40s. In recent years, the restored *Ecstasy* has been welcomed anew as a celebration of physical passion, a lyrical, soaring expression of nature whose beauty is echoed in the charms of its exquisite young star.

Eyes Wide Shut

Enquiring minds want to know

Directed by Stanley Kubrick; starring Tom Cruise,
Nicole Kidman (1999)

by Rob Nelson

WHEN STANLEY KUBRICK'S **EYES WIDE SHUT** WAS FINALLY, posthumously released in the summer of 1999, it didn't tell us very much about the sex lives of its then-married stars, Tom Cruise and Nicole Kidman. But it did prove definitively that the late director was one seriously perverse dude. Not *sexually* perverse, mind you: This unrivaled master of the Steadicam and the low-angle stare was far too much of a control freak to get jiggy, and indeed there's nothing of a carnal nature in his purportedly erotic parting shot that couldn't be found in one of the uncut Madonna videos from earlier that decade. Nor does such abstinence point to the auteur's sagging artistic virility near the end of his life, since even the young Kubrick of *Lolita* favored fucking with the viewer's head.

Even more than the postwar European cineastes who slyly titillated ticket buyers in exchange for the privilege of being inscrutably profound, the hermitic Kubrick lived to make intellectual sport of audience expectations. In this sense, his final work is the checkmate of a transcontinental chess tournament between Art and Commerce—the producer-director's strategy being to play both sides himself, without often leaving his Hertfordshire manse. Two of the pawns in this final match were Cruise and Kidman. And primarily on account of their box-office draw—a force exponentially increased by the apparent promise of catching them *in flagrante delicto*—*Eyes Wide Shut* opened big its first weekend. It was no surprise, and no faint praise, either, to note that the film was missing from most multiplexes only a month later. Not since Jean-Luc Godard's *Contempt* earned its title by making a Brechtian bore of Brigitte Bardot had a sextravaganza so systematically contrived to turn us off.

Based on the 1926 novella *Traumnovelle* by Arthur Schnitzler, *Eyes Wide Shut* is a ruthless tease and a deadpan farce—a sarcastic shaggy-dog story with a somnambulist's pace, a largely joyless film about joylessness, and as abstract and ambiguous (and brilliant) a study of marital "adventure" and reconciliation as Roberto Rossellini's *Voyage to Italy*.

But might there be a smidgen of '90s Hollywood in here too? Always an expert subverter of movies both high- and lowbrow, Kubrick may have been thinking of *Indecent Proposal* when he prepared *Eyes Wide Shut*. After all, the would-be water-cooler debate here involves whether Kidman's seemingly bored Central Park West homemaker tells her doctor hubby (Cruise) about her attraction to a naval officer in the interests of honesty or as a way of justifiably exacting a psychic toll. Then there's the matter of whether the doctor's subsequent search for love in all the wrong places is predicated on his justifiable need to get even with *her*. As for the heroine's fantasy, this (apparently) erotic dream is reenacted as a slurred succession of black-and-white images reeling through the mind of her (apparently) jealous husband; only the wife's prior confession of lust prevents the "love scene" from resembling a rape.

Such apocalyptic detonations of the viewer's desire were nothing new for a director whose swan song was widely and, in a way, quite accurately reviewed as "disappointing" and "not sexy." *Lolita* was an adult entertainment about child molestation; *Dr. Strangelove* was a screwball comedy about nuclear war; *2001* was a space odyssey almost entirely devoid of action; *A Clockwork Orange* and *Barry Lyndon* were ornate portraits of violent pathology; *The Shining* was a supernatural horror film about alcoholism and writer's block; and *Full Metal Jacket* was a war movie with a lone woman as the enemy. So . . . next up from the man who made HAL–9000 would be a double-star vehicle about "jealousy and sexual obsession"?

But of course. The auteur's interest in taking on and then twisting the iconography of arguably talented celebrities was hardly unprecedented. (See Ryan O'Neal as the pathetic social climber of *Barry Lyndon*.) Plus, human devolution begins in the bedroom, and so does *Eyes Wide Shut*, which flirts immediately with its promise to get up close and personal with the stars before revealing their characters (if not themselves) to be abundantly shallow. "Honey, have you seen my wallet?" asks Cruise's Dr. William Harford of Kidman's Alice, who's naked even before the main title appears and is ensconced on the toilet soon after. ("She didn't wash her hands," one observant moviegoer was heard to remark on opening night.)

Well aware of his actors' personae as developed onscreen and in the *National Enquirer,* Kubrick gleefully toys with the public's perception that Kidman is merely the woman behind the man—and that the man, heaven forbid, might not be a ladies' man. Indeed, no sooner has the mentally cuckolded Bill hit the streets in search of risky business than the top gun gets gaybashed by some drunken frat boys who in any other film would represent Cruise's core audience. A Tom Cruise character called a "faggot" by his fellow real men? What kind of sick summer blockbuster is this?

To the Cruise faithful, overheard dissing the star's latest film after an opening-night screening, what seemed simply "stupid" and "unbelievable" might really be that their hero has to rely on a stereotypically limp-wristed and eye-batting hotel clerk (Alan Cumming) for information about the movie's ostensible mystery. Or that during a decadent orgy, the passive, politically correct protagonist feels tempted to heed the calling of an impatient cabdriver. Or that before the night is through he politely pays almost a thousand dollars for services tangentially related to the procurement of sex without actually getting off. Or that his would-be sexual transgression carries all the excitement and danger of a sweaty man's late-night run to the porno store while his wife is at home sleeping. Or that he finally breaks down and *cries* at the sight of . . . a painted mask.

During the big orgy set-piece (another deadening ritual in a movie that's full of deadening rituals), Kubrick riffs on the ticket buyer's own recent transaction by having one of Bill's fellow patrons ask whether he's having a good time. "Well," our hero wearily replies, "I've had an interesting look around." And there, in a nutshell, is the experience of *Eyes Wide Shut.*

Eyes Without a Face

Don't make me over

Directed by Georges Franju; starring Pierre Brasseur,
Alida Valli, Edith Scob (1959)

by Kenneth Turan

FROM ITS EXPRESSIVE TITLE TO ITS BRILLIANT, UNSETTLING
images, *Eyes Without a Face* (*Les yeux sans visage* in the original French) is an
elegant shocker no viewer has ever forgotten. One of the least known of the
acknowledged classics of horror, it's a model of insinuating, understated terror, an experience no one should even think of missing.

Directed by Georges Franju, *Eyes* was released in 1959, when its pulp
subject matter and disturbing imagery—not to mention its undercurrent of
erotic tension that is more potent for being almost subliminal—led many European critics to dismiss it. In the United States, its fate was worse: It was
dubbed and released under the improbable title *The Horror Chamber of Dr.
Faustus.*

Although this film (Franju's second feature, made at age forty-seven) and
1963's *Judex* have a small and passionate following, Franju, who died in
1987, remains underappreciated here. The cofounder (along with the better-
known Henri Langlois) of the Cinemathèque Francais, Franju worked for
years as a director of documentary shorts, including the slaughterhouse-
themed *La sang des bêtes* that earned him the respect of the younger French
New Wave filmmakers. A surrealist who believed with compatriot Jean
Cocteau that "the more you touch on mystery, the more important it is to be
realistic," Franju's ability overcame all obstacles. "What is artificial ages badly

and quickly," he wrote. "Dream, poetry, the unknown must all emerge out of reality itself. The whole of cinema is documentary, even the most poetic. What pleases is what is terrible, gentle, and poetic."

Eyes is a series of images that burn themselves into your subconscious. It was shot by the great cameraman Eugen Shuftan, who won an Oscar for black-and-white cinematography for the very different *The Hustler* two years later. Every visual is carefully thought out and brilliantly composed, creating a world simultaneously real and surreal. With its ability to go deeply into our fears, this is a motion picture that captures the texture of nightmare as convincingly as it's ever been done on film.

The idea for *Eyes* was developed by several writers, including first assistant director (and future director) Claude Sautet, and also Pierre Boileau and Thomas Narcejac, whose novels became Henri-Georges Clouzot's *Diabolique* and Alfred Hitchcock's *Vertigo*. A young woman, her eyes untouched but the rest of her face "a vast open wound," has disappeared from a clinic where she was taken after a terrible automobile accident. Meanwhile, her father, the celebrated Dr. Génessier (Pierre Brasseur, more impassive and unbending than he was in *Children of Paradise*), lectures on the potential of the heterograft, the transplanting of living tissue from one human being to another.

It turns out that the doctor's ideas are more than theoretical. Helped by his diabolical assistant Louise (*The Third Man*'s Alida Valli), this brilliant madman has been kidnapping young women in Paris, removing the skin from their faces, and attempting a transplant on the visage of his daughter Christiane (Edith Scob), hidden away in the attic of his château. How the relentless doctor (who tinkers with a pack of constantly howling dogs in his spare time), the devoted Louise, and Christiane most of all manage to cope with the effects of his horrific experimentation is the frame for this singular film.

Despite its gruesome plot, one of the hallmarks of *Eyes* is its relative austerity. In general, there is little that is blatantly horrific that Shuftan's discreet black-and-white camera allows us to see. The reason, Franju explained, is that he envisioned *Eyes* as "an anguish film. It's a quieter mood than horror . . . more internal, more penetrating. It's horror in homeopathic doses." In part because of this delicacy, Franju's and Shuftan's remarkable gifts for the visual make this the spookiest of movies, filled with elegant and poetic images that express longing, terror, and despair. Aided by Maurice Jarre's unsettling music, everything that appears onscreen—from the doctor's shiny black Citroen and Louise's shinier black raincoat to the birdlike Christiane's oversize Givenchy housecoats to the final image, one of the most unforget-table ever created—is meticulously calculated to create unease.

A departure from the film's visual discretion is its most classic horror scene, an unflinching look at one of the doctor's blasphemous face-peeling operations. Though in terms of blood and special effects the sequence is pris-tine by today's dubious standards, it remains disturbing enough to make the skin crawl and keep crawling.

Even more psychologically unsettling are the sequences that show Chris-tiane floating around the château like a dispossessed ghost, saying things like, "My face frightens me, my mask frightens me more." For over her rav-aged face she wears one of Franju's most telling inspirations, a thin plastic mask with holes cut out for her untouched eyes, a neo-Noh object both ex-pressionless and expressive that creates the powerful sense of poignancy and loss that is the film's most impressive achievement.

While other motion pictures have obvious predecessors and successors, *Eyes* stands apart from all others, a film alone. But be warned. Like a nightmare that never ends, this is a vision of madness, loneliness, and, yes, horror, that demands to be viewed over and over again. It is that haunting, and that good.

Possession: What You Missed

by Gerald Peary

Few people know about Andrzej Zulawski's sexually bizarre *Possession* (1981). Those who do cling fervently to the 81-minute American tape version while cursing the unavailability of the Ukrainian-born, Polish-based director's 127-minute cut. What are they missing in those additional 46 minutes? I've seen it: even crazier, more excessive stuff!

If your taste is off-off-center kooky, *Possession* simply cannot be missed. Over the top? Try sailing out of the stratosphere. It's a rabid Polanski baying at the moon and Rosemary greedily balling a horned monster so she can have the devil's infant. It's Hitchcock bloody and buck naked, the *Psycho* bodies piling up and left to rot, a sliced Marion next to a diced detective Arbogast.

Here's a bit of the story: A wired young Brit, Mark (Sam Neill), comes home to Cold War Berlin after an espionage assignment in Russia. His French wife, Anna (Isabelle Adjani), doesn't want him anymore. She's wild-eyed, tormented, determined to leave him even though they have a son. What's up?

Mark, a frenzied, crazy-acting man, only gets loonier as he races about West Berlin trying to figure out how and why he's lost his wife, and to whom. "He makes love to me all night," brags Anna of her mystery beau. Is it Anna's German lover, Heinrich (Heinz Bennent), another of the movie's space shots? No. Anna has moved far beyond her merely mortal boyfriend—enter *The Twilight Zone*—to a supernatural lover apparently spawned from her very id.

In a dandy visual payoff, Anna's new amour turns out to be a large, lizardy, bloodsoaked thing with wormy tentacles. To visit with it, to eyeball it, is, for a guy, to die. Each time some bloke sees this gross-out sex creature, he's driven into a mad, whirling-dervish fit, and a spellbound Anna scotches him.

These brutal scenes are definitely inspired by Catherine Deneuve's stoned-out executions in Polanski's *Repulsion*. But Zulawski pushes further. There are doppelgangers of Mark and Anna that I don't begin to understand. There's a long scene in the Berlin metro of Anna swooning like a suicidal Ophelia on her way to an operatic miscarriage.

Don't worry: Even the 81-minute version preserves the scene that everybody waits and waits to see. Mark walks into the bedroom of that empty apartment behind the Berlin Wall where Anna's trysts take place. His wife's on her back, naked as Lady Godiva. She doesn't even notice him because she's so enraptured—so wrapped up—with that which lies on top of her . . . writhing! Writhing! ∎

The Fabulous Baker Boys
Blues brothers

Directed by Steve Kloves; starring Michelle Pfeiffer, Jeff Bridges, Beau
Bridges (1989)

by Jay Carr

YOU REMEMBER **THE FABULOUS BAKER BOYS.** IT'S AN AFTER-
hours nocturne of dead-solid serendipity, ultra-romantic without being the
least bit sentimental, weaving in and out of the lives of its failed musicians
like a sax or piano around a throbbing bass line. Its signature key, and catalyst, is Michelle Pfeiffer's torch singer, poured into a low-cut, claret-colored
gown, sprawling atop the ebony lid of a grand piano, making love to Jeff
Bridges at the keyboard by making proxy love to her hand mike.

In less expert hands, the song she's singing, "Making Whoopee," would be
self-immolatingly campy. Here it's simultaneously bittersweet, sultry, improb-
ably full of promise. After the New Year's Eve gig they've performed is over
and the celebrants have crawled off, Pfeiffer and Bridges make love in the deserted hotel banquet room against a party's-over backdrop of confetti turned
to litter, balloons that have descended from ceiling to floor, empty ringside
tables. The scene is sexy because you feel Pfeiffer's sexually confident singer
relaxing into the comfort her skin tells her is on the way when Bridges's fin-
gertips begin massaging her neck and back. There's a dollop of solace.

Never more than at this moment do we become aware that we're watching a movie about bruised survivors deciding how much of their hearts to
expose. But apart from gauging how much vulnerability to allow, there's a
wonderful sexual tension and release in the scene (which discreetly fades to

black). That's because we feel their coupling is the end stage in a mating dance that began building the night before, with their fumbling awkwardly in their adjoining suites, trying to figure out how to play the next few minutes, ending unconsummated as a hot trumpet solo to "Do Nothing Till You Hear from Me" wryly mocks their inaction. So the segue to "Making Whoopee" is not only earned, it's sweet. The coupling offers a sense of release because we have shared its long build.

The film's title is nothing but ironic. *The Fabulous Baker Boys*, brothers Jack and Frank, played by real-life siblings Jeff and Beau Bridges, are lounge losers, having spent fifteen years barely hanging on. The dark, kitschy, crumbling Seattle-area lounges that hire them are the dinosaur burial grounds of nightlife—perhaps of all life. Offering a wonderful counterpoint between a fragile interior world of feelings and the visual tonalities, tropes, and iconography of moody, bluesy '40s movies about musicians, *Baker Boys* is a string of riffs on pent-up feelings, powered by three enormously simpatico performances.

Jeff Bridges's Jack climbs into his tux each night with a slept-in smile, zombies his way through the act, pretends to be a solid citizen like his worrywart brother, Beau Bridges's Frank, when he'd rather play jazz in cellar clubs. Jack spends a lot of time avoiding his feelings. Frank spends a lot of time disguising his feelings in his focus on suburban stability. Jack, in his picturesquely seedy downtown loft, dresses in hipster black. Frank, offstage, wears fuzzy cardigans, blinkers himself by preferring to believe that he's the one keeping irresponsible Jack on track. Frank ignores the fact that the clearly more talented Jack has submerged his dreams to keep Frank happy.

Among other things, *The Fabulous Baker Boys* is a story of brotherly love. The siblings' feelings for each other are never superseded by the uneasy romance instigated by Pfeiffer's diamond-in-the-rough singer (with the tongue-in-cheek name of Suzie Diamond). Not that that's all she instigates. There's a wry dregs-of-showbiz humor in the portrayal of the brothers' sagging lounge act and the venues it plays. The act has turned into living Muzak because that's what the customers want. You can't help smiling as the commodification of their art is epitomized by their umpteenth version of "Feelings," through which they soldier on with cosmic ennui.

When the brothers decide to stave off obsolescence by hiring a singer, and Pfeiffer stumbles in on a broken heel an hour and a half late for her audition, they're more ready for change than they consciously know. We know, and they're about to find out, that beret-wearing, cigarillo-smoking, flair-filled Suzie, Seattle's answer to Sally Bowles in her ankle-length, camel-hair polo coat, is about to reconnect them to the world of vital impulse.

Suzie knows enough to know that it isn't enough to be confident in her sexual magnetism; to put a song across, she must be hot-wired to the feelings she's singing about. Once she unfurls a rendition of "More Than You Know" from which you can see wisps of smoke curling, it's as if the film and the Baker Boys' going-nowhere lives have found their compass. No matter how the brothers handle the jolt from their comfortable routines, you sense their relief at having something to fight about apart from who came in late on "Little Green Apples."

Writer-director Steve Kloves knows his *Casablanca,* and extends its cabaret mythology. He savors his characters, including the minor ones—like the endearingly tinny-voiced non-starter played by Jennifer Tilly. His emotional generosity, apart from the buoyantly disarming performances he draws from Pfeiffer and the fabulous Bridges brothers, even connects smartly with the sublime insouciance of the fabulous Epstein brothers' script for the gin-mill magic of *Casablanca.*

Kloves not only has the big, important stuff in place. He doesn't miss a trick with the minor-key material either. When Suzie describes a job doing voice-overs for vegetable commercials, Jack asks, deadpan, "Which vegetables?" Suzie ripostes: "Carrots. Peas. All the important ones." From every backlit scene of rain-slicked back-alley heartbreak to every shot of the yin-yang piano lids, fitting together but not fitting together, there's a lot of fabulousness to go around here—even the morning after.

Femme Fatale
Girl out of time

Directed by Brian De Palma; starring Rebecca Romijn-Stamos,
Peter Coyote, Antonio Banderas (2002)

by Stephanie Zacharek

IN BRIAN DE PALMA'S **FEMME FATALE**, THE DEADLY BLONDE
schemer of the title lives—or, more accurately, dreams—nearly a tenth of one
lifetime in just a few seconds. Laure Ash, played by Rebecca Romijn-Stamos,
is an American in France who makes a living off her wicked ways as if they
were secretarial skills: Thievery, deceit, and lace-trimmed stockings (panty-
hose are for pantywaists) are the tools of her trade, the shorthand squiggles
of her heartlessness. Although she's on the run from two thugs she's double-
crossed, Laure has a chance to sink into a hot bath and, like any working girl
worn out from earning a paycheck, she grabs it. The warmth of the water
lulls her to sleep, and in that miniature dream-lifetime she adopts the identity of a demure French widow (a woman who has tragically lost her husband and child); meets a rich, charming American (Peter Coyote) on an
airplane; marries him and moves to the States; returns to France seven years
later, where she seduces a clueless, gorgeous, underemployed photographer
(Antonio Banderas); and nearly pulls off a ransom scheme that would leave
her in luxury for eternity. Within those seconds, Laure lives more of a life
than most of us get around to in ten years, and the possibilities of that life are
orgasmically thrilling. To hell with *la petit mort*, those few seconds of bliss
most of us settle for. Laure will have the big life or none at all, even if it lasts
less than a minute.

Femme Fatale is such a meticulously calculated picture that it could have been made by Laure herself, as if, exasperated by the thick, milky stupor of the male gaze (or at least sick of hearing about it as a theory), she has hijacked the camera for her own glory.

Femme Fatale is an intensely sexual picture from the first frame. In its beautifully sustained opening sequence—which has all the pageantry and subterranean sensuality of an Ecclesiastical procession—Laure stalks and seduces a serpentine model named Veronica, played by Rie Rasmussen. (Her goal is to drive Veronica wild with ecstasy while removing the gold-and-diamond snake brassiere coiled languidly around her breasts. Their assignation takes place in a Cannes Film Festival ladies' room stall, whose rippled glass doors allow us to see, tantalizingly, practically nothing.) Much later, Laure performs an extraordinarily saucy striptease in a grungy Paris dive. (Her sole motive: to start, just for fun, a fight between a meaty lowlife she's met there and Banderas. She perches on a pooltable, dressed in bra, panties, and shiny, stiletto-heeled pirate boots, giggling with juicy glee as the men beat the crap out of each other.)

While the soft-core trappings of *Femme Fatale* are great fun, they're not the heart of the movie's eroticism. It's Laure's voraciousness that makes the picture thrum. She's its lifeblood, and De Palma neither flirts with nor judges her; an accomplished trickster himself, he identifies with her too much to condescend to her. Laure, like all great characters, seems to exist outside a world of the author's invention. She isn't the archetypal femme fatale, that convenient repository for male fears of womanly treachery and dominance; in other words, she's not a fantasy a man can easily control. She's too wild for that. She never puts us at ease, and yet we desperately want her to win every conniving little game. As Romijn-Stamos plays her (in a performance that has been deeply and unjustly underrated), Laure is a Hitchcock blonde by way of Debbie Harry, an haute rock 'n' roller who makes champagne-colored cashmere look as dangerous as black leather. If Laure were a double agent, her code name could be "Blondie," an almost-anagram for her chief rule for living: Her lie is her bond.

Laure is irresistible to men because of her ability to conform so perfectly to what they want to see in her. With Banderas, she plays the vixen who's so highly sexualized she can't be bothered with foreplay: "You don't have to lick my ass—just fuck me!" With Coyote, she plays the sorrowful French widow who, hoping to make a fresh start in America, does not yet speak good English. As he struggles to tell her how wonderful he thinks her native country is, her eyes mist over, as if scanning some imaginary horizon for the soul of her lost child. She needs to leave France, she tells him just before she moves in for the soft-sell kill: "I lost my bebe zere!"

And yet Laure's code of honor is highly attuned—it simply has nothing to do with her libido. She may have complete control over men, but she's not the stereotypical "man's woman" who has no use for members of her own sex. In fact, her only true allegiances are to women—to Veronica, the snake-bra girl, her partner in crime, and to Lily, the grieving widow she impersonates in her almost-life. The great joke of *Femme Fatale* is that it pretends to play to male fantasies when it's really dashing them mercilessly. The picture is filled with men who desperately want to be the center of Laure's universe, and instead of siding with the suckers, De Palma keeps the focus on Laure. (How could we possibly look away from her?) Even Banderas, who feigns indifference, is hopelessly ensnared.

But Laure will be no one's fantasy but her own—just as her bath-time dream, her minute of imagined life, belongs to her alone. Laure is a metaphor for many things, chiefly our perception of the "bad girl" in movie history. But she also represents the intense privacy of our sexuality, an essential unknowability that we can't share even with our most intimate partners. That's not a particularly comforting state of affairs, which is why, in our efforts to connect with others, we rail against it: We try to become the person of our lover's dreams, and they ours. What is Laure but an exaggerated version of that same impulse? A dream girl in café-au-lait Hermès one minute and Batman-sleek Gaultier the next, she tells you everything you want to hear. Not listening between the lines is what gets you in trouble.

Why Vertigo?

by Amy Taubin

"Can you explain," asked Brian De Palma, his tone both earnest and plaintive, "why I'm still obsessed with *Vertigo*?"

It was 2002, the same year *Vertigo* took the No. 2 spot on *Sight and Sound* magazine's "Ten Greatest Films Poll," finishing just behind that warhorse *Citizen Kane*. I was interviewing De Palma prior to the release of his most delirious and liberating *Vertigo* homage, *Femme Fatale*, and I was a bit startled—because if De Palma didn't know the answer after all these years, who would?

Here's the rap I use on twenty-year-old film students who just don't get *Vertigo*: Film is the most fetishistic art medium, and *Vertigo*, the most fetishistic of films, speaks directly to what is perverse and irresistible in cinema—that it is a substitute and shield for what is referred to as "real life," and that if you are invested in the substitutes and shields that cinema promises and occasionally delivers, then this film is the mirror of your psyche.

There's an incredibly revealing statement by Hitchcock in the invaluable book *Vertigo* by Dan Auiler. Auiler quotes a letter Hitchcock wrote to Maxwell Anderson, whom he was trying to enlist to do a rewrite of the *Vertigo* screenplay. "I should make it clear," Hitchcock wrote, "that the structure has been organized on the basis of telling two stories. First the 'front story,' which is the one the audience is looking at, and second the 'big story,' which is the conspiracy and which is only revealed to the audience in the final scene." (In fact, Hitchcock made a last-minute decision to reveal the conspiracy to the audience half an hour before James Stewart's deluded protagonist Scotty finally figures out he's been played.) The problem, Hitchcock went on to explain, was to make the "front story" so seductive that the audience's attention never wavers from it. In other words, the narrative is constructed so that the audience is involved in a fetishistic relationship with the film, just as Scotty is with Madeleine (Kim Novak), a woman who is not what she seems. We fall for the ravishing images, the swooning score, the passionate depiction of love, loss, and déjà vu which comprise the front story in order to shield ourselves from the ugliness of the "big story"—which is about a husband who murders his wife for her money, manipulates two people (Madeleine and Scotty) into becoming accessories to murder, and gets away scot-free.

It's the cold, hard truth of the "big story" and the way Hitchcock reveals to us our propensity to disavow it by fetishizing the love story (and we do it whether we've seen the movie once or fifty times) that accounts for the devastating power of *Vertigo*. ■

La Femme Nikita

Good grooming

Directed by Luc Besson; starring Anne Parillaud, Jeanne Moreau,
Tcheky Karyo, Jean-Hughes Anglade (1990)

by David Edelstein

THE POSTER IS A POWERFUL COME-ON: A YOUNG WOMAN IN A
supine crouch, with short black hair and a little black dress hiked all the way
to the tops of her thighs, her long stems ending in a pair of ladylike heels. Big,
dark, gamine eyes—and a big, dark gun. This was 1990, early in the "chicks
with dicks" era of action films, and the image was more striking than it would
be today. The actress, Anne Parillaud, had a whiff of what would come, later
in the decade, to be called "heroin chic": women on the runway programmed
to walk the walk and pose the pose, but with a vibe that made them seem
hard and faraway—untouchable. The combination of subjugation and resistance is tantalizing. And it's that combination that infuses *La Femme Nikita*.

In France it was called, simply, *Nikita*, but the American retitling was inspired. Written and directed by Luc Besson, the movie is a *Pygmalion* story
(that's Shaw's *Pygmalion*, not the myth) about the way in which the feral
junkie and murderer Nikita—the name itself is tough and unyielding—is
taught to dress and make herself up and act like a lady. The twist is that it's a
secret government agency that schools her, that a failure to accept "feminiza-
tion" would mean immediate death, and that the job she's being groomed to
do is assassinate people she has never seen for reasons she doesn't know.

It's a ludicrous plot. But as a dramatization of the ways in which society
both empowers and shackles *la femme*, it's unusually potent. At first, Nikita

resists her training, but two things bring her around: fear of death, of course, and a sixtyish woman named Amande, played by Jeanne Moreau. The woman resides in a plush, Old World suite above the high-tech warehouse agency compound—a place where you can almost smell the musky scent of perfume, cosmetics, and age. Besson exploits the faded allure of Moreau, who once drove Jules and Jim mad with desire. Now, she gazes at her wrinkled hands and says, "They were pretty once. But that's the past." She explains to Nikita, "There are two things without limits: the feminine and the means to exploit it."

And so, in Besson's parable, Nikita has unlimited power within the most rigid constraints—power that is hers only if she surrenders her autonomy and individuality to a patriarchal state. This would be quite a feminist message if Besson didn't madly objectify and fetishize his leading lady, with whom he was sleeping. The film's real focus often seems to be the aforementioned leggy crouch with gun, and the tremulousness of Parillaud's flesh in her bra and panties as she points a long, long rifle at a target. Nikita is at once a messenger of death and a damsel in distress.

The two images cited above are the heart of *La Femme Nikita*, and the sequences that surround them are the film's biggest turn-ons. The stage is set for the first—the crouch—when Nikita's agency mentor, Bob (Tcheky Karyo), takes her out to a posh restaurant for her birthday; it's the first time she has emerged from the compound since she was brought there years earlier. Bob's birthday present turns out to be a semiautomatic, and he abandons Nikita with instructions to shoot a man at a nearby table and make her escape through a window in the bathroom. That window is bricked up: Part of her test is to cope with obstacles and misdirection. When she returns to the agency in a teeming rain, having proven herself a bravura escape artist in a tense shoot-out in the restaurant kitchen, stockings ripped, eye make-up running, she kisses Bob passionately, then announces that she'll never kiss him again. She knows he's smitten with her, and she has learned to use her femininity as a weapon. The man to whom she does give herself sexually—a sensitive grocery-store cashier, Marco (Jean-Hughes Anglade), whom she seduces a short time after being sent out into the world—will never know her other side, the one primed for phone calls out of the blue and brusque directions to kill.

In the second seminal sequence, Nikita abruptly receives orders during a blithe, romantic Venice holiday. She must shoot from the hotel bathroom—

in her skimpy underwear, with her lover on the nearby bed and no lock on the door. She peers through the scope at a group of people across the canal and waits to hear, through headphones, which one she must shoot. It turns out to be the lone woman in the party, and Nikita hesitates while the male voice tells her over and over to fire. She has been depersonalized, forced to murder her own kind with an ostentatiously phallic weapon. It is a kind of rape—of her soul, if not her body. But her body is violated, too, by the camera. While she writhes in indecision, the audience is permitted to ogle her toned legs and trim backside.

The "chicks with dicks" genre is fascinating because it leaves women feeling empowered (it can even be called inspirational and progressive) while catering to the same voyeurism that has always been central to movies' appeal. A pioneer, Diana Riggs's Emma Peel in *The Avengers*, was knocked unconscious almost as often as she karate-chopped the bad guys. And before blasting the walking *vagina dentata* in *Alien*, the macho Sigourney Weaver had to be shown in her scanties. Even in this genre, the "male gaze" remains unobstructed. Besson, at least, maintains a tension in *La Femme Nikita*: Under our salacious gaze, his heroine squirms. After a gruesomely botched mission, she leaves both her men, vanishing into the city and out of our grasp. Along with Marco and Bob, we are left with a gnawing desire and a feeling of emptiness.

In 1993, *La Femme Nikita* was remade as an American thriller with Bridget Fonda called *Point of No Return*, and that title is a fair testament to the film's flaccidity. It is, beat for beat, set-piece for set-piece, a copy of the original, but Fonda is all wrong. She's a better actress than Parillaud, but she has a soft and needy presence: There's no erotic tension between her subjugation and her fierce self-containment. The allure of that *La Femme Nikita* poster is nowhere in evidence. Perhaps, as Besson so vividly demonstrates, we need our sex objects to be elusive—to keep reminding us that they can never be wholly under our control. Perhaps the woman in the little black dress is never sexier than when she trains her weapons on us. All of them.

Forever Mine
Why do birds sing so gay?

Directed by Paul Schrader; starring Joseph Fiennes,
Gretchen Mol (1999)

by Charles Taylor

FOREVER MINE IS ONE OF THE LUSHEST AMERICAN MOVIES
ever made. Its tenderness and sweeping romance represent the most fluid
and openly emotional directing Paul Schrader has done. From Angelo
Badalamenti's ravishing score to the glowing pastels of John Bailey's cinematography to the sensuality of the performances by Joseph Fiennes and
Gretchen Mol, *Forever Mine* is awash in the heightened emotion that's the
lifeblood of movies. It's that most movie-ish of genres, a film noir romance,
yet there's nothing ironic or self-conscious about it. Schrader tells the story
as if he were encountering this sort of outsized romanticism for the first time,
and he makes us feel *we're* encountering it for the first time. *Forever Mine,*
which moves with the grace of a great soul ballad, offers a pleasure unique to
movies and rock 'n' roll: the sense of being swept up and carried along by
something bigger than yourself. At its most basic, *Forever Mine* is about how
the music of romance becomes sweeter but also more painful with the years.

So how come you've never heard of it? The company that financed it went
under before a distribution deal was finalized, and its assets were taken over
by its Dutch insurers, who sold off its remaining unreleased films as a package to the highest cable bidder. *Forever Mine* has shown up at film festivals
and on cable, and DVD copies can be found, but one of the greatest American movie romances is still waiting to be discovered.

It opens in 1987 on a flight to New York. A well-dressed man with a partially disfigured face sits in first class, a thin beard his attempt to hide his deformity. He seems formal, distant. Something about him—the expensive clothes, the flashiness of his associate in the next seat, the suggestion that, if pushed, he could become dangerous—says "drug dealer."

The faint strains of Timmy Thomas's "Why Can't We Live Together" come over the soundtrack and the present dissolves. The man's pained, remote visage is replaced by his younger self, clean-shaven and smooth-faced, his body language now open and expectant. The closed-off confines of the airplane have given way to the sunny vistas of 1973 Miami Beach, a world of possibilities. You can feel the sun and the undulating melody of Thomas's lone hit as a balm.

The young man is Alan (Fiennes), a cabana boy at a plush beachfront resort who carries his dreams so close they're like an invisible cloak. One day, Alan is blessed with a vision, a beautiful blonde woman rising from the waves in a white bathing suit as if Neptune were giving forth his greatest treasure. She's Ella (Gretchen Mol), a honeymooner vacationing with her politician husband, Mark (Ray Liotta). As soon as Alan sees her, he knows it's his purpose in life to be with her.

Forever Mine is a story of false accusation and revenge as epic as *The Count of Monte Cristo* (on which it's based), and also as simple and unwavering as the torch Alan carries in his heart. It's the story of how he and Ella fall in love, are separated, and reunite years later when Alan steps back into Ella's life in another guise. More than that, *Forever Mine* is about the tango between purity and corruption, duty and dreams, masks and true identities.

The film takes place in 1973, when Nixon's presidency was beginning to crumble, and in 1987, when the Reagan era was about to segue into the Bush era and a far more insidious (and accepted) corruption than Watergate. Which is to say that all of *Forever Mine* takes place in a time when rogues rule, a time not conducive to heroic ideals. Alan and Ella are like the lovers atop the Berlin Wall in David Bowie's "Heroes," beautiful and foolish enough to proclaim that their love will overcome all obstacles.

The ruler of the roost here is Ella's husband, Mark. He's the sort of weasely small-timer with just enough juice to scotch the lovers' hopes and dreams. A fixer who's worked his way up from crooked construction deals to a seat on the city council, Mark bridges the movie's two eras. He seems to have spent the six years between the fall of Nixon and the rise of Reagan biding his time, waiting until his greed for power could be brought out in the open. (Jowly and with his hair slicked back from his wavy widow's peak, Liotta even looks a little like Nixon.) A ferretlike, volatile actor, Liotta carries his old gangster and thug parts into the role; he's still playing a criminal, but the kind who's achieved respectability.

Within the conventions of love stories and film noir, *Forever Mine* paints a complex view of the '80s. Schrader gets at the way the decade blurred political, corporate, and criminal life, and posits the reckless emotion embodied by Alan and Ella as an opposing force. Love stories traditionally put obstacles in the paths of its lovers; here those obstacles are the seductions of the decade itself. The film's tension derives from the lovers' temptation to succumb to the corruption that's in the air. Ella has tried to get Alan out of her mind and settle into the shellacked role of supportive political wife. Alan hasn't come close to forgetting Ella. But there's a danger he'll lose himself on the road he's chosen to reclaim her. Having trusted the advice of his friend Javier (Vincent Laresca) that the way to power and respect is through dealing drugs, Alan has stepped into a new identity as the international "banker" Esquema. He reenters Ella's life when Mark, about to be indicted for corruption, calls on Esquema to broker a deal with government attorneys. The stage is set for the characters to live up—or down—to their truest selves.

The soundtrack (songs like David Ruffin's "What Becomes of the Broken Hearted") functions like a statement of principles for Alan and Ella. The longing of the songs, their combination of the ethereal and earthly, and the way they hold out the possibility of loss, waft through the picture like Alan and Ella's unspoken vows. The love scenes between Fiennes and Mol are some of the most sensual in recent movies. It's not just the atmosphere Schrader establishes as they walk in the moonlight or sway to music in a beachside bar; it's the sustained sense of erotic discovery that exists between these two actors. In bed and out, Fiennes and Mol are so tuned into each other it's as if their hearts are transmitting invisible telegrams. Schrader makes us feel there's something at stake in their love.

The cruel irony of Gretchen Mol's career is that she was touted as the next big thing before any of her movies had been released, only to have those movies flop, while a performance that had the potential to make her a star went unseen. Ella is the movie's crucial role, a character torn between the wild romanticism and cold practicality represented by the two men, and Mol is superb. She combines delicacy with pragmatism, making you understand the need for security that attracts Ella to Mark, but also her knowledge that she's sold herself short. In one of the loveliest scenes, Ella reads *Madame Bovary* to a group of senior citizens and Mol transforms it into Ella's story. Mol could have settled for being the next glamorous movie blonde, but instead she puts tremulous flesh on the bones of that familiar icon.

Joseph Fiennes is often written about as if he is the matinee idol while his brother Ralph is the serious actor. There's an element of truth in that, and it's why Joseph is so pleasurable to watch. He's got fire in him (while his brother displays ever more washed-out masochism). Alan lives so far inside his code of romantic valor, his belief that you live or die by love, that he's removed from ordinary life. He asks Ella, "Why do birds sing so gay?"—quoting Frankie Lymon almost unconsciously, as if song lyrics were the same thing as everyday speech. But he doesn't come off as crazy or scary. The movies teach us to trust beauty, and Schrader and his production team surround Alan with the sort of beauty—the fairy-tale-palace look of the hotel where he works; the silky perfection of the songs issuing from the radio; the stunning sight of Ella rising from the sea—that makes his ardor a natural response to the world around him. The two parts of the performance work beautifully: As Alan, he foreshadows the determination he'll show as Esquema, and as Esquema, he harks back to Alan's vulnerability. Fiennes is a genuine romantic hero because whether he's Alan the cabana boy or Esquema, he has a knight's dedication to his one true love.

Schrader stirs up that sort of feeling without parodying it or making it seem like a mere movie conceit. (And it's a measure of his bad luck that he achieved this in a time suspicious of that sweeping emotion.) Fiennes's performance is his guiding light; Schrader allows himself to be seduced by Alan as much as Ella is. At first, he watches Alan from the outside, fascinated that anyone could be so steadfast. By the end, he's made the same leap of faith Ella has. Like his lovers, Schrader has surrendered to the music.

Frankenstein Created Woman
Lab work

Directed by Terence Fisher; starring Peter Cushing,
Susan Denberg (1967)

by Chris Fujiwara

THE FOURTH IN HAMMER FILMS' FRANKENSTEIN SERIES,
Terence Fisher's underrated film finds Baron Frankenstein (Peter Cushing)
working on the theory that the soul stays within the body for at least an hour
after death. The execution by guillotine of his assistant, Hans (Robert Morris), and the subsequent suicide of Hans's lover, the deformed and crippled
Christina (Susan Denberg), enable the Baron to test his theory. He captures
Hans's soul and transplants it into Christina's body, while also correcting her
physical flaws and making her beautiful. At first, Christina has no consciousness of either part of her dual identity, but her first view of the town
guillotine unleashes Hans's vengeful, destructive nature, which takes hold of
her and drives her to kill the three young men who committed the crime for
which Hans was executed. Having completed this mission, Christina commits suicide again.

Hammer films are known for exploiting their actresses' physiques, and
Fisher's Dracula films for the studio marked a breakthrough in the explicit
association of vampirism with sexuality. But the director has rarely, if ever, received his due as a specialist in erotica. This neglect is understandable: Decorous and controlled, Fisher's horror films critique but also celebrate the
containment of the body and the repression of desire. His heroic figures, like
Peter Cushing's Van Helsing and Sherlock Holmes, are apparent celibates—

self-possessed, determined men of reason and close cousins to Cushing's ruthless, obsessed Baron Frankenstein. But in opposition to those stalwarts, Fisher's films offer an array of characters representing the attractions of Eros. None is more provocative than Christina in *Frankenstein Created Woman*.

Not that her function is to bring the Baron, metaphorically, into the Swinging Sixties. Publicity photos showed Denberg (a twenty-two-year-old Austrian model who had earlier graced Robert Gist's outlandish film version of Norman Mailer's *An American Dream*) on a lab set, wearing only a white loincloth and bandeau, while Cushing's Baron hovers, adjusts her garments, or lifts her in his arms. His face is a thin-lipped mask of dispassion on which anything might be read. No scenes corresponding to this photo session appear in the film; when it comes time for the Baron to have his way with his subject's body in the lab, the scene chastely dissolves from him outlining his plans for her dredged-up corpse to a close-up of the resuscitated Christina's bandaged face, some time having elapsed. The lab-bikini photo shoot is the Hammer version of Denberg's August 1966 *Playboy* spread. It constructs for the film an alternate narrative (Frankenstein Makes Playmate), but one that confronts the erotic relationship between Frankenstein and Christina no more directly than the film itself. The question remains: Did they or didn't they?

The Baron presents himself as beyond all interest in the body (which is, of course, a supreme sign of sexual power). "Bodies are easy to come by, souls are not," he explains. He makes Hans's soul visible as a disc of white-yellow light hanging in midair between two umbrella-shaped reflectors. Nothing gives the ascetic Baron more pleasure than the sight of this soul. He's so abstracted from the physical that when Christina asks to see herself in a mirror, he replies, "What on earth for?," unable to comprehend why she should take any interest in her own appearance.

To lure the three young men to their doom, Christina wears a startling, low-cut blouse and adopts a bland pose of infinite sexual availability. To the first man, she is a prostitute, met loitering on the street in the middle of the night. To the second and third, she is a sexual adventuress, a libertine—a more advanced kind of prostitute. Money is never discussed. She offers, in addition to her body, the illusion that she gives it for nothing—which might flatter the beneficiary's estimation of his own charms, or might imply that she lacks all self-esteem, an erotic provocation in itself.

It's not insignificant that Christina never asks for payment from her client-victims. Money is a major theme throughout *Frankenstein Created Woman*: Neither the Baron nor his loyal collaborator, Dr. Hertz (a delightful comic performance by Thorley Walters), has any, and Hans must barter an overcoat for a bottle of champagne with which to celebrate the Baron's return from the frozen land of the dead. The three young men dress and behave like decadent aristocrats, but they can't pay the innkeeper for their wine.

If Christina is beyond money in a world consumed with commerce, it's because she practices a sacred rather than a commercial form of prostitution. She doesn't sell her body, she sacrifices it. With the three young men, she fuses feminine roles. Merely by sitting still and staring while the second victim wipes spilled wine from the lap of her skirt, she gets him to pounce on her and kiss her. With the third victim, she assumes a maternal tenderness, offering him food and solicitously leaning over him while he lies with his head in her lap. The first victim, lying in bed waiting for her, claims not to believe that she is real; indeed, she offers herself to all three as a dream girl, a male fantasy of the thoroughly malleable and maulable woman.

Christina's parting words to her "creator" are "Forgive me." Even in speaking this line, her ambivalence is dazzling. Frankenstein was more cruel to her than the men in her former life, such as her father, who wouldn't let her go out in public, or the three young men, who danced under her window singing, "You'll be a virgin till you're dead"—and yet she asks him to forgive her. The irony of Fisher's film is complete. Christina knows that, under patriarchy, her worth is measured by what she can be to, and for, men. She has tested this from two directions—as the ugly girl of no value and as the beautiful girl of infinite value. Her second suicide is both a protest and an acceptance—a duality perfectly captured in her "Forgive me." Her farewell look toward the camera conveys both pity and the ironic remorse of the prostitute about to take herself off the street for good.

The Garden of the Finzi-Continis
The walls come tumbling down

Directed by Vittorio De Sica; starring Dominique Sanda, Helmut Berger (1970)

by Desson Thomson

TO WATCH **THE GARDEN OF THE FINZI-CONTINIS,** VITTORIO DE Sica's saga of an aristocratic Jewish family faced with Mussolini's anti-Semitic laws, is to revisit a personal, distant past. I don't mean Ferrara, Italy, in the late 1930s, in which the film is set. I speak of my younger moviegoing days in 1970s Washington, when you could duck into the Circle Theater on Pennsylvania Avenue virtually any night and catch two art-house classics for a buck. (A $10 booklet gave you access to twenty films.)

Though the theater stank of things you didn't want to think about, having to do with the drunken souls sleeping in the front row, there were magical worlds on the screen above their snoring heads. The daily double feature was selected from a wealth of American cult classics (*Five Easy Pieces, Harold and Maude*) or European art films, such as *The Garden of the Finzi-Continis*.

De Sica's film was always a draw for me, but not so much for its artistic quality; it's estimable for its restraint, subtlety, and visual lyricism, but I've always found it vaguely stuffy and pretentious. I enjoyed it for quite another reason. I guess you could sum it up in two words: Dominique Sanda. She plays the central character in this drama, and she is also its erotic center.

Garden is suffused with the sexual potency of all those fairy tales about imprisoned damsels: Rapunzel, Sleeping Beauty. At the heart of those stories is a delicate, usually royal soul in her sexual and romantic prime who's either locked away in a castle or trapped under a spell. Her external situation is a metaphor, too, for her spiritual state. She sleeps inside herself. She awaits the undoing of the spell, or an act of simple goodness, or a plain old rescue so she can start living and loving.

What she's waiting for is a lover.

In *Garden,* that fairy-tale princess is Micòl (Sanda), the daughter of the Finzi-Continis. She has lived all her life inside a compound of wealth and privilege, with servants, tennis court, and an extensive, beautiful, walled garden. As Mussolini clamps down on the rights and freedom of Jews throughout Italy, Micòl's cloistered world gets smaller. She and her brother Alberto (Helmut Berger) continue to entertain their childhood friends—both Jewish and gentile—at their tennis court. (Their access to public courts is now restricted.) They dare not step outside for fear of detention. Micòl, who has bloomed into delectable womanhood, is a prisoner in her own castle.

Among the visitors are two men vying for Micòl. One is her middle-class, Jewish, childhood friend Giorgio (Lino Capolicchio), who feels a sense of entitlement to her heart. The other is a newcomer, Bruno Malnate (Fabio Testi), a darkly handsome gentile with socialist sympathies and supple, inviting arms. A friend of Alberto's, he comes often enough to attract Micòl. Giorgio senses that growing attraction, but the harder he presses his case, the more she retreats.

At one point, Giorgio and Micòl run into the gazebo to escape a sudden downpour. They sit in an abandoned street carriage while the rain beats down. Her white tennis shirt is soaked to the skin and radiantly transparent. Her face and hair are wet too. But when Giorgio tries to touch her, she pushes his hand away and runs back into the rain. Watching this scene, I have always felt an abstract possessiveness about Sanda; I'm glad to see her reject Giorgio. He's not right for her—too earnest, too wimpy. If it can't be me, at least bring on Malnate!

That rejection in the gazebo is just the beginning. Later, unable to contain himself, Giorgio kisses her passionately but she freezes like a doll, staring straight ahead. Half buried in shadow, she is beautiful yet chilly. Those unblinking eyes could be made of bright blue glass. When Giorgio forces himself on her, she complains she can't breathe. She tells him to leave. Forever.

"Lovers are compelled to overwhelm one another," she says to him. "But the way we are, alike as two drops of water, how could we overwhelm or tear each other to pieces? It would be like making love with a brother."

There it is. He disgusts her. She wants to be ravished, but not by him.

Giorgio is banished from this Garden of Eden. But he cannot keep away, so he scales the garden wall one night like he used to when he was a boy. He sneaks toward the gazebo and discovers Micòl naked in the darkness. Aware of his gaze, Micòl switches on the light to reveal herself in all her nudity. In front of her, Malnate sleeps peacefully.

It's a staggering moment. Not only is Micòl sleeping with Malnate, but she shoves the evidence in Giorgio's face; it's an act of pent-up eroticism and bare aggression.

It's also the harbinger of tragedy much greater than romantic and sexual rejection. In the coming Holocaust, Micòl's upscale, unattainable beauty and power will count for nothing. Like Giorgio, who comes from a middle-class Jewish family, the privileged Micòl is bound for extermination.

There is an inherent acceptance of cruelty in most fairy tales. Characters suffer, are killed, or lose love as a matter of course. Their tragedies are seen as a normal trademark of life. This gloomy atmosphere pervades *Garden*. And yet, there remains that frisson of cloistered sexuality—Micòl's puckery lips, blisteringly azure eyes, and ivory-smooth skin carry more heft for me than all that thematic sadness. Despite the bittersweet denouement, in which Micòl finds a moment of humane grace with Giorgio's father, there is really only one thought coursing through my head: Oh, for one night with that Italian princess in the gazebo, rain drumming on the roof, our tennis racquets tossed to the floor. Her shirt soaked. Just the two of us. Please.

Gilda

The girl can't help it

Directed by Charles Vidor; starring Rita Hayworth,
Glenn Ford, George Macready (1946)

by Jami Bernard

"ARE YOU DECENT?" ASKS GILDA'S NEW HUSBAND, HARDLY
awaiting her answer as he enters her boudoir with another man. "Me?" she
asks, flinging her flaming hair over her shoulders and cocking her glowing
face at the camera in one of cinema's most provocative screen entrances.

Decent? Gilda? Hardly! I remember the first time I saw that double-
entendre entrance, the first time I had ever seen a Rita Hayworth picture, in
fact. It was at a revival theater on Manhattan's Upper West Side. I remember
which seat I sat in; I can still taste that day. I was transfixed by Hayworth—
her glow, her hair, her audacity, and by the very idea that a movie could so
drip with sex and innuendo.

In Charles Vidor's strange, hot melodrama, Hayworth plays a girl so bad
that an awkward ending was tacked on to bank the flames. Those things you
think she did, she did none of them, we're told—"it was just an act, every bit
of it"—but this disclaimer is wedged in so haphazardly that we are free to
disregard it. Gilda is a slut. The girl can't help it.

It's not because she is bought and paid for that Gilda is the odd man out
in *Gilda*. The homosexual subtext between casino owner Ballin Mundson
(George Macready) and his trusted assistant Johnny Farrell (Glenn Ford) is
so thick you could run it through with a sword sheathed in a cane—the same
sword that Ballin shows Johnny when they meet one night on the Buenos

Aires wharf and which they later toast as their "friend." They promise that no woman will come between them, and Johnny subsequently rises to the rank of casino manager. It's the beginning of a beautiful friendship.

That goes sour when Ballin returns from a mysterious trip with a new wife in tow. One look at Gilda tossing her hair back in the bedroom and Johnny acts like a scorned lover, which perhaps he is—it's clear from the fast-and-furious double entendres that Johnny once knew Gilda quite well himself, and that it ended badly. Hate is such an exciting emotion, as Ballin points out and as everyone continues to affirm like a Greek chorus. The words "hate" and "love" are interchangeable in this screenplay, attributed to Jo Eisinger, E. A. Ellington, Marion Parsonnet, and an uncredited Ben Hecht. Expressions of longing are spit from tongues of fire. It is possible to read the movie the traditional way, with Johnny torn between loyalty to his employer and to his reawakened passion for the girl he's clearly been trying to forget. Gilda lifts a toast to the woman who brought him to this impasse: "Let's hate her!"

But it's hard to ignore the gay subtext, which describes a scenario in which Johnny really does hate Gilda for getting between him and his twin objects of desire, the boss man and his sword. When faced with whether to bail out Gilda when she's heading for trouble at the bar or to attend to Ballin, Johnny hesitates, then runs upstairs to the office. "Now we know," sighs Steven Geray's omniscient washroom attendant.

There's a third possibility. Just as Ballin can be considered a closet homosexual who makes nighttime visits to the waterfront, Johnny can be viewed as a closet heterosexual who is frustrated because Gilda has an uncanny ability to arouse him. She looks at his pants meaningfully when they dance, and in their charged flirtations Gilda taunts Johnny about his masculinity; hence the slap he gives her after her aborted public striptease to "Put the Blame on Mame."

Whichever direction the love triangle takes, *Gilda* is a coyly sadistic exercise where sex is a weapon that's constantly being unsheathed. Gilda flaunts her body and walks off with just about any guy who'll buy her a drink. (Being the boss's wife, you'd think her drinks would be free.) Johnny dutifully chauffeurs her to these hotel assignations out of some weird loyalty to Ballin, regarding Gilda as just so much "laundry."

"Did you teach her to swim?" Ballin asks suspiciously when Johnny brings Gilda home after-hours armed with some lame excuse. "I taught her everything she knows," he snaps, and we're back in double-entendre-ville. In any case, it's more likely that Gilda taught Johnny everything *he* knows, which would explain why he can't get over her. More than lust, pride is this movie's crown jewel.

Some of the dialogue is priceless. When haggling over just who would love to dance with whom, Gilda dismisses Johnny with, "The young man would love it, but he can't afford it." There are also dreadful clunkers, usually in the service of Gilda's unattractive self-effacement, wrapped in the guise of boastfulness: "If I'd been a ranch, they would have named me the Bar None."

The perfervid dialogue and sexual permutations become irresistibly frenzied and ridiculous. The movie is out of control. Johnny treats Gilda horrifically—refusing to sleep with her when they're later married, keeping her under house arrest with a portrait of the presumably dead Ballin gazing down sternly from the mantel.

However you look at this crazy movie, Hayworth's sexual magnetism carries the day. Even Glenn Ford looks like his testosterone is all bunched up in his face.

And then there's Hayworth's famous striptease. All she removes are two black satin gloves and a necklace. It's Gilda's willingness to go all the way that sticks. But the number that gives more bang for the buck is her earlier nightclub rendition of "Amado Mio," clothes intact, midriff bare. Hayworth undulates so subtly you marvel at the mechanics, and the movement is hypnotic, bewitching. The camera takes the point of view of a patron at a ringside table; you understand now how Ballin met Gilda, sitting at just such a table in just such a nightclub.

Everything we see as erotic or romantic about *Gilda* is in fact a bit perverted, even from behind the scenes. Hayworth was shy little Margarita Carmen Dolores Cansino from my own hometown of Jackson Heights, Queens. Her remarkable abilities to dance and seem sexually knowledgeable brought her a lifetime of older men who turned her into the fiction of Rita Hayworth. They changed her name, dyed her hair, went at her with electrolysis to raise her feral hairline. Columbia studio boss Harry Cohn was obsessed with her and hid microphones in her dressing room to monitor her conversations with Ford, who had been brought onto the picture late. Her husbands included Prince Aly Khan and Orson Welles. "Every man I've known has fallen in love with Gilda," Hayworth famously complained years later, "and wakened with me." Bad girls do pay a price.

Connie Nielsen: Empress Mine

by Charles Taylor

How many contemporary actresses could be believable as an empress? Not the bloodless Helen Hayes model of nobility that remains as boring as ever in Glenn Close, Meryl Streep, and all the other practitioners of "great lady" acting. But someone beautiful, regal, sexual enough to make you believe her subjects would know that hers was an empire worth dying for. Who? Angelina Jolie and Maggie Cheung, definitely. And then, and then?

Connie Nielsen. No one else even comes close.

We can carp all we want about the privilege of beauty—though if the notion offends us we probably should steer clear of movies—but when an actress carries herself with the combination of stateliness, strength, and tremulousness that the Danish-born Nielsen does in Ridley Scott's *Gladiator,* those privileges are well-earned.

As Lucilla, trying to keep clear of the machinations of her brother, the dangerously unbalanced emperor (Joaquin Phoenix), Nielsen balances cunning and fear in a way that feels cracklingly alive. She gives Lucilla's sense of encroaching danger a nearly sexual excitement as she struggles to maintain calm with the breathlessness of a woman on the verge of seduction. Nielsen invites our protection and makes it seem ridiculous that mere mortals might provide it.

And so the unconsciously sexual challenge Connie Nielsen seems to ask of her male costars in movie after movie is, "Are you worthy of me?" Nielsen's best work is when she has a costar strong enough to match her: Russell Crowe in *Gladiator* (together they contribute much of the gravity, sense of loss, and generally adult sensibility of this fashionably maligned movie); Nikolaj Lie Kaas as the brother-in-law she has an affair with in Susanne Bier's *Brothers*, and Tim Robbins in Brian De Palma's *Mission to Mars*.

Among the glories of De Palma's space drama—a great film that earned the most vicious and stupid reviews in recent memory—is its fully believable portrait of a happy marriage. Nielsen and Robbins (in one of his most likable performances), as married crew members on a rescue mission to the red planet, play marriage as a relaxed, ongoing sexual duet. Canoodling while they're supposed to be conducting a drill, their ease is accentuated by zero gravity, which makes it look as if they're luxuriating in bed after lovemaking. The zero gravity adds even more to an ecstatic scene where they twirl through the air to Van Halen's "Dance the Night Away."

Then, having given us this effortlessly sensual connection, De Palma, with the cruelty of the artists who affect us most deeply, takes it away. In one of the finest scenes he's ever directed, one that reverses his great theme of the man unable to save the woman, Robbins saves Nielsen's life at the cost of his own. We're left with the sight of these two people staring at each other across the untraversable vastness of space, adrift physically but, with the convenient inadequacy of technology, able to talk to each other as if they were back in that cockpit nuzzling. It's a devastating tableau of loss, not its least affecting detail the face of an empress who has lost the brave explorer ready to conquer new worlds with her at his side. ■

Great Expectations
Another green world

Directed by Alfonso Cuarón; starring Robert De Niro,
Gwyneth Paltrow, Ethan Hawke (1998)

by Stephanie Zacharek

ALFONSO CUARÓN'S ARDENT REIMAGINING OF CHARLES
Dickens's *Great Expectations* is a love story about Florida and New York,
about the sea and the rain, and about the shifting, shimmery surface of memory. Ethan Hawke is Finn, a young painter with a shot at a glittering New
York career, but everything he loves best—and every force that has shaped
him—radiates from Florida, that moist, sunwashed not-quite-paradise where
he spent his childhood. Finn is accustomed to the sea: He's been raised by a
fisherman and odd-job handyman (Chris Cooper) who loves him like a son.
And when Finn was very young, he encountered a shadowy, terrifying con
(Robert De Niro) who bullied him into engineering an ocean getaway in
Finn's little boat.

But the most powerful and mysterious tidal pull on Finn is that of his
childhood love, Estella (Gwyneth Paltrow), a willowy beauty as dazzling and
elusive as the bright flash of a minnow. She flickers in and out of his life with
tantalizing frequency, yet she's always beyond reach. Finn and Estella are separated for years at a stretch; each time they reconnect, she feigns interest in
him and then withdraws suddenly, leaving him crushed. She's so seemingly
cruel that we begin to think the Estella that Finn is in love with doesn't
really exist—she might be as illusory as the stippling of sun on the waves.
But Finn has captured her essence in so many of his paintings and drawings,

seeing shivery waves of passion and warmth that have so far eluded us, that we begin to believe in her too. Finn's renderings of Estella (the deft hand behind them is that of the painter Francesco Clemente) are collectively almost a character unto themselves: So vivid they almost breathe, they're the closest we, or Finn, can get to touching Estella.

That right there is the key to *Great Expectations*: One of the most romantic pictures of the 1990s, it recognizes that the erotics of memory are far more powerful than the things—and people—we can actually touch. Even the look of the picture suggests that the lushness of memory can brighten the colors of real life. Cuarón's color scheme is rapturously verdant, from the overgrown mini-jungle of the Florida villa where Finn first meets Estella to the tree-leaf canopies of Central Park to the jewel-green tones of Estella's clothing. And Emmanuel Lubezki's cinematography is glowing and translucent, suggesting both the shimmery clarity of pure water and the warmth of the sun. When *Great Expectations* was first released, the people who didn't like it (and there were far too many of them for my taste) would often ask belligerently, "What's with all the green?" Most obviously, green is the color of springtime and rebirth, but I think Cuarón's meaning is even more subtle: Memory isn't something dead and desiccated—like the cloistered, withered existence of Anne Bancroft's Miss Dinsmoor (the Miss Havisham figure)—but an organism that's inexplicably and joyously alive. Its photosynthesis sustains us even when, maybe especially when, the lights are out.

In Cuarón's universe, memory isn't something dreamy and dewy. It's visceral and vital, and it speaks in a roar like the ocean. The most erotic scenes in *Great Expectations* aren't even overtly sexual. In one sequence—actually, one languorous, miraculously unbroken shot—Finn abruptly leaves a hoity-toity art-scene party and rushes out into the rain to follow Estella to the restaurant, several blocks away, where she has gone with her fiancé. He approaches their table—he's wet and they're rich, a class divide he'll never be able to bridge no matter how much money he makes (to them, he'll always be wet)—and asks Estella to dance with him. Dancing is a ritualized series of steps that can be a clunky routine or a kind of poetry, depending on the skill and the souls of the people engaged in it. And dancing was the chief activity of Finn and Estella's childhood, the thing that brought them as close together, physically, as they could be. The restaurant in which Finn confronts Estella isn't a dancing kind of place, but she nevertheless rises from her chair and allows herself to be enfolded in his arms. The two drift out of the restaurant (and away from the disbelieving eyes of Estella's fiancé, played by Hank Azaria), for the shelter of the rain outside. And we recall that their first kiss also took place under the benediction of water: The very young Estella and Finn are bent over a bubbling water fountain, and she surprises him, in a flash of impulsive erotic innocence, by seeking out his lips with hers.

Cuarón films that first kiss as the kind of thing you're destined never to forget, an event that shapes your whole life even before you've gotten around to living it. From that moment on, Finn is fated to keep Estella alive in his memory, and the Estella of memory (if not the Estella of the flesh) needs him in order to live. Because memories have no shape unless we provide the vessel for them. They're amorphous, vaporous ghosts that depend on us for their survival. Cuarón understands what Charles Dickens and Johnny Thunders both knew: You can't put your arms around a memory. The best you can do is to give it a home.

Hercules and Hercules Unchained

Is your figure less than Greek?

Directed by Pietro Francisci; starring Steve Reeves (1959, 1960)

by Armond White

IT TOOK HOLLYWOOD TO TURN HERCULES, THE GOD OF GREEK myth, into a role model. When U.S. producer Joseph E. Levine got a look at American bodybuilder Steve Reeves in the 1959 action film *Hercules* by Italian director Pietro Francisci, his account ledger went *schwing*! Levine knew he had found an exploitable genre to pitch against the slowly waning Western. By dubbing the film and importing it to American audiences, Levine made the most of a novelty. *Hercules* epitomized the new synergy of international coproductions; it balanced the postwar European cinema's accepted cheesecake appeal to men by offering beefcake appeal to women; it also excited the teen market for fantasy and adventure.

It's movies like this, simplistically conceived and almost innocently executed, that epitomize the way pop culture can be used for unexpected, personal purposes. *Hercules* wasn't any more committed to reviving classical mythology than *The Seventh Voyage of Sinbad* was designed to cultivate appreciation of Oriental legend, yet these kinds of movies (including so-called Biblical epics that verge on gladiatorial spectacles, from *Samson and Delilah* to *Quo Vadis* and *Ben-Hur*) can always be found to surreptitiously indulge other appetites. For a kid unconscious of larger, anthropological matters, who knew Greek mythology only from comic books and oral fable, *Hercules* represented the discovery of new narrative possibilities. In the age of *Sputnik* and the threat of atomic bombs, *Hercules* transported the imagination toward less daunting warfare. More remarkably, it presented a seductive principle of manhood.

The idea was summarized in the theme song for the 1963 Saturday morning cartoon series *The Mighty Hercules,* sung by Johnny Nash:

> Hercules, hero of song and story
> Hercules, winner of ancient glory . . .
> Softness in his eyes
> Iron in his thighs
> Virtue in his heart
> Fire in every part of the mighty Hercules!

In Steve Reeves's outsized musculature, *Hercules* offered a model of how a man could be physically attractive. This wasn't a matter of fan-magazine handsomeness but of a painstakingly achieved flesh-and-blood ideal. Coming from the world of pushing weights and pumping iron, Reeves was a walking advertisement for a new type of Method. Clift, Brando, and Dean represented a new sexual sensitivity; they refined the psychological process of male introspection—continuing what Gary Cooper and Jimmy Stewart had done in previous eras and were just then adding to Hollywood's last hurrah to the Old West. But Reeves represented the benefits of *working out.* By playing Hercules, he wasn't simply the exemplar of brute force that described the '80s action heroes Sylvester Stallone, Arnold Schwarzenegger, and Bruce Willis; Hercules was committed to accomplishing good works for the city-state and very simply rescuing damsels in distress as when, in the first film, Reeves stops Sylva Koscina's runaway chariot.

More than chivalrous, the muscle-bound, big-screen Hercules was a paradigm of masculinity—especially for youth looking to define themselves. Thus, a hero of legend automatically becomes a figure of contemplation, and that's because he doesn't belong to the real, everyday world. Boys could emulate Hercules on the playground and imagine him in fantasy as an extension of how the movie so spectacularly eroticized him. He was an ideal of both fun and ambition. You could want to be like him so much as to find some way to actually *be* him. The next step, short of psychosis, is love—the sexual expression of that ideal through longing, exercise, devotion.

This is not to deny that movies provided subtler role models, such as the lessons in nobility Henry Fonda embodied in *Young Mr. Lincoln*. But the *Hercules* movies offered sensual excitement that was equally justifiable. Perhaps it was best expressed in the title of Joseph E. Levine's 1960 sequel, *Hercules Unchained*. In this episode, Hercules shows his diplomatic skills on his way to Thebes, attempting to prevent a war; still, his essential appeal is physical. The sword-and-sandal movies of this period played their part in the sexual revolution by allowing the uninhibited display of male anatomy. Nothing is especially risqué; *Hercules* and *Hercules Unchained* show as much skin as in a televised wrestling match, which is part of the fun. Scanty costuming allows for as much scopophilia as any of that era's "adult" European art films. Steve Reeves's hard-flexing thighs are no less inviting than Silvana Mangano's downy but firm ones in *Bitter Rice*.

Earlier heroic film figures rarely bared their bodies (was John Wayne ever seen shirtless?). But the *Hercules* movies arrived at a moment when male pulchritude was permissible. For the right curious teenager, here was an unimpeded view of veiny, developed calves below billowing tunic skirts. Given Hollywood's hypocritical restriction on sensuality, such as William Holden's shaved chest in *Rachel and the Stranger* (1948) eventually giving way to the jolt of his hirsute pectorals in *The Bridge on the River Kwai* (1957), the sight of Reeves's gleaming, tanned pecs amounted to a culturally transgressive event. The *Hercules* movies guaranteed a socially sanctioned revue of masculine sexuality. This genre created a sensually stirring objectification of men— a peek at the tough and tender parts of society's authority figures—that no other film genre would entertain.

Beefcake was as much a required element of these action films as the sword fights. Looking back, one can muse on the relation between these open displays of flesh and the covert enticement of the bodybuilding magazines that doubled as pornography during the same period. But the Hercules films were delightful for their uncloseted (unchained) appreciation of normal male concupiscence. Even in the 1963 *Jason and the Argonauts*, where director Don Chaffey followed a variation on the Hercules legend, there is a similar exhibition of tough-guy flesh. Nigel Green plays Hercules, this time with ginger-colored pelt, giving the god a look of seasoned strength. In this version of the myth, muscle and skin are contrasted with the ferrous and brass solidity of Ray Harryhausen's creatures—the sculptural representation of male prowess that admits a nightmarish possibility of malevolence. The lure of masculinity is questioned. Harryhausen's dark, menacing role model stretches one between attraction and repulsion. Adolescent fascination is not simply exploited by Hollywood routine; young boys are forced to think about power and the use of force.

Hercules movies become the best kind of boys' adventure. They relate tumescence to conscience.

Horror of Dracula
Down for the Count

Directed by Terence Fisher; starring Christopher Lee,
Peter Cushing (1958)

by David Edelstein

HORROR FILMS HELPED MANY OF US TROUBLED BOYS MUDDLE
through adolescence, providing a socially acceptable outlet for our loathing
of our bodies, females, parents and teachers, and alien others—pretty much
everyone, come to think of it. I'm grateful for those movies. But as I've gone
back to the ones that shaped my character and predilections, I've discovered
something about them more frightening than monsters and death—they're
amazingly misogynistic and reactionary.

It's only big news if you absorbed their lessons before you could think
them through. *Horror of Dracula*, one of the biggest turn-ons of my youth, is
especially flabbergasting to revisit because its scary sexual politics weren't apparent to my eleven-year-old self. Probably they weren't apparent to the post-
pubescent moralists back in 1958, either, who denounced its liberal dose of
blood and heaving cleavage. If they'd looked deeper, they'd have embraced
the movie as an exhortation to keep our women under lock and key.

Directed by Terence Fisher, *Horror of Dracula* remains a crackerjack vampire thriller, probably more responsible than its predecessor *Curse of
Frankenstein* for the wave of period British horror pictures, most of them produced by Hammer Films, that lasted into the '70s. Old-fashioned Hollywood
scare movies were dead by the end of WWII; now, Hammer seized the opportunity to inject bright red blood into classic formulas. These were

painfully low-budget movies, but thanks to resourceful production designers, cinematographers, and some of the best character actors on either side of the Atlantic, they were plush and colorful—the better to appreciate ripe flesh tones and gore.

As written by Bram Stoker in the early twentieth century, the Dracula story was xenophobic and apprehensive about female sexuality. Women were helpless to resist the allure of the Eastern European count who brought plague and death to our civilized shores, not to mention undermined our civil methods of courtship. I sympathize: In college, many of us looked with similar fear and contempt on the wealthy, self-assured "Eurotrash" that lured away our women. At least my postfeminist female classmates refused to buy into that self-serving perspective—unlike the heroine of the '20s stage adaptation of *Dracula*, who laments her surrender to the bloodsucker with the cry, "I am unclean!"

The most famous screen Dracula, Bela Lugosi, was a matinee idol in 1931, but thirty years on, the whey-faced Eastern European vampire was camp. ("I vant your blood!") It was Christopher Lee who brought a dose of newfangled sexuality to the king of the undead. Born Christopher Frank Carandini Lee to an English father and an Italian mother, he was discouraged from a career in film on the grounds that he was too tall (6-foot–5) and foreign-looking. Although later very much a men's-club Englishman (and something of a pompous Colonel Blimp), Lee spent years playing Nazis, Slavs, Asians, Arabs, swarthy buccaneers, and finally, in 1957, Frankenstein's monster. But it was his Dracula that made him an international sex symbol.

Lee's entrance in *Horror of Dracula* is surprisingly matter-of-fact. To Jonathan Harker, a guest in his castle, he is courtly and slightly brusque, his countenance stiff, his gestures mechanical. This is Dracula? But if there was never a Count so wooden in conversation, there was never one so bestial when the fangs came out. A young woman in a revealing negligee begs Harker to take her away, and when he assents and gives her a cuddle, she goes for his jugular. Enter Dracula: hissing, fanged, eyes bloodied—a jealous hellspawn.

Dracula is last seen bearing away the woman's supine body, but when Harker discovers her the next day, sleeping in a coffin beside her master's, she looks none the worse for wear and even rather pleased. After Harker drives a stake into her copious bosom, she transforms into a withered crone: Take that, harlot! Alas, he is too late to deliver a killing blow to the awakened Count.

To replace his mistress, Dracula goes after Harker's demure fiancée, Lucy, who begins to suffer symptoms of anemia. But with the loss of blood comes a new voluptuousness. Suddenly secretive, Lucy lies in bed awaiting the entrance of her lover from the terrace—preceded by leaves that swirl as if animated by her desire.

Morality's last line of defense is Professor Van Helsing, played by Peter Cushing. And it was Cushing, not Lee, who fired my imagination as I watched *Horror of Dracula* on TV at two in the morning at the height of the counterculture. That's my bloodcurdling realization: that it wasn't the Dionysian superman who inspired me, but the agent of repression and what he stood for—a holy alliance between science and the Church (especially the Church of the Inquisition). Cushing had come of age in repertory with Laurence Olivier (he was Osric in the film of *Hamlet*) and emulated Olivier's crisp attack and penchant for athletic effects. Unlike Olivier, though, he had natural warmth. He was fluid and mellifluous, and his manner rounded out his often steely and fanatical characters. When Cushing drove a stake into a woman's heart, you had no doubt he believed it was in her best interests.

After the vampirized/sexualized Lucy has been excitingly put down (a cross burned into her forehead, a stake driven through her heart, her angelic purity returning in death), the object is to keep Dracula away from Lucy's sister-in-law, Mina. No such luck. While Van Helsing and Mina's ineffectual husband stand guard outside, the vampire emerges from the cellar, where his coffin has been sitting all along. Flushed and breathless, Mina gazes on the totemlike Dracula, who backs her onto the bed, tenderly nuzzles her neck, kisses her breasts, and finally delivers the bite. There is a high-pitched shriek: not from Mina, but from an owl in a tree outside, warning the clueless men that their woman is lost to them.

That's the big sex scene of *Horror of Dracula*, but the true consummation is the first and last meeting of Van Helsing and Dracula, in which the vampire prepares to chomp down on his unconscious nemesis—who suddenly breaks free, leaps onto a long table, and hurls himself onto the heavy drapes, which give way to an incinerating shaft of sunlight. Lee's deaths in all the Hammer *Dracula* movies were elaborate production numbers, but none was as brilliantly staged and edited: As Van Helsing makes a cross out of two candlesticks and drives the writhing vampire into the burning light, it's clear that *this* is the payoff we've been waiting for—the money shot that elicits a surge of gratification.

Ah, there is nothing like delivering righteous death blows to deviants. Holy water scalds the infidel in *Brides of Dracula*. In *Dracula, Prince of Darkness*, a posse of monks holds down a writhing, flame-haired vampiress in low-cut negligee and drives a huge stake into her bosom—to the pealing of church bells. As the counterculture brought new and more defiant sexual freedoms, it provoked an equally intense lust for punishment.

In 1979, screenwriter W. D. Richter and director John Badham concocted a *Dracula* that turned the sexual message of the original on its head. The men were now fusty and repressive, allied with the coming age of cars and machines, while Dracula (Frank Langella) was a nineteenth-century Romantic with vine leaves in his hair. The heroine (Kate Nelligan) wanted him not with her most unclean self, but her most soulful and liberated. Even allowing for the maladroit special effects, this *Dracula* wasn't satisfying. Those of us who'd come of age with Hammer Films didn't just want to see the vampire die; we wanted to see his sexual power die too and his female followers suitably shamed. We wanted what we had in *Horror of Dracula*: sex and chastisement.

In the Cut

To the lighthouse

Directed by Jane Campion; starring Mark Ruffalo,
Meg Ryan, Jennifer Jason Leigh (2003)

by Sheila Benson

WHAT MAKES MARK RUFFALO'S MALLOY, A LOWER MANHATTAN
police detective complete with obligatory Zapata mustache, so hot? That's
easy: He's a smart, unsimple man who's good at what he does; very, very
good, in a way that combines precision with intuition. Watching a man
working well—at anything—carries a special jolt for me: My father was an
artist, quiet and funny and effortless at what he did, and being there when he
worked built an unspoken bond. Here, Malloy's limitless confidence seals it
for me. ("Never apologize," Jane Campion directs Ruffalo on the DVD. "You
never apologize.")

Sex is generally a package deal with Malloy's brand of confidence. Listen
to him lay it out to Frannie Avery (a magically liberated and shattering Meg
Ryan), the NYU English prof he's met in the course of a particularly grisly
murder investigation. On their first date, while they're still working out the
percentages of a flirtation, he tells her he'll do anything she wants sexually—
short of beating her up—no problem. As he's running that list, he doesn't
lower his voice the way men do when they're talking dirty. He's not. This is
simply his area of expertise. (Frannie's, by happy coincidence, is words and
the power of language.)

After Malloy makes love to her the first time, without even kissing her
mouth, Frannie asks wonderingly, "How did you do that?" And he's able to

lie back with a cigarette and tell her—probably the first woman who's cared to ask—the story of the summer he was fifteen and what the married "Chicken Lady" taught him, and exactly how she went about it.

He's not grandstanding. This isn't Crash Davis's *Bull Durham* manifesto, which begins with "The soul, the cock, the pussy" and ends with "long, soft, slow, deep, wet kisses that last three days." That was pretty much a barnburner for a lot of women, but it always felt like *screenwriting* to me. *In the Cut* feels like a connection, however fragile, between two people willing to venture beyond the expected.

Campion has always known that sex begins in the mind, and Susanna Moore, who wrote the original, disturbingly erotic novel and collaborated with Campion on the screenplay, also knows, absolutely. Moore has said she wanted to write about sex with *In the Cut* "because nobody'd gotten it right." She got it so right within the first eight pages it was a punch to the solar plexus.

That would be the moment when Frannie blunders onto a blow job in progress in the basement recesses of a seedy Village bar. She's sure the shadowy man has seen her in the doorway from the way he sweeps aside the girl's long hair, as if to give Frannie a better look. All she can really see is the small tattoo on the inside of his wrist; when she sees one later on Malloy's wrist, he says wryly that he's in "a small club." Still, after this same girl is found in Frannie's garden—"disarticulated," to use Malloy's precise term—it gives her something new to worry about.

As she has been since *Sweetie*, Campion is in peak form. Her peripheral characters reinforce Frannie's ironic world view: a hulking, gentle NYU student whose blood-spattered term paper is a spirited defense of John Wayne Gacy, and a creepy ex-boyfriend who is as barking mad as his ratty dog; if he isn't a serial killer, at least he's a serial annoyer.

Campion and Moore depict them with the same care they lavish on the hyper-macho sparring between Malloy and his partner, Rodriguez (Nick Damici), and the hilariously brutish way they use it to exclude outsiders, i.e., women. You get the strong impression that narrative is the least of Campion's concerns here. What really intrigues her is the shimmering dream world of Frannie and Pauline (Jennifer Jason Leigh), her magnificently messed-up half-sister. (Seeing the soft, brilliant interplay of their scenes, you wonder just when Leigh—a complex, exquisite, intelligent actress—became shorthand for "victim.")

Frannie and Pauline are muzzy mirror images. Their father, a career diplo-
mat married five times and counting, had a talent for abandoning wives and
children, creating a wide streak of wariness in both daughters; it just takes
different forms. Pauline specializes in crazy obsessive fantasies that keep her
from real relationships. Frannie has dreams in which her father's desertion of
her mother becomes murder. It's no wonder there's a Babes in the Woods
quality to their entwined lives.

Frankly, I could hang out in their world forever. Dion Beebe's lenses give
it the steamy lushness of an urban hothouse. Frannie's tiny private garden
turns pinky-white in a petal storm; out on the streets the summer heat reflects off the moist bare skin of women in slip-dresses. The light runs and
darts, and Pauline's apartment glows with jewel-colored votives and tinkling
wind chimes.

Most men, meaning about 90 percent of our critical voices, had no pa-
tience with *In the Cut,* primarily (I suspect) because of the Campion/Moore
generosity toward this inner world of women which mucked up what was
perceived as a thriller. Who was this *English teacher* for chrissake who takes
subway-placard poetry as some kind of received message? And what's with
all the overwrought symbolism, in and out of dreams?

Yes, dreams are hardly subtle, and I have to say I cringed at the explicit
red chalk lighthouse on Frannie's blackboard—not just for her class on Virginia Woolf but, I fear, as a motif for "fate." That's okay—on the DVD commentary, even Campion thought it was one phallus too many. And though I
absolutely buy that long, blood-stained walk home, ignored by every pru-
dent motorist in New York, the sequence needed to be longer, to let us join
her emotional journey before she surrenders to Malloy—completely.

Lovers of the novel may miss Moore's shocking conclusion, which takes
the device of the unreliable narrator right over the edge as Frannie, our first-
person voice, bleeds out from the killer's surgically expert knife. Campion
(let alone any sane producer) is entirely too much an optimist for *that.*

Campion's unarguable triumph is the utter honesty of Ryan's and Ruffalo's
work. (Leigh has already established a career on this dangerous edge.)
Stripped for once of the need to be lovable, Ryan is unguarded, open, a tena-
cious mixture of damage and hope, while Ruffalo, obliterating his bruised lit-
tle-boy persona, makes Malloy a complex, rounded hero for *these* times, and
worthy of every lickerish look he's likely to get.

The Female Gaze

by Carrie Rickey

The Question has always nagged me: Are there male and female styles of filmmaking?

John Berger theorizes that male artists (like Goya) frame women as sexual objects while female artists (like Cassatt) frame them as social subjects. Sociolinguist Deborah Tannen says men speak and hear a language of status and independence while women's language is about connection and intimacy. Laura Mulvey's essay "Visual Pleasure and Narrative Cinema" argues that Hollywood presumes a male spectator.

One way of answering the Question is by way of the Joke—told by Hollywood execs whenever "the female gaze" comes up. It's a She Said/He Said.

Her side of the story: He was in an odd mood when I got to the bar. We weren't connecting. Was it me? Back at his place, I expected the break-up conversation, but he turned on the TV. I said I was going to sleep, hoping he'd get the hint I was upset. After ten minutes he joined me and we had sex. Thought he might open up after such an intimate exchange, but he was still distracted. Cried myself to sleep.

His side of the story: Played badly today—shot 93. Felt kind of tired. Got laid though.

When male execs tell the Joke, it's to illustrate how women gum up the narrative while men get to the point. Female execs draw a different conclusion: There are times when the audience wants to know what's going on inside a character's head. In other words, the male gaze is the weather report; the female gaze takes in the microclimates of mood.

From decades of considering the Question, I submit that when the gaze is female:

- **The protagonist's psychological turning point takes place in real time.** Thus the supercharged atmosphere of Isabelle Huppert's first orgasm when a soldier pleasures her on a train in Diane Kurys's *Entre Nous*, a humid sequence shot in a continuous take. And Holly Hunter's discovery of the Brave Nude World when she leaves her instrument to explore Harvey Keitel's in Jane Campion's *The Piano*—a breathless scene where neither she nor the camera stops for air. And we see Frances McDormand emotionally factor that her son's probable pain at her having a threesome with his fiancée will outweigh her pleasure in Lisa Cholodenko's *Laurel Canyon*, a swelling erotic bubble pricked by conscience.

- **Nudity is matter-of-fact rather than idealized.** Consider Keitel in *The Piano*, tense as an animal being appraised at a livestock auction. Or contrast the locker-room sequence of Robert Towne's *Personal Best* with that of Gurinder Chadha's *Bend It Like Beckham*. Towne's camera eroticizes female forms in conventional T&A fashion while Chadha's celebrates the T&A of toughness and agility. Similarly, Penny Marshall's *A League of Their Own* and Gina Prince-Bythewood's *Love and Basketball* celebrate the power of the female form over its beauty.

- **Characters are more likely to be flawed than omnipotent.** Consider *Lost in Translation, Bend It Like Beckham, Look at Me*. Like the lady said, sometimes getting inside a character's head makes everything more resonant. When the weather report is insufficient, bring on the microclimate. ∎

In the Mood for Love

A fine romance

Directed by Wong Kar-wai; starring Tony Leung,
Maggie Cheung (2000)

by Rob Nelson

WONG KAR-WAI'S **IN THE MOOD FOR LOVE** IS THE SEXIEST FILM
I've ever seen, and there's not a single sex scene in it. Prurient types might
moan that the movie is all foreplay and no fuck. But what's wrong with that?
Isn't foreplay the most creative part of sex—when you most relish your partner, savoring and suspending the intimate pleasures ahead? Too many
movies come on like the kids in *American Pie:* They don't know how to take
their time; they're all "kiss kiss bang bang" in the words of Pauline Kael, who
didn't call her most alluring book *When the Lights Go Down* for nothing.
When they go down, those lights, our excitement invariably goes up: Anything and everything remains to be seen. (Or felt. Or fantasized.)

At Cannes, where Wong's time to diddle with his own hotly awaited *objet
du désir* ran out, the recorded announcement of a screening's imminent start
always sounds like the sweetest pillow talk: *La séance commence.* That seductive, trancelike moment of infinite possibility is where Wong's film endeavors
to linger as long as it can—which turns out to be 97 minutes and 57 seconds. (Some might call this a work of tantric cinema.)

In the Mood for Love follows a man and woman in early '60s Hong Kong
who are maybe in love and will maybe act on that love, despite being married to others (who've had an affair of their own). In the end, the central relationship appears unconsummated, the better for Wong to suggest that the

deed can still be done later. When a Cannes critic asked whether as many as hundreds of hours of footage (some explicit) hadn't made the final cut, Wong's typically droll reply—"Not at this moment, no"—played with the notion that the master of melodramatic procrastination was still scheming to keep his *Love* affair alive. (Now it's clear that Wong wasn't really kidding: In his work since, the director has nostalgically revisited nearly all the same themes, separation anxiety among them.)

Despite the insinuating title, *In the Mood* is about more than sex—about more than love, even. The movie is really about the art of living, insofar as it's explicitly about choices—the seemingly unlimited number of them. And the romance of putting them off. And the ache that accompanies their passing. (One scholarly essay on Wong's oeuvre is aptly titled "The Erotics of Disappointment.") No less than the shooting and cutting of the film, courtship here is experimental. Half an hour into the movie, Chow Mo-wan (Tony Leung) and Su Li-zhen Chan (Maggie Cheung)—gorgeous neighbors in a cramped apartment building—are walking home after drinking tea in a café, having just confirmed their suspicions that their spouses are having an affair. "I wonder how it began," Li-zhen muses, possibly setting another affair in (slow) motion. Mo-wan gently reaches for her wrist and, cradling it in his hand, asks, "Shall we stay out tonight?"—imagining what her husband might have said to his wife. A moment later, in another hypothetical variation on the earlier proposal, Li-zhen playfully twirls a finger in the general direction of where Mo-wan's belt meets the bottom of his tie, and blushes.

This is foreplay, certainly—although, even more tantalizing, what sort of foreplay isn't clear. Are the two seeking to discover how they were cheated? Are they getting revenge? Falling for each other? All of the above? Do we have to decide now? In a way, the only pressing issue in the picture is: Should they or shouldn't they? Wong takes this question to heart and clutches it tight: Every cut and camera movement seems to draw the director, his characters, and his audience into a kind of shared lament for the infinitesimal choice that has just been made and can never be made again. Avoiding the urge to go all the way, stylistically speaking, the film stops short of blatant eroticism (or surrealism), preferring to flirt with its own flamboyantly sensual mise-en-scène. There's the heroine's wardrobe of high-collared, tight-fitting, floral-print *cheongsams* (her person, like her passion, pushing the bounds of societal stricture); a winking tease of a tune from Nat King

Cole ("Quizás, Quizás, Quizás"—meaning "perhaps, perhaps, perhaps"); and, for the food fetishist, a shot of rare steak dipped in spicy yellow mustard as hot as the kiss you taste for days.

As with the deepest love, the movie's true feelings are communicated without words. (Small wonder the film was shot without a script.) Just after Mo-wan and Li-zhen have brushed past each other on a narrow stairway, the image of rain falling beneath a street lamp comes like a tiny orgasm or a drizzle of tears. The overripe array of reds, golds, greens, purples, and pinks—sometimes all in a single shot—is enough to make you swoon. And yet Wong's hyperexpressive style is about control as well. Indeed, what better approach than restraint for a film about the agony of ending an affair, about the regret over all the other Loves that must be left unmade? At Cannes, Wong admitted to identifying with the characters' excruciating indecision: Only at the eleventh hour did he opt to excise a sequence of Li-zhen and Mo-wan engaged in, as he put it, "hanky-panky." (My press book from the festival contains a single image of the two in bed together—which, in the context of the finished film, is almost too haunting to behold. The DVD too includes a deleted bedroom scene. I can't bear to watch it.)

Like the mournful violin that wails against the rigid 3/4 beat of Michael Galasso's score (the sound of desire not quite repressed by convention), In the Mood for Love grieves every tick of the metronome while holding itself in check, awaiting every unlikely outcome of the lovers' platonic trysts. An impossible love it is. But for 97 minutes and 57 seconds, at least, everything is open.

In the Realm of the Senses
Sex and nothing but

Directed by Nagisa Oshima; starring Eiko Matsuda,
Tatsuya Fuji (1976)

by Peter Brunette

I WAS OVERWHELMED AND GROSSED OUT BY THE EROTIC
Japanese masterpiece *In the Realm of the Senses* when it came out in 1976.
Seeing it again recently on DVD, I realized that it still shocked me, but different parts, and for different reasons. The biggest surprise was the grand seriousness of its themes, which I had missed the first time around.

Its claustrophobic story, based on true events of 1936, is the essence of simplicity, as in the porn films with which it shares kinship. Sada (Eiko Matsuda), a young serving woman and sometime prostitute, enters into a sexual relationship with her somewhat older master, Kichi (Tatsuya Fuji). They fuck, fuck, fuck, then enjoy some fellatio. Later shots show a classic porn image—semen dribbling from the woman's mouth—and, a fresh conceit, an egg inserted into her vagina. After that they fuck some more. Seeking ever more stimulation, they decide to go to the "end" in the little strangling game they play to enhance his erection. In the film's infamous finale, Sada castrates her now dead lover and leaves with his genitalia in tow.

In the Realm of the Senses was directed by Nagisa Oshima, whose art-house credentials are impeccable. Yet it immediately calls into question the border between art film and porn film. The entire enterprise, which at times seems frivolous, even silly, is undertaken in an atmosphere of classic Japanese cultural tradition, including the music the geishas play and the style of kimonos.

And the film clearly takes on issues that are larger than mere arousal and physical release.

Nevertheless, there is a perverse insistence on showing the penis in multiple close-ups, a ubiquity that, strictly speaking, advances neither plot nor themes. The vagina is a decidedly secondary character—although, interestingly, it is the woman who provides the movie's momentum, especially toward the end. And it is she who always properly places the penis for mutual pleasure while her lover passively looks on: At one point she fellates him while he smokes a cigarette.

Oshima's film offers the startling premise that sexuality can be not only the center of one's existence, but the whole of it. In the realm of the senses, indeed. The world becomes reimagined and reconfigured through the genitals, which are the true main characters in this curiously (and purposely) artificial drama. ("All that we do," says Sada, "even eating, must be an act of love.") The external world disappears—exchanged for a claustrophobic bedroom—so much so that it comes as a shock to see soldiers march by in a brief outdoor scene. This totalizing of sex, not the titillation of pornography, is why Oshima has decided that everything must be fully and continuously displayed. This apotheosis of the visual leads in some scenes to what could be called a collapse of the space of representation: Since fellatio is obviously hard to fake, the usual gap between represented performance and meaning disappears. Are the actors playing characters engaging in fellatio or are they simply engaging in fellatio? Or both? (One can only hope that fully fictive status has been restored by the time Kichi's genitals are removed in close-up.)

The figure of Sada is supremely interesting. When she says "I feel reborn" after their earliest sexual encounters, it's hard to know whether this is merely the male fantasy of the compliant female reduced utterly and anonymously to her sexuality, or the unashamed claiming of the right to female desire, the ultimate empowerment. Other fascinating questions arise, such as: To what extent is self-pleasure related to pleasing others? (As Jacques Derrida pointed out while discussing Rousseau, isn't sexual intercourse always a kind of masturbation?) Most importantly, the film addresses a conundrum of Eastern and Western philosophy: To what extent can two become one? Can there be complete surrender of the self through sex? And who really owns the penis that Sada so strongly claims as her own?

There is a great deal of *looking* in this film, always at someone else having sex, and almost exclusively by women. This recalls the urge to see, pushed by sexual desire, in Hitchcock's *Rear Window*. Like that earlier film, *In the Realm of the Senses* foregrounds and thus questions our own looking and our own visual/libidinal investment in the sexual activity we watch onscreen. One of the strangest things about the film, in fact, is how much of the most intimate sex takes place in front of others—leading to perhaps inadvertent comic moments, as when the geishas refuse to clean up their room because she is "always sucking him."

The narrative force of *In the Realm of the Senses* comes from the narrative arc of the sex itself, as in traditional porn films. Also, as with porn, the sex must never become repetitive, and thus boring; hence the logic and length of the film demand that the lovers become ever more adventurous. This accords nicely (and tragically) with the inevitable introduction of pain and its increasingly dangerous demands. There is one difficult, mercifully short scene, in which Sada pinches a boy's little penis and won't let go even when he screams. Yet it is difficult to imagine any other direction or outcome for this couple. When mutual obsession is so consuming, could there ever be a future for routine sex? When they agree that "to reach total pleasure you must go almost to the end," we know what to expect. What else is left for them to do? Here Oshima seems to be investigating the relation between pain and love, or, more globally, the quintessential balance between love and sex: Are they crazy in love or just crazy?

At the end, a voice-over tells us that Sada carried around her lover's genitalia for four days before she was finally arrested. Observers reported, the voice-over continues, that, "strangely, she seemed to glow with happiness."

In My Skin: Hack Work

by Gerald Peary

In My Skin (*Dans ma peau*) is a slasher film for art-house intellectuals, theorists of "the body," and swimming-against-the-PC-tide feminists. It's a kind of filmed performance piece written, directed by, and starring France's Marina de Van, who has acted for François Ozon (*Sitcom, See the Sea*) and cowritten some of his features (*Under the Sand, 8 Women*).

In My Skin tells the freaky but undeniably absorbing tale of Esther (De Van), a thirtyish Parisian research analyst who, one strange evening, enters a masochistic netherworld after she trips outside a party, bloodying her leg. Rather than wipe up or get medical attention, Esther lowers her pant leg. Once home, she examines her festering wounds, absorbed in the hurt of them, fascinated by the topography of bruises, scabs, and red drips. A doctor bandages her injury, but Esther revolts, going feverishly after the bandage with scissors to liberate her naked, maimed flesh. Grown antsy at her staid office, she races to a subterranean hideout where she can razor more of her body. Back at her computer, she reveals a stealthy, smutty smile.

As Esther becomes possessed, private and public space inevitably clash. At a formal business lunch, while her straitlaced colleagues drone on about the beauty of Lisbon, Esther hacks at her arm beneath the table. She's so transfixed that she can't hide what's happening from her horrified office pal, Sandrine (Léa Drucker), and her confused and threatened boyfriend, Vincent (Laurent Lucas). Why does she do it? "I don't know," Esther answers her boyfriend honestly. In her haze, she's like Catherine Deneuve's schizoid, murderous protagonist in Roman Polanski's 1965 classic *Repulsion*.

De Van the screenwriter-director offers no facile explanation for Esther's behavior, nor does she condemn it. When interviewed, she admitted an autobiographical connection: A traumatic childhood car accident left her with a deformed leg. "It reinforced my feeling of strangeness," she explained. "During my entire adolescence my body intrigued me." In contrast, Esther, the workaholic, has cut herself off from her body up until that fateful, epiphanic night. Self-mutilation, according to de Van, "is a very elementary and strong way to reconnect with the present, the moment, and with sensation. A reappropriation of the body comes with pain."

Interestingly, Esther never touches her breasts or genitalia when she's slicing away, never masturbating, no matter how blatantly sexual the charge when she's violating her flesh. *In My Skin* is a potent text for those debating what constitutes "pornography." There's a long, juicy section in which Esther's face goes down on her bleeding arm, and she licks and sucks it as if she's mouthing a ripe, wet vagina; does that qualify as porno?

Those who argue that horror-movie bloodsucking is displaced oral sex will adore *In My Skin,* especially since de Van, with her dark, shaped eyebrows and pronounced teeth, looks so prototypically vampiric. Dracula's daughter! ■

Intimacy

On a no-name basis

Directed by Patrice Chéreau; starring Kerry Fox,
Mark Rylance (2001)

by Michael Wilmington

EVERY WEDNESDAY AFTERNOON, AMID LONDON'S GRAY TORRENT
of people, a man and a woman who know almost nothing about each other,
not even names, meet in the man's dingy flat for fierce, quick, anonymous
sex. They tear into each other, but they barely talk. And they never arrange
to meet outside.

Described like that, bluntly and simply, director Patrice Chéreau's *Intimacy*
sounds like a porn movie. That the actors who play the couple—Kerry Fox
and Mark Rylance—actually have sex onscreen endows the film with an even
more exploitative aura.

But *Intimacy* is anything but pornographic, anything but blunt and simple; anyone who expects vicarious fantasy and arousal will be disappointed.
The movie is exciting, but not because it breaks taboos or turns us on. Defying expectations, it is about the emotions of the characters—about the
"who," "where" and "why" that they themselves scrupulously avoid.

Based on the novel *Intimacy* and the story "Nightlight," by Hanif
Kureishi—the Pakistani-British novelist, who also wrote the screenplay for *My
Beautiful Laundrette*—this is a surprisingly moving film. It's a real exploration
of modern sensuality, brilliantly written and acted, powerfully directed, done
with raw honesty and high style.

Rylance plays divorced barman Jay and Fox plays married actress/teacher Claire. Despite their nearly anonymous arrangement, Jay becomes obsessed with learning more about Claire, surreptitiously following her after one of their erotic sessions and discovering the seedy little pub theater where she's performing (as shy, repressed Laura) in a third-rate production of *The Glass Menagerie*. There he also meets Claire's husband, Andy, a gabby, relentlessly cheerful taxi driver played with lacerating skill by Mike Leigh's consummate regular Timothy Spall.

Jay and Claire's hidden lives both include families and children, though in Jay's case, it's a broken family. They also have confidantes: Jay has hanger-on Victor (Alastair Galbraith) and his sympathetic fellow barman Ian (Philippe Calvario), and Claire has middle-aged acting student Betty (Marianne Faithfull, Mick Jagger's one-time blonde angel). Away from the flat, their lives are messy, unfulfilled, and unsexy, which is partly why they don't discuss it. Jay, vulnerable and bitter, and Claire, trapped in a failed dream, are incomplete people drawn together out of emptiness and need.

The film is superb at showing how and why ordinary people can be driven to reckless passion.

As Jay learns more about Claire—intruding into her world and striking up an unlikely and dangerous friendship with Andy, teasing him with snippets of the truth—the erotic bonds begin to snap. Claire retreats; Jay pursues. Like Marlon Brando's Paul and Maria Schneider's Jeanne in *Last Tango in Paris*, Chéreau's London lovers have made a little cul-de-sac away from the real world. The truth, in this case, may drive them apart—but truth, Chéreau says, is inevitable.

It's unfortunate that Fox and Rylance received lurid press for their unfaked sex scenes; it obscures the excellence of their acting. (Fox won Best Actress at Berlin, where the film won Grand Prize.) The two of them command the screen totally, playing ordinary people transformed by passion. And though they aren't presented as erotic objects—some critics, with staggering obtuseness, even complained that they look too dowdy to be making love onscreen—you can't take your eyes from them, dressed or undressed.

The realism of the sex scenes doesn't titillate. It extends and enhances the burning, aching naturalism of the performances. Chéreau strives for a John Cassavetes–like rawness and vigor, and he frequently uses long, unbroken camera takes with lots of movement to maintain the emotion and intensity. But it's Fox and Rylance who generate that emotion. So do Spall and the other actors. (The weak link is Calvario's barman, whose role is the only near-cliché.)

Rarely has a cuckolded husband been done as memorably as Spall does Andy. Audiences may remember Spall as the quiet, decent family man in *Secrets & Lies* or the foolish gourmet in *Life Is Sweet,* but he's also good in loud, disruptive roles like this. Here he triggers one comic or dramatic explosion after another.

Fox was in her early twenties when she gave her great performance as New Zealand writer Janet Frame in Jane Campion's best film, *An Angel at my Table.* Here she's thirty-four and, like most women past their twenties, even more sensual and open, if deliberately deglamorized. Fox gives Claire a wild yearning, a salty knowledge, and an almost palpable frustration, as well as a mystery that makes her the most magnetic of the characters.

Rylance, best known in Britain as the director (until late 2005) of the Globe Theater and a prolific actor with the Royal Shakespeare Company, has a sad-eyed delicacy and crisp attack that usually get him typed as a shy neurotic (*Angels and Insects* and the Quay Brothers' *Institute Benjamenta*). Indeed, Chéreau initially cast him as the dissolute Victor, but the actor's pensive, knowing melancholy make him surprisingly right for Jay. His final scene is shattering.

Though it was made in Britain with a partly British crew, *Intimacy* fits right in with the recent line of startlingly candid or radical French films about sex (*Romance, Fat Girl*). Yet Chéreau has said he intended no parallels between his film and *Last Tango in Paris;* his model was Nagisa Oshima's 1976 *In the Realm of the Senses.* Obviously, Chéreau sees this affair as partly therapeutic and liberating, which may be what alienated some audiences and critics.

Yet Chéreau is no panderer; he's long been one of the most famous and admired theater and opera directors in Europe, the French equivalent of Sweden's Ingmar Bergman and Italy's Luchino Visconti. All his films are interesting, especially his spectacular 1994 adaptation of Alexandre Dumas's *Queen Margot.* But it's with *Intimacy* and 1998's *Those Who Love Me Can Take the Train* that he became a supremely confident filmmaker. Stories with huge ensemble casts, like *Train,* are his forte, but *Intimacy* succeeds with a smaller cast and a tighter, almost Bergmanesque focus: two people alone in a room. In that chamber setting, emotions and sensuality blaze and *Intimacy* lives up to its title. Vibrating with humanity, it's a potent portrait of love, ranging from the purely carnal to the impurely sublime.

Irma Vep

Phantom lady over Paris

Directed by Olivier Assayas; starring Maggie Cheung,
Jean-Pierre Léaud (1996)

by Charles Taylor

*"That's desire, and that's okay because that's
what we make movies with."*
—MAGGIE CHEUNG IN IRMA VEP

*"He waited until daybreak, but nothing happened
to disturb the peace and hush of the night."*
—MARCEL ALLAIN AND PIERRE SOUVESTRE,
THE SILENT EXECUTIONER

She enters unnoticed, her hair pulled back, no makeup. Amid a film office in the chaos of preproduction, she is as invisible as the character she will play, who blends into the night in her black bodysuit as she scampers over the roofs of Paris. She will exit the movie before it ends, 96 minutes later, like all and everyone that passes in front of a camera, leaving only an image behind. By then her face will seem the heart and soul of cinema itself, everything we try to imprint on our eyes and our hearts and our memories while watching a movie before it slips away from us, just as film runs through the projector. As always, we're left wondering how something we can't hold, something as intangible as shadows and light projected on a screen, can seem as real as life itself.

The eroticism of *Irma Vep* comes not just from the image of Maggie Cheung in her black latex catsuit, but from the film's awareness of how movie images come close enough to feel like a caress. Who's to say that the darkness of a theater doesn't replicate the darkness of a love nest, that the whirr of a projector doesn't have the sensual contentment of a purring kitten, that the passage of celluloid through a projector isn't like a silken scarf drawn along our skin?

Like no movie since *Vertigo*, *Irma Vep*, Olivier Assayas's film about the unmaking of a movie, captures the obsessiveness of a life spent chasing images—or watching them. Assayas understands the movie theater as a place of ravishment and worship, a place we approach with the appetite of voluptuaries and the fervor of true believers. But where Hitchcock found tragedy, Assayas finds comedy—and glory.

His holy fool is René (Jean-Pierre Léaud), a once-revered French director faltering in the era of big-budget commercial filmmaking, who has taken on the impossible task of remaking Louis Feuillade's 1915 serial *Les vampires*. "Not a French actress can be Irma Vep after Musidora, it would be blasphemy," he says, invoking reverence for the Frenchwoman who played the head of a gang of jewel thieves in Feuillade's series of ten 40-minute films. And so René casts the Hong Kong actress Maggie Cheung (appearing as herself).

Everyone, including Maggie, wants to know why. René's answer, and Assayas's, comes to us before we've heard anyone ask the question, in a clip from Johnny To's *The Heroic Trio*. A female superhero picture where Maggie shares the screen with Michelle Yeoh and the late, beloved Anita Mui, the movie seen here in the murky light of René's TV screen, *Heroic Trio* is faded and silvery like something that might have been made by a Feuillade contemporary. The three stars leap through the air, or just hover in it, pull deadly metallic foils from their sleeves as a magician pulls flowers from his, send poles careening across a room by telekinesis, use hair clips to slice oncoming bullets into harmless shavings.

For Maggie, the sequence is just the trickery of Hong Kong moviemaking. For René, it's a revelation. "It's because I saw you in a very, very cheap cinema in Marrakesh," he tells her, "and you, you are like a dancer, and also like an acrobat." When Maggie protests that what beguiled him was the work of stuntwomen and wires, René will have none of it. His voice drops to the whisper you use to address a lover or a deity: "You have the grace . . . you are mysterious like Irma Vep, you are beautiful like Irma Vep, and also you are magic like her."

René's vision of her doesn't get any further than that. Later he tells Maggie, "I have this idea of you in this part, in this costume . . . it's like a fantasy.

. . . But in the end, there is nothing for you to act." As it turns out, René's idea is everything. What he saw in Maggie survives his film's falling apart and makes nonsense of the pessimism that drives him to a breakdown. "You think you are at the core of the scene, but in fact you are just at the surface," René admonishes, and as if unconsciously proving him wrong, Maggie takes her leave by slipping out the window, a cat burglar in the making.

Irma Vep is about how the muse goes on to realize the vision she isn't even aware she shares. The comedy of the film comes from the distractions on the way to that realization, the distractions of moviemaking in the era of globalization. *Irma Vep* takes full measure of the age when movie love is divided between people like Nathalie Richard's Zoé, the frazzled costumer who harbors a passion for Maggie, who disdains the bigness and waste of American movies, and the ain't-it-cool-style movie geek who interviews Maggie, singing the praises of Schwarzenegger and Van Damme and hoping that the age of personal movies is finally over. Assayas disdains the puritans on both sides, and his heroes bridge that divide: René, a maker of small personal movies who finds inspiration in the star of a Hong Kong action film (there's special poignancy in the bedraggled visage of Jean-Pierre Léaud, who spanned the whole of the nouvelle vague from *The 400 Blows* to *Weekend*), and the star herself, whose work encompasses Jackie Chan and Wong Kar-wai.

Irma Vep is a love song to Maggie Cheung (she and Assayas were briefly married after the film). This is an actress whose work has ranged from smashing movie-star acting (in Peter Chan's *Comrades: Almost a Love Story*) to a mystery worthy of Greta Garbo (in Zhang Yimou's *Hero*) to the total immersion in a role that only a handful of actors are capable of (in *Clean,* on which she reteamed with Assayas). Here, Assayas is confident that he can find all those possibilities in her face alone. It's a face that expresses girlish embarrassment as she's being tugged into her catsuit, as well as—in costume as Irma Vep, done up in ghostly white makeup, her kohl-lined eyes huge—the allure that is at the heart of cinema itself.

Maggie starts out behind, showing up late for the shooting, not even sure why she was hired. The poetry of *Irma Vep* is how she catches up—not in the stiff, formal scenes René shoots, but in the way she penetrates to the core René talked about.

In one of the loveliest sequences, Maggie, dressed in her catsuit, stalks restlessly about her hotel room with its debris of Coke cans, fashion mags, clothes, CD booklets. How, she seems to be wondering, does she become something real, something more than just pop detritus? With Sonic Youth's "Tunic" (an ironic elegy to the ultimate pop detritus: dead rock stars) blasting on the soundtrack, Maggie begins to "live" the part. René has told her the constricting suit should make her feel absolutely free, that the camera will find her and reveal her. Leaving her room, creeping up the spiral stairs that surround the elevator cage (that essentially European bit of scenery familiar from *Charade* to *Last Tango in Paris*), Maggie sneaks into another guest's room and purloins a tangle of jewels from the bathroom sink. It could be costume jewelry or the most valuable stones. No matter. Making her way to the roof in a howling rainstorm, Maggie prowls over the city like the character she's named for, or like Fantômas, the fiendish criminal mastermind in the pulp novels of Marcel Allain and Pierre Souvestre who, masked and tuxedoed, towered over the Paris skyline. She's lit from below in blue-white light, as if the night itself were adding to her luminousness. Regarding the jewels in her hand, she lets them fall, glittering among the raindrops; the thrill has been in the thievery.

In that sequence, Maggie is everything René could have wished for in his *Irma Vep*, only he isn't there to see it. He has realized his dream, though, and it's that vision that ends the film. As in the beginning, the production is in chaos. René and Maggie have left the project. The remaining crew and the new director (played by Lou Castel who, years before, starred in Marco Bellocchio's *Fists in the Pocket*) gather to see the footage René had edited.

"He'll muck it up in the editing room," someone has said of René earlier. Except that René has found his movie in the editing room. No more than fragments, and yet everything. In the black-and-white footage, Maggie sneaks up grand staircases, stands on wintry rooftops. René has scraped bits of emulsion off the surface of the film, like a favored stuffed animal that has had the fur loved off of it. Lines scratched into the celluloid emerge from Maggie's eyes like death rays, wavy figures buffer her face, circles dance around or obliterate her features. René's purposeful desecrations seem to be telling us how quickly Maggie's face, this image he dotes on, will be gone from us, as soon as the film slips the reel and the lights come up. What we have in that stolen time before is everything and nothing, a ghost of a movie and its essence. What we have is Maggie Cheung's face. And it's enough.

Irréversible
The backward gaze

Directed by Gaspar Noé; starring Monica Bellucci,
Vincent Cassel (2002)

by David Sterritt

IRRÉVERSIBLE DOESN'T TURN ME ON SEXUALLY, AND I HOPE I
never walk through a dark underground tunnel with anyone who does re-
spond to it that way. It does turn me on culturally, though, suggesting grim
truths and evoking severe moods rarely probed in today's cinema. These are
often horrifying, and therein lies their value. Intellectually and emotionally,
transgressive filmmaking this powerful is a genuine turn-on in its own bel-
ligerent, take-no-prisoners way.

Written and directed by Gaspar Noé, the film deals largely with two men,
Marcus and Pierre, overwhelmed by hate for the rapist who has brutalized a
woman, Alex, pregnant by one of them. Told in reverse chronology, the
movie shows them hunting down and killing a man in the bowels of The
Rectum, a gay nightclub. Then it portrays the excruciating rape that infuriated them. Finally it depicts the main characters earlier that day, indicating
how these cataclysms grew from bestial urges embedded in their personalities and, by extension, in all of human nature.

All of this unfolds through vertiginous camerawork, with audaciously
long takes depicting the vicious Rectum murder (modeled on documentary
footage of a botched execution) and the rape in such obsessive detail that one
reviewer called the film "little more than a snuff movie with subtitles." Yet
what makes *Irréversible* important are the very things that repel most of the

people who assail it: the shock provoked by its exploration of sexual agony and homicidal mayhem; its strategic use of homophobic and misogynistic tropes; its gyroscopic camerawork, stylized sound and lighting, and climactic burst of stroboscopic editing; and its against-the-grain analysis of space, time, and destiny. All serve the film's purpose of portraying modern society as a self-narcotized hell plagued by existential numbness so profound that Noé feels compelled to attack it with a battery of nightmarish assaults.

The film is structured by bodily and literary concerns. We begin in the realm of the anal—The Rectum, a dark and filthy place—in search of a villain called Le Tenia, the tapeworm, whose violence turns out to be infectious. Le Tenia anally rapes Alex in the tunnel of a dark, deserted underground passageway. We then progress to what Sigmund Freud might call the more "mature" vaginal realm. Alex and Marcus make love, and a home pregnancy test shows Alex she is expecting Marcus's child. The finale of the film (and start of the story) is almost blindingly beautiful, with Alex relaxing in a sunny park surrounded by children at play. This journey also echoes Dante's medieval vision—starting in the pits of Hell, continuing along the tortuous slopes of Purgatory, and ending with an apparition too blazingly delirious for human comprehension.

Another clue to the film's meaning is a book Alex is seen with more than once: *An Experiment with Time* by J. W. Dunne, first published in 1927. Dunne theorizes that there are multiple states of time. Time 1 is the kind we're accustomed to in daily life—moving steadily forward, with states of the external world experienced in succession. Time 2 exists in a kind of fourth dimension where future, past, and present merge. Dunne suggests that we can access Time 2 in various ways, including through our dreams, when our faculties don't concentrate so intensely on the present moment.

Scientists have dismissed Dunne's space-time metaphysics, but his theories have been taken up by dilettantes, dabblers, and an occasional artist like Noé, whose *Irréversible* conducts a similar kind of experiment. "You want to hypnotize with a movie," Noé once told me. "If the hypnosis works well, the audience will get into your dream."

According to Dunne, dreams and trances give potential access to Time 2. In our dreams, he writes: ". . . nothing stays to be looked at. Everything is in a state of flux. . . . And, because of the continual breaking down of your attempts at maintaining a concentrated focus, the dream story develops in a series of disconnected scenes. . . . You are always trying to keep attention moving steadily in the direction to which you are accustomed in your waking observation . . . but attention relaxes, and, when you recontract it, you find, as often as not, that it is focused on the wrong place. . . . You start on a journey, and find yourself abruptly at the end."

Irréversible captures this flux with uncanny precision. The film is also shaped by a sense of helplessness in the face of a future as unchangeable as it is unavoidable, since (as Dunne suggests) it is *already here*. The coexistence of different time states is signaled in *Irréversible* by the appearance of elusive signs and omens: Moments in the film's first, most violent scenes are later replayed in an affectionate context, suggesting links between "romantic love" and the brutality of rape and violence. (Marcus teasingly tells Alex, "I want to fuck you in the ass," for instance, a line clearly anticipating Alex's anal rape.) Banter, play fighting, and real violence are all intertwined and continually present. Only human perception interprets them as distinct.

Irréversible is inflected by the philosophy of fatalism, which states that whatever happens *must* happen, and that people do only what circumstances compel. Noé's characters are predestined to an *Irréversible* fate, and this hellish state is just the way things are. Humans can't save themselves from their destinies, which—in the case of Alex, Marcus, Le Tenia, and other characters—are marked by destruction and disaster.

In this sense, *Irréversible* reflects twentieth-century "age of anxiety" thought, characterized by a breakdown of traditional meaning systems and feelings of disillusionment and alienation. In the past century as before, tragedies and fears have been attributed to external factors—the will of God, the devil, an Axis of Evil, the configuration of planets. Noé suggests that in the twenty-first century we can no longer blame violence and disaster on any cause outside the brutal nature of humanity itself. Hence the film's eruptions of misogynistic and homophobic hate. Noé isn't toying with current cultural taboos; he's unmasking strains of revulsion and rage that still surge through today's allegedly civilized societies. All that's new is the degree of repression with which they are disguised.

Such camouflage is the worst enemy of all, Noé tells us, since it conceals truths about human instinct and impulse while encouraging the urge to disavow them within hypocritical shells of numbness and denial. It's this existential deadness that *Irréversible* assails, using cinema's most radical resources to distress, disorient, and alarm an audience accustomed to movies as a narcotizing pleasure, not a galvanizing journey into its own most desperately hidden realities.

It Happened One Night
But could it happen again?

Directed by Frank Capra; starring Claudette Colbert,
Clark Gable (1934)

by Kevin Thomas

GREAT FILMS AND GREAT CHEMISTRY SOMETIMES EMERGE BY
happy accident. This was especially true during the heyday of the studio system, and such was the case with the timeless *It Happened One Night,* one of
the most joyous Hollywood pictures ever made. It is also one of the sexiest,
thanks to palpable star chemistry and a perfect balance of camaraderie and
erotic suggestiveness.

It took director Frank Capra and writer Robert Riskin a while to warm to
the romantic-comedy possibilities of Samuel Hopkins Adams's *Cosmopolitan*
short story "Night Bus," about a spoiled runaway heiress and a wisecracking
reporter down on his luck. Casting, too, got off to a slow start. When Columbia's Harry Cohn tried to get MGM's Louis B. Mayer to cough up Myrna
Loy and Robert Montgomery, Mayer refused—but surprisingly offered Clark
Gable, to punish him for malingering in a futile attempt at a pay raise.
Miriam Hopkins, Margaret Sullavan, and Constance Bennett turned Capra
down. Bette Davis and Gable's future wife Carole Lombard were indisposed.
Cohn then thought of Claudette Colbert, even though Capra had directed
her screen debut, *For the Love of Mike* (1927), which in Capra's words was "a
stinker." Hardly enthralled, Colbert held out for double her $25,000 Para-
mount salary and insisted the picture be shot within her upcoming four-

week vacation, never dreaming the Columbia mogul, still struggling to lift his studio out of Poverty Row, would agree.

After such inauspicious beginnings, magic. Gable exuded a cockiness tempered by humor, a virility cushioned by sensitivity and vulnerability, while Colbert's sleek sophistication was matched by her natural warmth and allure. They made a tremendously sexy couple, and in this film established the images that would dominate their respective careers.

Just when down-to-earth New York newspaperman Peter Warne (Gable) is riding out his latest pink slip in Miami, impetuous banking heiress Ellen Andrews (Colbert) is jumping from her father's Miami-moored yacht to run off with a middle-aged society playboy. They meet while boarding the night bus for Manhattan—she's traveling incognito, but he recognizes her and smells a story—and they clash immediately, setting off sparks that ignite one of the screen's great romantic adventures.

Proving that sex appeal in movies is more than just a happy arrangement of the right flesh, the script here is flat-out perfection, offering Capra room for an energetic blend of breeziness and sentiment. The film never seems talky: For all the subtlety, richness, humor, and gallantry of the characters, the justly famous repartee, and the memorable set-pieces, the dialogue never upstages the storytelling work of the camera. It Happened One Night is a supreme example of image complementing word, right up there with the best of Billy Wilder—e.g., Sunset Boulevard and Some Like It Hot. You remember not only the lines, but the faces.

Timing played a role in the movie's reception. During the depths of the Great Depression, It Happened One Night lifted audiences everywhere, becoming one of the most heavily booked movies of its era and for years to come. Gable's character is the embodiment of the confident, can-do attitude the country so desperately missed. His enthusiastic wave to a passing freight shows solidarity with the common man. Of course, Peter is none too common. He's clearly a top-notch, untrammeled reporter in The Front Page tradition, a man of wit and sartorial style, and, beneath his bluster, a lonely romantic.

Ellen, too, is humanized, to balance the heiress factor. The most inspired touch is when she admits to Peter—who has accused her of a lack of humility and a belief that money solves everything—that she has in fact spent her life being told what to do and when and with whom. Her existence has been a gilded cage tended by nannies, governesses, and bodyguards. It is through Ellen then that the film becomes a grand adventure, and it is understandable why she would fall in love with a man as protective, independent, and resourceful as Peter.

By instinct or design—probably both—Capra and Riskin allow Peter to score all the points until, after their bus gets stuck in a storm, the couple decides to hitchhike. By now Peter is acting like a know-it-all and expounds on the fine art of thumbing a ride. Ellen bides her time, amused, as Peter's carefully honed technique repeatedly fails. She announces she'll give it a try her own way. A car immediately screeches to a halt after Ellen lifts her skirt to show one of the shapeliest legs ever to face a movie camera, thus proving "the limb is mightier than the thumb."

The hitchhiking scene is one of an unusual number of memorable—and often sexually suggestive—moments. There's the gallant, symbolic Wall of Jericho—a blanket Peter strings on a clothesline between their motel beds—that won't come tumbling down (until the end) in order to protect Ellen's modesty and also to insulate Peter from his own growing affection for her. There's Peter famously taking off his shirt to reveal no undershirt underneath, a fashion statement so bold it was rumored to have depressed sales of men's underwear. There's Peter teaching Ellie proper donut-dunking etiquette or negotiating sleeping arrangements in a haystack. It's just one inspired sequence after another.

Although the movie is quite famous for its flirtations and coy glimpses of skin (Gable's chest, Colbert's leg), the most splendid sequence underscores the movie's celebration of our commonality. It's when one bus passenger after another spontaneously contributes to a rousing rendition of "The Daring Young Man on the Flying Trapeze," their voices accumulating and swelling. This infectious sequence may well represent the most potent moment of collective happiness in American movies.

The enchantment of that moment also marks the thaw between Peter and Ellie, although a slight melt begins earlier when a crass salesman (Roscoe Karns) makes a pass at Ellen: "Shapely is my name and shapely is the way I like 'em!" It's a great comic moment, and Karns's supporting performance is equal to that of Walter Connolly as Ellen's father who, for all his wealth, is just as solid and shrewd as is Peter.

It Happened One Night swept the Oscars, but it would be difficult, if not impossible, to make this movie today. Consider the isolating nature of TV, the ascendance of consumerism and self-absorption, and above all the disintegration of our once solid middle class. This movie celebrates the common man and our common language; Americans no longer speak the same language—certainly not the one Capra and Riskin so expertly captured. Peter and Ellen would not have discovered each other had they not paid attention, listened, to each other. *It Happened One Night* is eternally amusing and sexy, but when viewed today, it is also a surprisingly wrenching experience. It celebrates an era and a style of intimacy that no longer exist.

The Eroticism of Words

by William Wolf

Words in movies can be as or more erotic than explicit sexual action. Take the case of Molly Bloom's soliloquy—not the complete text, but twenty long and moving minutes of it delivered in voice-over by Barbara Jefford in *Ulysses* (1967), based on James Joyce's classic novel and directed by Joseph Strick. The soliloquy is sensual in its expression of Molly's sexual longings while her husband, Leopold (Milo O'Shea), lies in bed with her, his head at her feet as is his custom. They have not made love since the death of their infant son. Molly's desires and her recollections of sexual escapades and fantasies are erotic in themselves, made even more so by her candid use of words that had been barred from the screen until then.

In a stream of consciousness, Molly reflects on her romps with Blazes Boylan:

> I wished he was here or somebody to let myself go and come again like that I feel all fire inside me or if I could dream it when he made me spend the 2nd time tickling me from behind with his finger I was coming for about 5 minutes with my legs around him I had to hug him after O Lord I wanted to shout out all sorts of things fuck or shit or anything at all . . .

Imagining Stephen Dedalus:

I often felt I wanted to kiss him all over also his lovely young cock there so simply I wouldn't mind taking him in my mouth if no-body was looking as if it was asking you to suck it so clean and white . . .

Molly recalls in the famous "yes" conclusion how she surrendered to Bloom:

And I thought well as well him as another and then I asked him with my eyes to ask again yes and then he asked me would I yes to say yes my mountain flower and first I put my arms around him yes and drew him down to me so he could feel my breasts all perfume yes and his heart was going like mad and yes I said yes I will yes.

Like Joyce's book itself, the film ran into all sorts of attacks and censorship. At the Cannes Film Festival, certain French subtitles were obliterated with a grease pencil. Strick tried to stop the projection, only to be hurled down the stairs from the booth. The festival director at the time, Robert Favre le Bret, told Strick that it was quite different to hear words than to read them—the height of irony, since it was in France that Joyce's book was first published.

The Hollywood Motion Picture Code of 1930 banned a long list of words, sexual and otherwise, and language has played an important part in determining ratings in the system adopted in 1968 by the Motion Picture Association of America. But by 2005, a movie like *Closer* could include scenes of Internet chats in which characters type out explicit sex acts they wish to perform. ■

[Quotes from the film *Ulysses* are taken from Joseph Strick's shooting script.]

Kinsey

It's too darn hot

Directed by Bill Condon; starring Liam Neeson,
Laura Linney, Peter Sarsgaard (2004)

by William Wolf

KINSEY IS SERIOUSLY ABOUT SEX. YET IT IS NOT AN EROTIC
movie and isn't meant to be. More than half a century after the publication
of Dr. Alfred Kinsey's then-startling *Sexual Behavior in the Human Male*
(1949)—which came to be known simply as The Kinsey Report—and his
Sexual Behavior in the Human Female (1953), this film raised hackles of
morality extremists who attacked it ferociously. Perhaps that should not have
been surprising in the increasingly censorial atmosphere of the George W.
Bush administration, as this biographical drama about the doctor, his life,
and his work is unusually frank when it comes to heterosexual and homosexual relationships and sexual impulses in general.

Still, it is disturbing that in 2004 a candid film about sexual practices that
is neither prurient nor exploitative would come under attack. It is also disappointing that a film as well made and important as *Kinsey* resulted in tepid
box-office figures. Despite generally favorable reviews, the U.S. gross as of
April 2005 was barely $10 million. One can't put the blame solely on the
controversy; perhaps moviegoers have become blasé about sex and are not
interested in such a film unless it's titillating. And serious films tend to get
lost in the contemporary marketplace anyway.

Nonetheless, *Kinsey* stands as a milestone for its analysis of sexual behavior within a drama format. Liam Neeson, playing the doctor, gives a strong,

nuanced performance that reflects Kinsey's obsession with his research. Laura Linney received an Oscar nomination for best actress for her incisive portrait of Kinsey's wife, who played a major part in his work. She also exercised her own right to explore, and the character is shown having an unconcealed affair with one of her husband's assistants. Two of the biodrama's strengths are its acceptance of extramarital relations as a fact of life and its acknowledgment of homosexual impulses.

Writer-director Bill Condon uses a swift and canny approach to set the mood and tone of the film. It opens ironically, with Kinsey, the great interviewer, being interviewed. It's part of the training he devised to school his staff in the art of eliciting detailed sexual histories from their subjects. Dramatically and structurally, Condon's device serves the dual purpose of introducing us to Kinsey and establishing the man's nonjudgmental technique.

Among the most moving performances is that of John Lithgow as Kinsey's ultramoralistic father, a preacher whose tirades include:

Lust has a thousand avenues. The dance hall, the ice cream parlor, the tenement saloon, the Turkish bath—like the hydra it grows new heads everywhere. Even the modern inventions of science are used to cultivate immorality. The gas engine has brought us the automobile joyride and the even more pernicious menace, the roadside brothel. Electricity has made possible the degrading picture show. Because of the telephone, a young woman can now hear the voice of her suitor on the pillow next to her. . . . And let us not forget the most scandalous invention of all: the Talon slide fastener, otherwise known as the zipper, which provides every man and boy speedy access to moral oblivion.

This extremism is later manifested in a poignant father-son discussion when Kinsey Sr. reveals that at the age of ten, to stop him from masturbating, "I was outfitted with a tight strap that I wore at all times. It kept me from coming into contact with my genitals. . . . The condition was cured."

Some of the invective spewed at this movie is not far removed from the ravings of Kinsey's father. Concerned Women for America (CWA) charged on its website that the film is "an attempt to cover up sex researcher Alfred Kinsey's horrifying reality," and quotes CWA director Robert Knight: "Alfred

Kinsey encouraged pedophiles to molest children, all in the name of science. Instead of being lionized, Kinsey's proper place is with Nazi Dr. Joseph Mengele or your average Hollywood horror flick mad scientist."

Movieguide, which describes itself as "A Family Guide to Movies and Entertainment," posted an article under the headline "Help Us Stop Hollywood's Normalization of Perversion" in which it accused *Kinsey* of promoting "a pro-homosexual agenda" and "an extreme humanist worldview that attacks Christians and traditional Christian values about sexual morality."

More disturbing is the rejection of a spot for *Kinsey* by Public Broadcasting's WNET. Frank Rich wrote in a *New York Times* piece headlined "The Plot Against Sex in America" that the first explanation for killing the spot was that it was "too commercial and too provocative." But Rich noted that the real problem was the movie's content, plus fear of controversy and viewer complaints—all made clear in an e-mail from a National Public Broadcasting media manager and leaked to the press by the film's distributor, Fox Searchlight. Rich wrote: "Maybe in the end Channel 13 got too many complaints about its own cowardice, because by last week, in response to my inquiries, it has a new story: That e-mail was all a big mistake—an 'unfortunate' miscommunication hatched by some poor unnamed flunky in marketing." Rich forcefully observed: "When they start pushing the panic button over 'moral values' at the bluest of TV channels, public broadcasting's WNET, in the bluest of cities, New York, you know this country has entered a new cultural twilight zone."

The sexual explicitness and liberal attitudes in *Kinsey* are certainly sufficient to anger an army of prudes. In one scene, Kinsey introduces a woman who experiences orgasms with machine-gun rapidity; she turns out to be a grandmotherly type in her late sixties. And in a moving coda, a middle-aged woman—a heart-wrenching turn by Lynn Redgrave—captures what Kinsey's research accomplished for so many who had been living in the sexual shadows. The woman recounts how while married she fell in love with another woman, but bottled up her feelings. "I couldn't talk to anyone about my situation, so I found other ways to cope. I took up drinking. Eventually my husband left me, and even my children fell away. I came very close to ending it all."

When Kinsey gently asks what happened, she replies: "You did, of course." The Kinsey Report let people like her know they were not alone. "I mustered the courage to talk to my friend, and she told me, to my great surprise, that the feelings were mutual. We've been together for three happy years now. . . . You saved my life, sir."

[Note: Quotes from the film *Kinsey* are from Bill Condon's shooting script, published by Newmarket Press.]

Klute
Nine to five

Directed by Alan J. Pakula; starring Jane Fonda,
Donald Sutherland (1971)

by Desson Thomson

THE CUSTOMER IS BASHFUL ABOUT HIS REQUEST, SO HE
whispers it in the call girl's ear. She smiles professionally.

"Wow, that sounds so fantastic," she says with all the erotic conviction of
an automated phone voice. "Oh, that's so exciting. But it's going to cost you
more."

Moments later, the john is heaving and gasping on top of her, almost suffocating her with his bulk. "Oh, angel," she moans theatrically. "Oh, my
angel." She steals a glance at her wristwatch.

In this early scene, we realize that *Klute* is about sex, and it isn't. It's erotic
at first blush, but closer to antifreeze soon after. As the call girl Bree Daniel,
Jane Fonda wears a tight, nipple-friendly sweater, knee-high boots, and a
shag haircut that departed from the long-haired hot-chick style of the early
'70s. She's a sexual grunt in the same way John Travolta's Vincent Vega is a
gangster underling in *Pulp Fiction* or the weed-toking soldiers are mere can-
non fodder in *Platoon*. A failed actress, Bree takes a professional approach to
being a pro, enjoying her sense of control over her customers, the johns.
"You lead them by the ring in their nose in the direction that they think they
want to go in," she tells her analyst.

Who better to keep us mindful of the dutiful mechanics of sex and political pillow games than Fonda? After all, she gamely played the intergalactic

sexual being for her exploitative first husband, French director Roger Vadim, in the 1968 *Barbarella,* and at his request arranged for prostitutes, sometimes two at a time, to join them in bed. Was that pleasure for her? Hardly. But Fonda did it, she has said, with a sort of chilly detachment, as a desperate attempt to save the marriage.

Looking at *Klute* now, through the revisionist prism of time, you can almost anticipate Fonda's lifetime of detached reinvention to follow. Perhaps it's Bree's sangfroid glance at that watch. "Too much organization," Vadim once said of his wife. "Time is her enemy. She cannot relax. Always there is something to do." And he said this: "There is also in Jane a basic wish to carry things to the limit."

After *Klute,* the Fonda of *Barbarella* metamorphosed into the radical anti-war activist Hanoi Jane. Later came Exercise Jane in the woolly leg warmers, then Executive Jane, no longer the political wife of Tom Hayden but now the power-spouse of Ted Turner. Most recently, she has transformed into a sort of Hillary Jane Clinton, the autobiographical author with the frosty coif, confessing all about her years of bulimia as well as those long-ago twosomes and threesomes for Roger.

Jane Fonda is a serial survivor, never afraid to take things to the limit—or to start over again. In a man, this is called resourcefulness; in a woman, it's calculating and unfeminine behavior—or, in the more mundane, schoolboy's assessment: Jane is up for anything.

All these connotations and thoughts make *Klute* an especially delicious movie for constant and perhaps unsoluble reassessment. As a teenager in 1971, I remember going to the K/B Cinema in Washington, D.C., and watching Fonda with rapt appreciation. I was drawn in by her performance, which turned out to be one of her best. (She won an Oscar for it.) Bree Daniel was more than just a hooker, I thought, she was a person. I also remember the movie's erotic charge.

But watching it again more than thirty years later, I have to ask, where and when is it so? That wristwatch moment is surely a passion-chiller for any man, and Bree's confessions to her unseen analyst aren't designed to rev the sexual pulse. I searched and searched until I found two sensual moments.

The first occurs when Bree attempts to seduce John Klute (Donald Sutherland) by unzipping her evening dress. "Would you mind not doing that?" begs the detective, who has spent most of the movie trying to track Bree's would-be killer and sublimate his own attraction to her. There is something about her back, and her willingness to display it, that cannot be explained rationally. Let's just say I don't share Klute's seeming reluctance to see it.

The second moment is in the final scene when the stalker confronts Bree and plays a tape (remember reel-to-reel?) containing a traumatic recording from long ago, when a transaction between them turned brutally ugly. As she listens to her own distress on tape, Bree's head bends forward. Her cheeks become wet with grief. All of the Fonda brittleness and unflappability melt away. She softens beautifully. For that fleeting moment, Jane Fonda sits there, tender and warm-blooded. I feel a need to reach out and hold her.

The Last of the Mohicans
Manifest destiny

Directed by Michael Mann; starring Daniel Day-Lewis,
Madeleine Stowe, Russell Means (1992)

by Matt Zoller Seitz

A ROMANTIC DRAMA SET DURING THE FRENCH AND INDIAN
War, Michael Mann's *The Last of the Mohicans* is a primal epic of survival and
the overpowering urge to reproduce. Reworking the 1936 movie of the same
name, Mann and coscreenwriter Christopher Crowe transform their literary
source, James Fenimore Cooper's chaste frontier potboiler, into a passionate
tale of tough, simple men fighting and dying for land and women. In the
movie's political/historical background, native tribes, white settlers, and
British and French military forces compete for the mountains and forests that
they hope will someday be overrun by their descendants. *Mohicans* shows
that both the individual goal to mate and pass on genes and a civilization's
desire to possess and transform the land issue from the same biological urge.
As articulated in the original 1992 version, and detailed further in Mann's
2002 director's cut, the major characters are driven by the need to control,
protect, or perpetuate their bloodlines.

The film's central triangle sees Nathaniel "Hawkeye" Poe (Daniel Day-
Lewis), the adopted white son of Mohawk warrior Chingachgook (Russell
Means), competing with British Major Duncan Heyward (Steven Wadding-
ton) to defend and possess Cora Munro (Madeleine Stowe), Duncan's pre-
sumptive fiancée and the daughter of a British colonel. A secondary triangle
echoes the first: Nathaniel's adoptive brother Uncas (Eric Schweig) pairs off

with Cora's sister, Alice (Jodhi May), then loses her to Magua (Wes Studi), a Huron warrior whose wife and child died in an attack ordered by the Munro sisters' father, Colonel Edmund Munro (Maurice Roëves).

The sustained comparison between two prizes—land and women—is established in the spectacular opening sequence. After a terse, scene-setting title card, Mann reveals the story's geographical and metaphoric prize: the wilderness of upstate New York (actually filmed in North Carolina). Shooting in CinemaScope with long lenses, director of photography Dante Spinotti flattens and abstracts the blue-green mountains to emphasize their rising, falling curves, then pans elegantly from right to left, inviting us to caress those curves with our eyes. The next shot is a static panorama of converging mountains that unexpectedly tilts down, swooning into a triangular valley shrouded by mist.

Then we meet our heroes—Nathaniel, his adoptive father Chingachgook, and Chingachgook's blood son Uncas, stalking and killing a deer. After blessing the deer's carcass, the hunters visit friends in an isolated cabin—the married couple Alexandra and John Cameron (Tracey Ellis and Terry Kinney) and their young children. Alexandra remarks, "Why is Uncas with you? He should have settled with a woman, started a family by now." Nathaniel says they'll winter in "Kentuc-kee" and jokes that they'll "find a Delaware-speaking woman for Uncas. She will say, 'You are the one!' and bear him many children!" Upon repeat viewings, these lines ring with sadness; Chingachgook and Uncas are the sole survivors of a once proud bloodline—the last of the Mohicans. Uncas will find a mate, then perish defending her.

Mann and Crowe's script repeatedly invokes blood and bloodlines, hearts, wombs, marriage, and "seed." Early on, when Cora rebuffs a marriage proposal by Duncan—an emblem of the boring old England she left behind—the English officer's arrival is heralded by a long shot of his carriage traversing a bridge; the bridge's arch and the arch's reflection in the river create a perfect egg shape in the center of the frame.

When our native tracker heroes save the Munro sisters from a Huron assault, Cora cozies up to Nathaniel and admits that the American frontier is "more deeply stirring to my blood than any imagining could possibly have been." Cora's beauty and bravery mark her as an ideal frontier wife, transforming Nathaniel from single warrior to committed mate so rapidly that neither has time to contemplate the change. "I don't call myself subject to much at all," Nathaniel jokes in an early scene, a slap against government that also alludes to his lack of romantic attachments. But midway through, in one of the simplest and most powerful statements of commitment in American cinema, he tells Cora, "You be strong, you survive. . . . Stay alive, no matter what occurs. I will find you."

Nathaniel's monologue about the origin of the stars reinforces the film's symbolic architecture, which is intensely concerned with sex, reproduction, and legacy. "My father's people say that at the birth of the sun and of his brother the moon, their mother died," he tells Cora. "So the sun gave to the earth her body, from which was to spring all life. And he drew forth from her breast the stars, and the stars he threw into the night sky to remind him of her soul."

Magua, whose own bloodline was destroyed by Munro, vows vengeance against the colonel's family: "When the Grey Hair is dead, Magua will eat his heart. Before he dies, Magua will put his children under the knife, so the Grey Hair will know his seed is wiped out forever." Sweet, stoic Uncas seizes a chance to extend his own endangered bloodline by protecting helpless Alice. But late in the film, after the Munro sisters have been kidnapped by a Huron war party, a Huron chief imperils Uncas's dream, giving Alice to Magua so that Magua can pass on his bloodline and "heal his broken heart." During the film's climactic mountaintop battle, Magua cements his claim on Alice by killing Uncas in hand-to-hand combat (and in a powerful yet ambiguous gesture, beckons Alice with a hand stained by Uncas's blood). But Alice leaps off a cliff rather than become his mate.

Incidental characters and situations reinforce the film's sense of biological urgency. Throughout *Mohicans,* men and women struggle to reunite after violent separations, or to prevent their mates or offspring from being wiped out. A dramatic crest occurs in the final act when a Huron chief orders that Alice be given to Magua and Cora be burned to death. Nathaniel reflexively offers to die in Cora's place. But Nathaniel's romantic rival, Duncan, who serves as translator in the scene, manipulates the proposal so that Duncan is the one volunteering to die. Duncan perishes so that his beloved Cora—the woman who resisted his marriage proposal—might survive.

Mohicans is less an action picture, romance, or war film than it is a fierce and beautiful dream about fighting, rutting, dying, and leaving behind some trace of yourself. That so many of the characters fail to accomplish that last part gives the picture a rare feeling of melancholy. This sadness is most pervasive at the end, when surviving characters Nathaniel, Cora, and

Chingachgook stand on a mountaintop surveying the land so many people died to possess.

"The frontier moves with the sun and pushes the Red Man of these wilderness forests in front of it until one day there will be nowhere left," Chingagchgook says. "Then our race will be no more, or be not us."

"That is my father's sadness talking," Nathaniel says.

"No, it is true," his father replies. "The frontier place is for people like my white son and his woman and their children. And one day there will be no more frontier, and men like you will go too, like the Mohicans. And new people will come, work, struggle. Some will make their life. But once, we were here."

Last Tango in Paris
Power play

Directed by Bernardo Bertolucci; starring Marlon Brando,
Maria Schneider (1972)

by Peter Brunette

LIKE MANY CRITICS MY AGE, I WAS NEARLY STRUCK DUMB BY
the sexual power and joyfully perverse *attitude* of Bernardo Bertolucci's *Last
Tango in Paris*. So when Marlon Brando, without whom one cannot even
begin to imagine this film, died in 2004, I decided to pay a little homage of
my own and watch the film again. Wow. What mostly struck me was how
much I was still struck by it, more than thirty years later.

Countless Brando impersonators have uttered the famous phrase, "Go get
the butter." The line is spat out by Brando's character, Paul, when he is about
to indulge in some anal sex with his love slave, Jeanne, played by the much
younger and supremely sexy Maria Schneider. The butter aside, what got to
me most on my recent viewing (I must have repressed it back in 1972) was
the scene in the kitchen, much later, when Paul demands that Jeanne find
the nail scissors, trim her nails, and—this is in the dialogue—stick her fingers up his ass. This was pretty intense for a Catholic kid growing up in the
'50s in Pittsburgh. It still is.

What remains more disturbing than the sex itself are the sexual *situations*, and the shifts in power that are achieved through a variety of humil-
iations instead of money shots. (The idea of a couple meeting regularly,
anonymously, in the neutral territory of a rented apartment solely for the
purpose of sex is such a powerful one that it was repeated in Patrice

Chéreau's *Intimacy* in 2001.) The wounded Paul, still trying to understand why his wife committed suicide, is harsh and demanding, yet Jeanne seems to draw sustenance from his brutal treatment of her. When he anally rapes her—surely this is the word for it, despite some ambiguity—he demands that she repeat half-comprehensible phrases like "Holy Family Church of Good Citizens," and "the will is broken by oppression," the first overt appearance in the film of Bertolucci's characteristic linking of sexuality and politics. Later, when Jeanne puts her fingers up Paul's ass, Bertolucci seems to want to equalize the lovers, since both have now been anally penetrated, though it is important to remember that it is Paul who gives the directions and who demands Jeanne's total capitulation by promising to "swallow vomit," "smell pig farts," and so forth. "Will you do that for me?" he shouts. "I will do more than that," she answers.

From the beginning of their encounters, Paul insists on no names, wanting to keep their relationship as elemental (pure?) as possible. ("Everything outside is bullshit," he hollers.) He insists she realize that every person is essentially alone, and that one can survive only "by looking death in the face, by going right up his ass." This motif of the elemental, the brutal but natural—as opposed to the safely middle-class—is embroidered when Paul and Jeanne imitate wild beasts, grunting and snorting, a humorous scene in an otherwise pretty serious movie.

Jeanne's attraction to the aging Paul is, it is suggested, due to unresolved feelings toward her soldier father, who served in France's various colonial adventures. (Another of Bertolucci's abiding interests is psychoanalysis.) At the very end of the film, Paul puts on her father's military cap, collapsing the two figures, just before Jeanne shoots him with her father's ancient gun. (The doubling motif also shows up in the identical robes Paul's wife had bought for him and her lover, Marcel, played by Massimo Girotti.) Paul's motivation (in addition to the obvious) stems from an all-consuming loneliness, which obviously predates his wife's suicide.

One big draw of the film for me was, and is, the sheer size of Maria Schneider's breasts, and the multiple full-frontal shots of her forest of pubic hair. She seems utterly at ease and fully compliant, every heterosexual male's dream. As was typical for movies of the era, there is not a single shot of Brando's genitals, which also says something about the gender politics between the story's characters and in the larger society of the time. But, though we don't see much or any of Brando's body, references are made to the (real-life) problem he had keeping weight off his midsection. Any glimpse of his body might have uncomfortably echoed the fleshy-creatured Francis Bacon paintings of the film's opening credits.

Bertolucci's lifelong fascination with sexual dynamics and their relation to power and politics (*Before the Revolution, 1900*) is in evidence here, often expressed through the manipulation of the visual and references to the act of seeing. Mirrors abound, with their suggestion of the instability of personal identity and visual perception. Equally ubiquitous are shots of characters taken through the distorting glass of bathroom windows—which also, not coincidentally, refer back to the Bacon paintings.

Bertolucci's larger political point is made through the unavoidable comparison between Jeanne's two lovers. On one hand, there's Paul in all his wild, brutal, painfully vulnerable vitality. On the other, there's Jeanne's fiancé, Tom—played by Jean-Pierre Léaud, who uses an over-the-top, stylized manner that isn't, frankly, completely successful. In a clearly self-reflexive gesture pointing to Bertolucci's presence, Tom is making a film of his relationship with Jeanne, but it's a "reality" soaked in the movies, as when he ebulliently compares her to Joan Crawford, Ava Gardner, and so on. This often silly, completely bourgeois "cinematic" relationship is at odds with the "real" relationship that Paul represents. (This will be Paul's second defeat at the hands of middle-class values, the first being when his mother-in-law insists on a proper church burial for the wife who has killed herself.) When Tom films Jeanne picking out a wedding gown, Jeanne talks about how well they embody that focus of contemporary advertising, the perfectly happy young couple.

By the end of the film, Paul has fallen in love with Jeanne and is now more than willing to name names and make plans for the future. They go to a sad dance hall where a tango contest is taking place (like love, Paul points out, the tango is an elaborate ritual), and get sadly drunk while the "last tango" plays. Jeanne is completely turned off; the balance of power has clearly shifted in her favor. Though she masturbates Paul in a dark corner of the dance hall as a kind of farewell gift, it isn't enough for him, and he pursues her through the streets of Paris (a constant presence in the film) until death intervenes. Rehearsing her story for the police, Jeanne says aloud, "I don't know who he is," "I don't know his name." Both statements, on several levels, are utterly true.

Last Tango with Grandma

by Desson Thomson

My grandmother died Friday, September 7, 2001, a few days before the world changed forever. She was spared that trauma. But she did not escape the indignity I dealt her one spring evening in 1973.

That was when she visited my boarding school in England to give her fifteen-year-old grandson a night out in London. I was dressed in my school uniform: navy blazer, tie, white shirt, gray dress pants. I told her I wanted to see a movie in the West End, something arty. Yeah, I was that kind of kid.

We found a theater playing *Last Tango in Paris*. You probably know the movie. Not minutes into it, Paul (Marlon Brando) and Jeanne (Maria Schneider), complete strangers, decide to share a Paris apartment. Soon they are entwined around each other, rutting against the wall. Paul, still standing, has his long coat wrapped around her. She clamps her legs around him like a cat trying to slither up a thick, slippery tree. When the noisy encounter is over, Jeanne rolls naked and exhausted across the floor toward the camera.

This would have been ecstasy for a fifteen-year-old boy under most circumstances. But I was sitting next to Martha Gertrude Daniels, who wore a crucifix around her neck, sang hymns in church with quiet conviction, and faithfully took communion every Sunday. Throughout the movie, she never budged, her lips taut with shock.

I knew the critics, including Pauline Kael, were raving about this movie, but I hadn't actually read the reviews. I slipped lower and lower into my seat, transfixed by the sensuality onscreen but too flushed with embarrassment to enjoy it. I winced as Paul ordered Jeanne to get the butter. I cringed when he joked about his penis or informed Jeanne matter-of-factly that she'd be playing soccer with her tits when she got older. This might be funny one day, I thought. But not now.

I kept remembering the last movie my grandmother took me to see: *The Sound of Music.*

I remember nothing else about that outing except deep shame as we trudged silently out of the theater. We never spoke of that night again. I have seen *Last Tango* many times since and have even given myself permission to enjoy it. But there isn't a moment when I don't catch an eerie image in the periphery of my vision: It is a pair of lips, taut, appalled. ∎

Laura

Portrait of a lady

Directed by Otto Preminger; starring Gene Tierney,
Dana Andrews, Clifton Webb (1944)

by Emanuel Levy

WITH TIME, OTTO PREMINGER'S **LAURA** GETS RICHER IN
texture, deeper in meaning, and more problematic than most noir films of
the 1940s. An intense meditation on the nature of love and control, *Laura*
tackles such taboos as voyeurism, fetishism, and necrophilia a whole decade
before Hitchcock's masterpiece *Vertigo,* which bears some thematic resem-
blance to the 1944 film in its disturbing depiction of obsessive love initiated
by an encounter with a portrait and a presumably dead woman.

A troubled production from beginning to end, *Laura* serves as a case study
for the notorious battles between strong directors and even stronger execs,
such as Darryl F. Zanuck, head of 20th Century–Fox. Initially, Preminger was
only to produce, but when Zanuck rejected Rouben Mamoulian's dailies, Preminger got his wish to direct as well.

Laura achieved status as a classic for several reasons. It was one of five
films that French critic Nino Frank identified as film noir when he coined
the term in 1946 to suggest similarities between a cycle of dark Hollywood
pictures and the hard-boiled detective fiction published by Gallimard as part
of its "Série Noire."

Contributing to the film's distinctive mood is David Raksin's lush tune, to
which, at the behest of Fox, lyrics were added by Johnny Mercer months

after the film's release. The haunting theme song that resulted made *Laura* even more popular at the box office.

Finally, Preminger had to fight to cast Clifton Webb in the crucial part of Waldo Lydecker, the shrewd columnist and Laura's mentor, due to Fox's concerns that Webb was too effeminate. Preminger won, and *Laura* became the first major film for the British thespian, who overshadows the other actors with his idiosyncratic and deliciously nasty performance.

The story line is deceptively simple. Detective Mark McPherson (Dana Andrews) is investigating the murder of Laura Hunt (Gene Tierney), presumably killed with a shotgun. He interviews Lydecker, an acid-tongued radio and newspaper commentator who knew Laura well. Together they visit Ann Treadwell (Judith Anderson), Laura's aunt, who is infatuated with Shelby Carpenter (Vincent Price), Laura's fiancé.

Thematically, *Laura* depicts a cynical world in which every player has motive and capacity for murder. Given such a premise, the ostensibly happy ending—Laura and McPherson embark on a new life together—is strange and incoherent. That's why purists fault *Laura* for being more of a romantic melodrama than a quintessential noir, whose innate pessimism usually leads to loss and defeat.

Structurally, *Laura* is divided into two equal parts. In the first half, the audience believes that Laura is dead, and in the second, that she is alive. The transition occurs when McPherson falls asleep in Laura's apartment beneath the gaze of her portrait, and she walks through the door. You can see the influence of the seminal *Citizen Kane,* whose story of the investigation of a complex figure and convoluted temporal structure likewise depends on flashbacks. In both films, the characters' pasts reveal crucial cues to their present problems.

Manipulation of point of view is a common component of the detective film. One thing that makes *Laura* intriguing is that even though Lydecker is a prime suspect, he narrates the first half, giving the impression that he's the protagonist. Lydecker's opening line, "I shall never forget the weekend Laura died," indicates a subjective POV. He then relates how he met Laura, helped her career in advertising, and succeeded in choking off her romances with other men.

McPherson plays a phlegmatic, unimportant role in the first half. But once the camera transfers the POV to him, most scenes begin with McPherson arriving at the scene or already on hand. For the sake of clarity, the POV then stays with the detective, but in the final scene, when Lydecker is disclosed as the killer, the film abandons individual POV entirely for an objective perspective.

The most controversial issues here are voyeurism and fetishism, exhibited by both Lydecker and McPherson. Despite divergent personalities, the two men share an obsession with Laura and a need to control her as an object of desire. They embody different values and temperaments, yet both are in thrall to an elusive woman who reveals little of herself. The Laura that each creates is therefore a product of fantasy.

Laura remains an enigma throughout the film. Her only act of independence is to go to the country for a weekend (during which the murder occurs) in order to resolve her feelings for Shelby Carpenter. On her return, she resumes a passive role and is again manipulated, this time by the detective. Early on, Lydecker tells Laura: "You have one tragic weakness. With you, a lean, strong body is the measure of a man, and you always get hurt." So it's not surprising that Laura ends up preferring the dull but virile cop over the effete art critic. Anti-intellectualism runs through all Hollywood genres, not just noir; *real* men aren't interested in literature, art, or music, all signs of effeminacy or homosexuality.

McPherson falls in love with a dead woman through her diary and portrait. In the creepiest scene, McPherson, motivated by insatiable curiosity and desire, examines Laura's possessions. He stares at her portrait, has a drink, considers her bed, handkerchief, perfume, and clothes, reads her diary, and falls asleep in her easy chair, all signals of sexual fantasy. Is McPherson only able to love the ghost of a woman, a dream expressed in a painting?

Laura not only allows but encourages viewers to transgress the Production Code's prohibitions against voyeurism and fetishism. Raksin's score underlines the romantic-fantasy element of McPherson's exploration, and the whole movie, lavishly photographed by Joseph LaShelle, has a sumptuously dreamy and supernatural atmosphere. Preminger's gliding yet probing camera is the perfect visual analogue to Lydecker's perversions and McPherson's obsessions.

All the important ideas are conveyed in the interactions between McPherson and Lydecker, although it's bizarre that the detective spends so much time with his prime suspect. Lydecker brings into the open McPherson's la-tent fantasies when he asks: "Have you ever dreamed of Laura as your wife?" And he continues to taunt him: "You'd better watch out or you'll end up in a psychiatric ward. I don't think they've ever had a patient who fell in love with a corpse."

Like most noir protagonists, McPherson is a flawed hero. He constantly plays with a pocket baseball game; it "keeps me calm." He explodes at a party and punches Carpenter. There's mention of a gunfight in which he was injured and which might have left mental scars. His brusque manner often crosses the line; while interrogating Laura under glaring lights, he leans over her aggressively in a scene replete with sexual connotations: "Now, did you really decide to call the marriage off, or did you just tell me that because you know I wanted to hear it?" McPherson conceals a smile and a sigh of relief when Laura declares that she doesn't love Carpenter.

Though tough, McPherson is defensive where women are concerned. Asked by Lydecker if he's ever been in love, he replies: "A doll in Washington Heights got a fox fur out of me once." When they inspect Laura's apartment, Lydecker says: "Look around, is this the home of a *dame*?" expressing resentment over McPherson's vulgar description of his Laura.

In the final reel, the unloved and unwanted Lydecker is reduced to a sadistic madman seeking revenge. His first shotgun blast was meant to mutilate Laura's face, and he uses the same gun for his second try at her.

First seen in the credit sequence, Laura's portrait becomes a permanent fixture, even a character. The camera concentrates on Lydecker and McPherson's focused gaze on it, and their gaze guides the viewers' perspective, which in turn is reinforced by the painting's composition. Laura seems to be looking at them—at us—from any place in the room.

Despite the "happy ending," ambiguity prevails. When Laura and McPherson walk off together, the camera doesn't follow them but tracks back to the shattered clock, and the film gives Lydecker the final words: "Goodbye, my love." The clock, a symbol of their asexual, intellectual relationship, is Laura's last link to Lydecker; by destroying the clock, she is free. But is she really? Laura's departure with the detective suggests yet another unhealthy relationship with a "lean and strong" man. As Lydecker observed, it's Laura's "one tragic weakness."

Laurel Canyon
Everybody in the pool

Directed by Lisa Cholodenko; starring Frances McDormand, Christian Bale, Kate Beckinsale, Natascha McElhone (2002)

by Carrie Rickey

HIPPIE PARENTS AND THEIR CONSERVATIVE SPAWN HAVE BEEN comic foils at least since denim-clad Michael Gross rolled his eyes at Michael J. Fox's Brooks Brothers suits on television's *Family Ties.* But that sitcom parent and child had only a political generation gap to span. In the primally charged *Laurel Canyon,* the wild-maned Jane (Frances McDormand) and her carefully coiffed son Sam (Christian Bale) stare at each other across the wider, deeper, more fraught chasm of the sexual generation gap.

The distance between Jane, a juicy rock-music producer with a taste for threesomes, and Sam, a stony Harvard med grad doing his residency in psychiatry, is partly a product of different ages and values. But in larger part it is the product of the son's lifelong refusal to accept his mother, herself accepting of everyone in the world but Sam. The film dives into a pool both metaphorical and real, where the son's if-it-feels-conflicted, don't-do-it vibe butts up against his mother's philosophy of anything goes. Warmed by sexual heat, this pool is also where libertine Mama literally skinny-dips with virtuous Sonny's fiancée, Alex (Kate Beckinsale), before ultimately learning to respect Sam's boundaries.

Lisa Cholodenko's superlative, drolly observed film about this free spirit and her tightly wound son has more twists than Laurel Canyon, the pass carved out of schist and scrub that snakes through the Hollywood Hills.

Though a relatively discreet, R-rated film, its erotic payload and emotional payoff favorably compare with more graphic product.

For Cholodenko, Laurel Canyon is a place both geographical and sexual, where lush flowers mask prickly underbrush. Like the figures in Joni Mitchell's "Ladies of the Canyon," Jane comes wrapped in siren songs and gypsy shawls. She's the flower-child-turned-earth-mother who nurtures everyone but her grown son.

For his part, Sam arrives swaddled in clinician's detachment and disapproval of Jane's lifestyle, not to mention lovestyle. You don't have to be a psychiatry resident to see that Sam is pathologically jealous of Jane's surrogate children, the many musicians she cossets and occasionally enjoys affairs with. One of them is Ian (the supremely charismatic, hunky, and humpy Alessandro Nivola), whose new album Jane is producing. Another is the ex-beau to whom she gave her beach house in Malibu, which is why she and Ian's band are still in the vine-swathed Laurel Canyon house. Never mind that Jane promised it to Sam as a love nest for him and his Boston Brahmin fiancée, a Harvard grad working on her biology dissertation (on the sex lives of fruit flies). As the young doctors hypothesize theories of sexuality, the mature musicians are busy fucking.

When Sam and Alex arrive at the Laurel Canyon house, they are startled to find Jane, Ian, and the boys in the band hanging out and hung over. Sam went to med school precisely because he couldn't live on his mother's diet of forbidden fruit and cigarettes; his form of rebellion is to overthink and sublimate the urges his mother wouldn't think twice about acting upon. But it's that very atmosphere Sam ran from that proves to be an aphrodisiac for cerebral Alex. Exposure to Jane, whose erotic energy is electromagnetic, has the brainiac wanting to live more in her body—and wanting to reveal it too. Beckinsale's Alex is the art-film version of that porn-film cliché, the repressed girl in a bun who discovers sex and loosens her hair. Within days of arriving at Villa Bougainvillea, Alex has exchanged concealing clothes for gauzy ones. Before long she is nude-bathing with Jane and Ian in the pool, sharing open-mouthed kisses with her future mother-in-law and extended foreplay with the musician.

As Alex unzips her libido, Sam grows even more buttoned up, finding the structure he needs in his work and a confidante in his fellow resident, Sara (Natascha McElhone), to whom he is intellectually and sexually drawn.

The film offers the quasi-incestuous frisson of a young woman attracted to her fiancée's mother, and also implicitly suggests that Jane's ideal partner is the same age as her son and that Sam's ideal partner has the same temperament as his mother. To Cholodenko's credit, she doesn't take sides, maintaining a different-strokes-for-different-folks appreciation of her characters without privileging one sexual arrangement over another: She notes that Jane would rather do it than talk about it and that Sam prefers to talk about it rather than do it, and that both could intensify their pleasure by considering the consequences of sex.

The movie samples erotic flavors from vanilla to rocky road, all while exploring the psychology of sexual taste. However, it does suggest the superiority of a certain sexual venue. In Laurel Canyon, a bed has limits of space that limit the imagination, and a phone is a great sex tool for fantasy and foreplay. But it is the pool—that fluid, forgiving place where one can stick a toe in, wade, or take the plunge—that is the ideal site of sexual baptism and cleansing, reconciliation and renewal.

The Long, Hot Summer
Burn, baby, burn!

Directed by Martin Ritt; starring Paul Newman,
Joanne Woodward, Orson Welles (1958)

by James Verniere

BOOKENDED BY BURNING BARNS, MARTIN RITT'S **THE LONG,**
Hot Summer features the first screen matchup of Paul Newman and Joanne
Woodward, plus more enflamed penises per acre than perhaps any main-
stream American film released in the 1950s.

Ritt's third film starts and ends with burning barns, but it's really about
bodies in heat—the sultry, wet heat of the South and the heat of lust and
longing. It's based on William Faulkner's 1940 novel *The Hamlet* and 1939
short story "Barn Burning." But the action seems a far cry from Faulkner's fictional Yoknapatawpha County when this 1958 release begins in the contem-
poraneous South with the arrival of a handsome stranger (Newman) in the
hamlet of Frenchman's Bend (it was shot in Louisiana).

In the novel, the young drifter's name is Flem Snopes (he is a member of
Faulkner's morally debased, upwardly mobile Snopes clan). No doubt "Flem"
was unacceptable for a character played by the matinee idol Newman, and
the more glamorous, suggestive, if not ejaculatory tag Ben Quick was bor-
rowed from a minor Faulkner character.

As Gabriel Miller notes in his insightful study *Fanfare for the Common
Man: The Films of Martin Ritt*, *The Long, Hot Summer*, which was adapted for
the screen by Ritt's collaborators Irving Ravetch and Harriet Frank, Jr.,
seems more like an adaptation of Tennessee Williams (not to mention

Erskine Caldwell, whose scandalous Georgia-set novel *God's Little Acre* also reached the screen in 1958). Many characters and scenes will especially remind viewers of Williams's 1955 stage sensation *Cat on a Hot Tin Roof,* also brought to the screen in 1958 with Newman in a lead role.

According to Miller, the title was changed to avoid confusion with Shakespeare. But I can think of other reasons to change the title from *The Hamlet* to the more Williamsesque *The Long, Hot Summer.* Considering how catchy and suggestive it is (Jimmie Rodgers had a hit with Sammy Cahn and Alex North's eponymous theme song), I'd say it was a flagrant Freudian sales pitch to 1950s audiences longing to catch a streetcar named desire.

Speaking of Williams, *The Long, Hot Summer* even has its own Big Daddy, the Rabelaisian Will Varner, owner of much of Frenchman's Bend's real estate and business, if not its citizens, and played by a heavily made-up Orson Welles, then forty-two. Welles, whose Falstaffian performance is pure, hickory-smoked ham, challenged Ritt's authority, according to Miller, until the alpha males agreed on a truce.

Figuratively speaking, the film is replete with big, swinging dicks. Even the bloated, cigar-chomping Will Varner is perpetually tumescent, openly cavorting with Minnie Littlejohn (a luminous, pricelessly funny Angela Lansbury), whose surname could be a pet name for a penis. When Will's not draining beer bottles on Minnie's porch, he's inhaling her homemade piccalilli and ripping into her corned beef. His appetites suggest a gluttonous sexuality.

The other women in Will's harem are his headstrong, unmarried daughter Clara (Woodward), the epitome of the repressed schoolmarm of boys' wet dreams, and daughter-in-law Eula (a dazzling Lee Remick), a sexpot from whom Will (like Big Daddy of *Cat*) wants grandchildren. Eula is married to Will's ne'er-do-well son Jody (Tony Franciosa) and is so desirable that the young men of the town come to the Varner place at night to howl and call her name in the darkness. While Jody is duly priapic in his wife's presence, he has not impregnated her and is apparently equally ineffectual in other areas of endeavor, the weakling son of a strong, overbearing father.

The film is an erotic comedy pitting lowborn sharecropper Ben against Varner's impotent heir Jody and the refined, bloodless Southern aristocrat (an excellent Richard Anderson) who has been courting Clara indifferently.

Ben, described by Varner as "a big stud horse," is also a human battering ram sent to conquer the fortresslike Clara and thus provide Will with a strong line of descendants (in this sense, the name Quick also connotes something vibrant and alive, as in "the quick and the dead"). Newman, one of the handsomest leads in movie history, was busy in 1958, also appearing in Arthur Penn's *The Left Handed Gun* and Leo McCarey's *Rally 'Round the Flag, Boys!* He brings urbanity, humor, and a sense of social justice—things he also would bring to *Cool Hand Luke* (1967)—to Ben Quick, as well as an impressive set of abs (a porkpie hat Ben wears at a picnic apparently was admired and coopted by Jude Law for the misconceived *Alfie* remake).

In one spectacularly suggestive sequence, Newman's Ben stands barechested outside Clara's bedroom looking at a mirrored reflection of her in her childhood bed and calls her name, gently but also lewdly, imitating the horny town boys. In case we don't get the point, Ritt cuts to a church steeple, gleaming white and erect in the morning sun. In other scenes, Ben irradiates Clara with his beaming—if not leering—smile, and relishes a seeming ability to see through her clothes. Newman's libidinous masculinity, wit, and intelligence are reminiscent of Clark Gable, and the chemistry he and Woodward generate recalls the legendary Gable–Vivien Leigh flare-ups in *Gone With the Wind* (1939), as well as Gable's even sexier work with Claudette Colbert in *It Happened One Night* (1934).

Woodward's tightly bunned-and-buttoned teacher oozes erotic longing from her pores, something Woodward also managed in her Oscar-winning performance in *The Three Faces of Eve* (1957), when she lets one of Eve's "other" personalities seduce Eve's cloddish husband. Notably, Woodward's Clara is even more desirable than Eula because she is better educated, more refined, more curious about life.

Even Woodward's scenes with Welles ooze sexuality insofar as Will, in an effort to mitigate his offensive words, repeatedly compares his daughter with his late wife, reminding Clara of the powerful physical attraction they had shared. Vocally, Welles's performance could be described as one long, bestial grunt.

The Long, Hot Summer earned Newman the best actor prize at Cannes in 1958 and was the first of many Ritt-Newman collaborations, including *Hud* and *Hombre*. Ritt had taught Newman, Woodward, Remick, and Franciosa at the Actors Studio, something that probably set Welles apart and may have helped set the "generations" apart onscreen as well.

Ritt, who believed directing was "80 percent casting," assembled one of the sexiest lineups of his time for *The Long, Hot Summer,* and it makes the film more than just a hugely entertaining Southern-gothic erotic comedy. By their humid example, they paved the way for every American growing up in the 1950s to a long, hot summer that has never ended.

The Makioka Sisters

Incandescence

Directed by Kon Ichikawa; starring Yûko Kotegawa, Yoshiko Sakuma,
Keiko Kishi, Sayuri Yoshinaga (1983)

by Peter Rainer

KON ICHIKAWA'S **THE MAKIOKA SISTERS** MAY JUST BE THE
most beautiful-looking film I've ever seen. It's a ravishment of color and texture and flesh. I don't think there has ever been a movie this beautiful that
was so meticulously controlled. Ichikawa shows us the patterning in a square
inch of kimono, gives us the squeak of fabric shifting against fabric, reveals
the architecture of a cherry blossom and skin that glows like pearl. The
movie is such a nonstop sensual experience that you sit there from the first
frame in a state of pure, beaming ecstasy.

I don't want to give the impression that *The Makioka Sisters* is simply a
gorgeous exercise in style, devoid of human content. I'm not sure how he's
done it, but Ichikawa, with his great cinematographer Kiyoshi Hasegawa,
gives his characters a novelistic richness while also displaying them as poetic
emanations. The women, the four Makioka sisters from Osaka, are so beautiful that they seem anointed; their brightly colored kimonos and lustrous
skin are jaw-droppers. This movie gives you such a feeling for the scintilla-
tions of flesh that it's not only a visual experience, it's a tactile experience too.
In an early scene, the youngest of the sisters, the headstrong Taeko (Yûko
Kotegawa), sees the glowing, bare ivory shoulder of her second-oldest sister,
Sachiko (Yoshiko Sakuma), as she dresses before a mirror. No other response
is possible: Taeko reaches out to touch the flesh, as we do.

The movie, set in 1938, is adapted from a classic novel by Junichirô Tanizaki, whose work Ichikawa adapted in the more overtly erotic 1959 *Kagi* (*Odd Obsession*). Ichikawa has a direct pipeline to Tanizaki's way of seeing. This passage from Tanizaki's *Naomi*—his first important book, written in the '20s—could as easily be a description of an image in *The Makioka Sisters:* Naomi's "delicate skin, though still moist, was a pure vivid white. . . . Her face was glossy, as though a membrane of gelatin had been stretched across it. Only her eyebrows were still wet. Above them, on her forehead, the cloudless winter sky was reflected in pale blue through the window."

Imagine the visual and tactile beauty of this passage extended 140 minutes and you have some idea of the experience of this movie. Ichikawa's feeling for the sheer sensuality of things gives the movie an eroticized shimmer. The film is about the fate of the four Makioka sisters, raised in wealth by their merchant father but now, their parents dead, their wealth depleted, struggling to maintain their dignity and social position. Tsuruko (Keiko Kishi), the oldest, is married to a banker (Juzo Itami, director of *Tampopo*), who made the pragmatic, unfavorable decision to sell the family shop in order to make ends meet. Now the offer of a promotion to a bank in Tokyo threatens to pull the family from its roots. Sachiko lives in the suburbs of Osaka with her docile husband Teinosuke (Koji Ishizaka) and the two youngest sisters, Yukiko (Sayuri Yoshinaga), a beauty for whom the family is trying to find a respectable match, and Taeko, a doll maker who, as tradition has it, is constrained from marrying until her older sister weds.

The four women are distinct and unique and yet, in some magical, unstressed way, sisters. (It's one of the most convincing sister acts in movie history). Tsuruko is old enough to be the youngest girl's mother, and that's the role she unself-consciously assumes. Of the four, it is she who most registers the regret and sadness at how little the Makioka name means in an increasingly Westernized Japan on the brink of war. There's nothing haughty about Tsuruko's pride: She's so extraordinary a creature that that pride seems only just—her birthright. *All* of the Makioka sisters move in a kind of radiant swoon: They are not fully aware of their incandescence, it startles them, they're humbled by its blessing.

A comic motif involves Yukiko's suitors—widowers, an expert in fish—and we look forward with glee to each meeting. Yukiko is the only sister who incarnates traditional Japanese female passivity (she won't even talk on the telephone). She is such a fairy-tale vision of femininity that she stuns each man she meets—they all want her. Her effect on men is comic, also poignant; the poor souls are mesmerized by their proximity to such purity. They know they may never pass this way again.

Taeko is Yukiko's opposite. She smokes, wants to make her dolls in Paris, and sometimes wears Western clothes. She was involved in an elopement scandal with a jeweler's son five years ago; her taste in men is wayward. Taeko seems the most lost of the sisters; she's caught in the limbo between family tradition and Westernization. She makes a pain of herself because she feels neglected, but her dissolution can't erase the imprimatur of her beauty. Even on the skids, she has a high gloss.

In form, *The Makioka Sisters* is something of a tragedy, but it's not a weak-kneed tragedy. It offers a serene acceptance of life's disappointments, like that other great Japanese family tragedy, Yasujiro Ozu's *Tokyo Story*. And, like *Tokyo Story*, it has such a deep, resounding feeling for the textures of every-day life that you really don't think of the film as being a tragedy at all. *The Makioka Sisters* is an astounding, revivifying experience. It reaffirms beauty as an innate and indispensable quality of cinema.

McCabe & Mrs. Miller
Winter lady

Directed by Robert Altman; starring Julie Christie,
Warren Beatty (1971)

by John Anderson

WHY IS **MCCABE & MRS. MILLER**—WITH ITS SNOW, RAIN, AMPLE
rumps, pendulous, perspiring breasts, and all-but-fragrant cast of characters—cited by so many as their favorite Robert Altman film? Why do
rheumy, feverish looks cross the faces of cinephiles as they consider the
damp squalor and gap-toothed charm of this great revisionist Western occu-
pying the middle mesa between *The Searchers* and *Unforgiven*?

At least on the surface of its mottled, grimy skin, *McCabe* would seem the
least sexy of the director's movies. Situated in the Altman oeuvre between
Brewster McCloud (1970) and *Images* (1972), it's one of a trio of genre-busters
the director produced in the early '70s—the antiwar war movie *M*A*S*H*
(1970), the romantic antiromance *McCabe* (1971), and the daylit noir of *The
Long Goodbye* (1973). What's odd is that in its cynical perspective of the Old
West, its reduction of human sexuality to a near toiletlike necessity, and its
portrayal of men as cowards and preFreudian neurotics, *McCabe* is also Altman at his most sincere. The milieu may be contrary to everything we've
been taught to think about the Old West, but the people are as real as any
Altman has put on screen.

Is that what makes it sexy, the director's uncharacteristic lack of guile? His
virginal innocence? (Uh-huh.) Or is it simply Julie Christie? No longer the
handbag-swinging Brit of *Billy Liar,* and yet to be lowered into the gassy

misogynist swamp of costar/lover Warren Beatty's *Shampoo,* she is, in *McCabe,* the most delicious mix of eroticism and intelligence since Garbo. Hers is the Best Lower Lip in screen history; it hangs, beckoning and unattainable, the ripest fruit on the loftiest limb. But her allure alone does not define the movie's charm.

In many ways, *McCabe & Mrs. Miller* is cinema as cold shower. Altman's screenplay, adapted from Edmund Naughton's *McCabe,* is largely about frontier prostitutes and the men they worked for/with/under. The mechanics of sex are described in the manner of Melville on whaling, with about as much gauzy, glamorous allure; in short, none. The mining town of Presbyterian Church into which John McCabe rides one sloppy day is a half-built work of exploitation, with no women save the "chippies" who are imported for a specific reason and treated slightly better than the horses.

Christie's Mrs. Miller, with her Cockney Britishness and taste for tea and opium, brings to John McCabe's whorehouse amenities of which he never dreamed—such as hygiene. She's the Brookstone of the Old West, full of stuff you never knew you needed so badly. She's also the closest thing to the unattainable virgin that the gossipy, fishwife-ish men of Presbyterian Church have. Once things are up and running, Mrs. Miller will cost five dollars rather than two.

But it isn't the allure of the top-shelf item that gets McCabe's engine running. Is it Leonard Cohen? Well, presumably McCabe can't hear Canada's great contribution to confessionalist pop poetry, but we hear the singer-songwriter all through the movie, whose effect is unimaginable without him. Cohen's songs—"Suzanne," "The Sisters of Mercy"—provide not only mournful, unvarnished emotion, but an ironic connection to present times, an elegiac note that all this we see will soon be gone. In fact, the West as pioneer icon is already deader than the three hit men who come looking for the uncooperative McCabe. Commissioned violence, rather than the one-man-one-gun rule of early John Ford, is another signifier of how the West was moving away from the haloed epoch of *Cimarron* and into the manifest destiny of Arnold Schwarzenegger. But I digress.

Wherein doth lie the attraction of Mrs. Miller for John McCabe: pimp, rumored killer, liar, petty and incompetent businessman, harbinger of doom for dignity, an unfinished man in an unfinished house that mirrors an unfinished country and the incomplete civilization of its inhabitants?

That McCabe manages to tickle her fissure of tenderness by being as suave as last week's saddle is itself a miracle.

Meanwhile, Mrs. Miller eats like a trucker, cuts McCabe down to size with a comment about his cologne, and is, perhaps by necessity, a castrating bitch. But McCabe is smitten by her competence, just as surely as he might be by her face or hips. She tries to be as tough as a man (and there are few tougher) merely because she's had to. It's her competence—she can run the brothel better than McCabe—that makes her a modern woman, and he a modern man for his ability to appreciate her. Is he threatened? Yes, but not so much that he blinds himself to the beauty of her formidable skills, specialized though they are to the fields of brothel-keeping and opium-smoking.

Altman has been labeled a misogynist many times, for good reason. (*Dr. T and the Women*—what was he thinking?) But you watch Mrs. Miller disassemble McCabe with that gun-smoking glance, quick-draw disdain, rapid-fire wit, and Altman seems like the most progressive of directors. Take his use of the oh-so-phallic steeple on the church where McCabe goes to hide, but can't. Is there a more blatant visual metaphor for the traditional male modus operandus and the way it can cut off a man from his community (which flourishes even as a gunfight rages on its margins), and how the result is often impotence? *McCabe & Mrs. Miller* is a sad movie, a Christ tale in a way—McCabe dies so the town can live, and so Mrs. Miller can flourish. It's a bouquet of flowers drawn in blood. But she's worth it. Does anybody disagree? And give Altman credit: He knows that a woman's sex appeal lies in what she can do, not in the advertising.

Swoon, Britannia

by Andy Klein

What is it about Brits?

Over several decades and several thousand films, I've had count-less reactions of sheer lust—and more complicated forms of infatua-tion—for actresses across a range of size, shape, nationality, race, age, talent, intelligence, and damned near everything else. So why is it that my *really* big crushes have been on Brits?

My first complete sexual/emotional swoon began the moment Julie Christie strode into John Schlesinger's *Billy Liar* (1963). There had been minor crushes before: I seem to recall Hayley Mills. But something crucial transpired in my life between *Tiger Bay* (1959) and *Billy Liar*—puberty. Goodbye, Pollyanna! Hello, Darling!

The attraction doesn't need explanation—I mean, it's *Julie Christie*. But there was something here that transcended even Ms. Christie's beauty, talent, Britishness, etc. Her character in *Billy Liar* was designed as the perfect love fantasy for adolescent film geeks: a gorgeous free spirit who somehow completely understood the pro-tagonist and *nonetheless* chose to go off with him. Virtually all my male friends were smitten. (The appeal of this fantasy was not lim-ited to adolescents. Christie—a last-minute substitution for Topsy Jane and onscreen for only a handful of scenes—instantly became a star.)

Christie remained foremost in my pantheon until 1988, the year of *A Summer Story*. Directed by Piers Haggard and adapted by Pene-lope Mortimer from John Galsworthy's wrenchingly awful classic

"The Apple Tree," *A Summer Story* is a much less formidable achievement than *Billy Liar*, which only makes more impressive the extent to which its star, Imogen Stubbs, supplanted Christie's grip on my fantasy life.

The plot was as simple and generic as the title: Back at the turn of the (twentieth) century, a well-off Londoner (James Wilby) falls for a poor farm girl (Stubbs). They have a torrid affair, he jilts her, she dies of a broken heart, roll credits. But part of what knocked me out was that Stubbs first comes across as merely pretty, and in a slightly odd-ball way; she was not drop-dead-gorgeous-everybody's-cup-of-tea beautiful like Julie Christie. Having heard the advance buzz, I thought, "Well, she's *okay*, but what's the big deal?" A half hour later, my heart wanted to leap on the next plane to London to throw itself, and myself, at her feet. Stubbs had somehow gone from merely pretty to achingly lovely. It wasn't one of those gee-honey-with-a-little-makeup-and-a-new-hairdo-you-wouldn't-be-half-bad transformations, either; it was strictly a matter of performance and presence.

Sadly (for me, anyway), I had neither the money nor the stalker personality necessary for such a quest. I settled for basking in Stubbs's radiance in later film and TV appearances, which grew far less common after she married that darned Trevor Nunn and started having kids.

Sigh. Seventeen years, and no other actresses have stirred me so deeply. Sometimes I try to imagine a movie with both Julie *and* Imogen in it, but I don't think my poor heart could take it. ■

Morocco
Mon Légionnaire

Directed by Josef von Sternberg; starring Marlene Dietrich,
Gary Cooper (1930)

by Stephanie Zacharek

BEFORE THERE WAS JIMMY PAGE, THERE WAS AMY JOLLY.
There's no greater image of the sexual magnetism a performer can exert
on an audience than Marlene Dietrich dressed in a man's tuxedo and croon-
ing a blasé siren's song in Josef von Sternberg's *Morocco*. The setting is Morocco, sometime, anytime, no time: This is a place to which people escape
when their hearts have been shattered beyond repair, not so much a location on a map as a part of the mind, or the imagination, that has decided to
shut down indefinitely. And so Amy Jolly—a woman we know virtually
nothing about, although we instantly fall for the lullaby coo of her voice and
her quizzically glittering eyes—has arrived here not to begin a new life, but
to erase an old one.

Tom Brown (Gary Cooper) happens to have arrived at the same place at
the same time for the same reason. He's a private in the French Foreign Legion, a country-boy lady-killer who's always either idly seducing the local
women or fending them off with jocular detachment. We know almost nothing about him either, except for what we can see in his eyes: Sometime earlier, a lady must have killed something off in *him*. He has come to the desert
to march through the dunes for very little pay, to accept impossibly treach-
erous assignments, and, in his few off-hours, to amuse himself in this or that

marketplace or nightclub while he's waiting for his time to die. What is there to live for?

But here comes Amy Jolly in gentlemen's evening wear, a lioness in wolf's clothing. She's just taken a job in the top club in Morocco, which is perhaps a bit more swank than the worst club in Berlin or New York or Paris. It attracts both the rich (including Foreign Legion officers and moneyed fat-cat charmers like Adolph Menjou, who's already fallen hard for Amy), who have, for whatever reason, temporarily found their way to this godforsaken land, and the not-so-rich (hoi polloi like the Legion's enlisted men, who sit cordoned off in the club's worst seats).

Tom Brown is one of the latter, although he doesn't fit in with them: He carries himself like a prince, and when Amy Jolly saunters onto the stage, he sizes her up just for a moment with the narrowed eyes of a sleepy lizard about to slip into a slithery dream. She surveys the audience, her captives, and although she's just taken the stage, she already looks bored with them. But once she catches sight of Tom, boredom evaporates; she's like a cat who's caught sight of herself—or could it just be her perfect counterpart?—in the mirror. She's suddenly alert, alive, ready to spring. She saunters through the club, procuring a flower from a dazzled female patron (she plants a kiss full on the blushing woman's lips) and, in a move that catches everyone off guard, tosses it to Tom. He holds it to his nose, coquettishly; later, we see that he's tucked it behind his ear.

Amy Jolly works her crowd like a rock star, but the only one she wants in her breast pocket is Tom. He responds with the outright adoration and confused desire of a teenage girl. He's her groupie, her slave, her Miss Pamela. He wants her, badly, and the biggest miracle of all is that she's picked him out of the crowd. His appraising gaze turns into a kind of bewildered erotic appreciation: Who is this creature, and what might she want with him? How can he get to her? And even if he can, will he know what do?

That's how Amy Jolly and Tom Brown meet. It takes the rest of the movie—including several awkwardly steamy conversations and a cold, confused betrayal—for them to recognize they're made for each other. (One of the great mysteries of *Morocco* is how a movie set in the desert can look so impossibly dewy.) But their moments in that club are the ones that shine. What passes between them isn't that standard-issue electrical current we so casually call love at first sight, but the wordless exchange of secret desires. Dietrich in a man's suit is sexy, and so is Cooper with a bloom tucked behind his ear: For a few brief moments, they're trading roles, trying one another's masculine and feminine traits on for size. Dietrich swaggers, and Coooper, with his shadowy eyes and long lashes (and even longer legs), yields.

Years later, the Replacements would sing, "You be me for a while, and I'll be you," not as a way of erasing differences between the sexes but of finding an empathetic center within the battle zone. What we see in the cabaret scene in *Morocco* isn't just a temporary trading of roles but a permanent merging of them: Who wants to be a man all the time, with the concomitant pressures and anxieties? And who wants to be a woman all the time, wondering if she's lovable or beautiful enough? At their first meeting, Tom Brown and Amy Jolly are already working out a pact, a way of dissolving their mutual sorrows and beginning anew. One takes the lead, the other follows, but that's just for today: In their fantasy-perfect partnership, they'll switch off roles from day to day (and from night to night) for the rest of their lives. Amy Jolly reaches out to the feminine in Tom Brown, and he to the masculine in her. They meet in a place where they can both wear the pants—until it's time to take them off.

Mulholland Drive
Dangerous curves

Directed by David Lynch; starring Naomi Watts,
Laura Elena Harring (2001)

by Peter Travers

LET'S GET OUR DEFINITIONS STRAIGHT: THERE'S CONVENTIONAL
erotic, in the centerfold sense. Then there's David Lynch erotic, in the sense
of dark and dangerous and being caught in the act of doing something secret.
Now we're talking!

That brings us to *Mulholland Drive*, as pure a vision of Lynch's impure
thoughts as exists. *Mulholland Drive* won the New York Film Critics Circle
Award as the best picture of 2001, though lots of critics turned off to what
turned Lynch on. "A moronic and incoherent piece of garbage," said Rex
Reed in the *New York Observer*. But to paraphrase Mae West, when it comes
to sex, coherence has nothing to do with it. Neither does all that drool on the
Internet from fanboys salivating when stars Naomi Watts and Laura Elena
Harring strip down and rub tits. You can't reduce *Mulholland Drive* to hot
lesbo action or a Freudian exercise. You have to let the movie pull you in.
Surrender to it. For visionary daring, swooning seductiveness, and colors
that pop like a whore's lip gloss, there's nothing anywhere like this baby.

After the credits roll over a brassy jitterbug contest, *Mulholland Drive*
opens in a sultry fever dream, with a woman twisting and turning in bed.
Then it's dark—Lynch dark, an inky black accentuated by Angelo Badalamenti's seductively unsettling score (his sound design has its own erotic
pull). It's night in Los Angeles. A limo slithers along Mulholland Drive, but

just as the driver stops to point a gun at the hottie (Harring) in the back seat, the limo is rammed by a carload of hard-partying teens. The only survivor is the back-seat brunette, who staggers down a hill in stiletto heels (the true femme fatale never wears flats), taking refuge in a Hollywood bungalow just vacated by a woman on her way out of town.

Cut to the L.A. airport. Bright sunshine. Perky, blonde Betty Elms (Watts) has just jetted in from Deep River, Ontario, to make it as an actress. An elderly couple from the plane wishes her well, but they give off a malevolent vibe, especially when they laugh. Lynch includes a shot of the pair grinning at the camera that creeps you out big-time.

A feeling of dread infects everything except Betty, who keeps smiling even when she settles into her aunt's bungalow and finds the brunette in the shower. Instead of reporting the naked stranger to the apartment manager (the late dance legend Ann Miller in a frisky cameo), Betty offers to help. The brunette calls herself Rita, after Rita Hayworth (she spots a poster on the wall for *Gilda*), but the limo accident has erased her memory of everything, including where she got the cash that's stuffed in her purse. So the girls play detective (Lynch's Angels?) and turn up no end of surprises, including a mysterious blue box and key, a dwarfish tycoon (Michael J. Anderson) with ties to Hollywood, a mobster (composer Badalamenti) who doesn't suffer bad espresso gladly, a bungling hit man (Mark Pellegrino), a threatening cowboy (Lafayette Montgomery), a crazed psychic (Lee Grant) and—oh, yes—a rotting corpse. And I haven't mentioned Adam Kesher (Justin Theroux), a hotshot director who passes up Betty for the lead in his movie because the mob has ordered him to audition a mystery woman named Camilla Rhodes and to shout out, "This is the girl!"

There are moments when you wonder if Lynch knows where he's going, such as the scene in which Adam catches his wife in bed with the gardener (Billy Ray Cyrus, of all people) and retaliates by smearing her jewelry with pink paint. But each vignette adds to the unease that envelops Betty and Rita. One such vignette, about a man who dreams of something terrible lurking behind the diner where the girls eat, has a shuddering impact.

But how, you ask, is unease erotic? Just wait. Harring makes Rita a ravishing blank slate on which Betty draws her fantasies. And Watts nails every subversive impulse under Betty's sunny exterior. Watch her in the audition scene—as perversely brilliant as anything Lynch has ever directed—when

Betty reads lines with Jimmy Katz, an older actor smarmed to perfection by Chad Everett. Earlier, with Rita, Betty had rehearsed the role of a good girl who is being sexually abused by her father's business partner. But with Jimmy, Betty assertively takes charge, breathing in his ear, biting his lip, eyeing his crotch, reading her dialogue—"Get out of here before I kill you!"—like a carnal invitation.

As Watts digs into the juiciest role for a young actress in ages (the Academy failed to salute her with a nomination), Lynch starts unveiling the method behind his madness. When Betty invites Rita to share her bed, their give-and-take is richly comic: "Have you done this before?" asks Betty. "I don't know," says the amnesiac, nonetheless open to suggestion. Later, Rita whisks Betty off to a decaying nightclub; no one does Hollywood rot like Lynch. Zombified musicians perform without benefit of orchestra. "*No hay banda,*" says the sleazy MC (Geno Silva). He introduces a singer (Rebekah Del Rio as herself) who breaks into a Spanish version of Roy Orbison's "Crying" that brings tears to the eyes of Betty and Rita (Rita is wearing a blonde wig now, shades of *Vertigo*). To add to the symbolism overload, the singer collapses midsong, though her voice goes on, and a blue-haired lady at the club whispers, "*Silencio.*"

Whew! You can do one of two things: Scratch your head and curse Lynch or realize that what's transpired so far is the dream of the woman from the first scene, a woman who might be Betty.

Might is the operative word. In the film's final third, as identities shift and the world is thrown out of balance, we are encouraged to link the pieces of this cunning puzzle devised by Lynch and cinematographer Peter Deming. The challenge is exhilarating. You can discover a lot about your secret self by getting lost in *Mulholland Drive*. It grips you like an erotic dream that won't let go. In this movie, even the title has curves.

The Mummy
Wrapped

Directed by Karl Freund; starring Boris Karloff,
Zita Johann (1932)

by Charles Taylor

"MY LOVE HAS LASTED LONGER THAN THE TEMPLES OF OUR
gods," says Boris Karloff's reincarnated ancient Egyptian priest Imhotep to
Zita Johann as Helen, the reincarnation of the vestal virgin whose love he
died for.

That line, from Karl Freund's 1932 *The Mummy,* could sum up any movie
about that romantic chestnut, the love that lasts beyond the grave. But *The
Mummy* is a horror film, and the genre allows for a particularly unsettling
twist on the theme of eternal love (a sexless concept if ever there was one).
As Imhotep, the mummy inadvertently brought back to life when a British
archaeological team excavates him, Karloff carries the whole meaning of the
movie in his lined, dried-out skin. His bandages appear to have fused with
his flesh; the result looks both dead and repellently alive. This is a horror-
movie vision of sexual desire abiding despite physical decay.

What makes *The Mummy* such a perversely erotic experience is the atmosphere is so thick and vivid, the mood so enveloping, that the picture
proceeds less by narrative than poetic logic. *The Mummy* is far stranger and
more exotic than other horror movies made at Universal in the same period.
There are no jumpy scenes. Like Karloff's Imhotep, the movie casts a spell
rather than using force. When this ancient wants to command obedience,
he simply raises his ring and fixes his subject with his hypnotic gaze. The

effect is placid, the tremors of unease nearly subterranean. Like everything Karloff does here, it's economical and precise. Dressed in a fez and floor-length robe that emphasizes his long frame, Karloff seems to glide. When he turns, he does so with his whole body, and when he sits, it's as if he simply deliquesces inside his robe to the desired height. Karloff transmits the cunning and helpless yearning beneath Imhotep's sedate surface. His performance is at the heart of why *The Mummy* is the most quietly seductive horror film ever made.

The beautiful unity of tone is surely thanks to Freund. As the greatest of German cinematographers, Freund shot some of the most revered German silent films, F. W. Murnau's *The Last Laugh* and Fritz Lang's *Metropolis* among them. Freund came to America in 1929, and *The Mummy* was the first of a handful of films he got a chance to direct. Of the early and often awkward talkies, *The Mummy* is one of few to convey what characterized the greatest silents—the sense of immersion in a shadowy otherworld.

The dialogue is often stodgy ("In the interest of science, even if I believed in the curse, I would go on with my work for the museum."), and there's David Manners playing another in his string of ineffectual suitors. But those slight defects blow away like the dust from Imhotep's disturbed tomb. Freund uses some astonishingly delicate lighting effects, many having to do with the eyes. There's a recurring close-up of Karloff in which his eyes at first appear in shadow, as if they were empty sockets, then are lit gradually until they might be glass marbles glowing from within. And when he turns those mesmerizing peepers on Johann—whose own eyes are dark and enormous—we see little beams of light form a nimbus around her head.

Our first look at Imhotep is a long stationary shot of him in his sarcophagus, still wrapped in bandages; we discover he has come back to life by the small glistening jewels of light we see when his eyes open just a chink. Freund patiently sustains entire sequences just as he does that shot. The film is only 72 minutes long, yet seems to unfold gradually, the deliberate pacing giving the eeriness time to sink in. We might be seeing the whole movie in the reflecting pool in which Imhotep conjures visions of the past and spies on the present. Yet there is a corner-of-the-eye quickness to some of the effects—a skull becoming visible beneath Imhotep's decaying skin—that vanish before the mind quite registers them. Perhaps Freund simply didn't want to disturb the mood he had so carefully achieved. Much of the movie's action is suggested, as when Imhotep's coming to life is suggested by a mummified hand reaching for an ancient scroll, then a bandage trailing slowly out a door, a shot Freund alludes to later when Helen, under Imhotep's spell, goes to him and we see the train of her white negligee disappearing around a corner.

Like Helen's somnambulistic midnight stroll under her ancient lover's spell, there's an unnerving sense of eroticized compulsion deep within *The Mummy*. The tragic inevitability of the picture calls for Helen to reject Imhotep's plans for her to join him in eternity. She's young and alive; she doesn't want a lover who embodies the decay that awaits her. You can find an echo of Helen's revulsion forty years later in Bernardo Bertolucci's *Last Tango in Paris* when Maria Schneider sees her lover Marlon Brando outside their Paris love cell and is repelled by the difference between her ripeness and his battered middle age. Wooing his reincarnated lover, Imhotep invokes the vanished temples of the Egyptian gods. The horrific sadness of Karloff's performance is the horror of being trapped in a ruin, the body as a crumbling chapel of love.

Habit-forming

by Peter Keough

No need to consult an analyst as to why I find a scene in Leo Mc-Carey's *The Bells of St. Mary's* (1945) stimulating. Sister Benedict, played by Ingrid Bergman, the sexiest woman to wear a wimple, picks up a Louisville Slugger and strokes its fire-hardened white ash length with hands encased in black silk gloves. It's the fetishistic covering that makes this hot, allowing a Catholic boy to imagine the forbidden fantasy of what lies beneath.

I think the straitlaced, right-wing McCarey was not unaware of this. Nor were the people at RKO, who proclaimed: "Ingrid Bergman has never been lovelier, hubbahubbahubba." But Bing Crosby's Father O'Malley doesn't know what he's in for when he arrives at his new parish gates fresh from *Going My Way*. Cryptically, the housekeeper wonders what it's like to be "up to your neck in nuns."

Quite an image, and O'Malley tops it off by promptly sitting on a pussy—one of the kittens from the parish cat's litter. The pussy gets its revenge; O'Malley makes his introductions to Sister Benedict and her charges, but the kitten has climbed into the padre's trademark straw boater on the mantelpiece. The pussy enters the hat, an inversion of the phallic order; no wonder the nuns are laughing.

Their "differences" notwithstanding, there's no doubt that O'Malley and Mary Benedict are meant for each other. So, of course, he must send her away, the spot on her lung in an X-ray merely a transparent excuse (this reminds me of the spotted milk bottles representing sinful souls in the Baltimore catechism).

They don't have that option in John Huston's *Heaven Knows, Mr. Allison* (1957). Corporal Allison (that great slab of manhood, Robert Mitchum) and Sister Angela (Deborah Kerr, already in the habit with Michael Powell's 1947 melodrama *Black Narcissus*) are stranded on a South Pacific island, alone but for periodic occupations by hostile forces.

He's blunt and earthy. She's prim and witty. Thank goodness for the Japanese. Every time the two are tempted, "that crazy war" comes storming in like a pissed-off superego. Allison's fantasy of Sister Angela's long, golden locks, and the crude comb he carves for them, are scenes that tremble with pathos and sensuality.

A tense truce persists until Sister Angela passes a jug of sake to Allison. Plastered, he points out the obvious—that they'll probably be marooned forever, Adam and Eve in a new Eden. Sister Angela plays hard to get, runs into a swamp in a rainstorm, and catches a fever. "I had to get you out of them wet clothes, ma'am," apologizes the sheepish marine, and we see that Sister Angela's hair, though short, is indeed a rich reddish gold. Cue the Imperial Navy!

It would take the sexual revolution for the taboo to be broken, and what a disappointment. There's no mystery about Sister Jeanne's hair in Ken Russell's *The Devils* (1971), an account of events in 1634 France that is *The Crucible* by way of Monty Python. Early on, Jeanne (Vanessa Redgrave, no Maria Falconetti here), head of a convent of Ursuline nuns, daydreams about washing the feet of Father Grandier (Oliver Reed) with her long golden tresses. Her unhabited state shows all, including a grotesquely hunched back.

Poor Jeanne. Her hots for Grandier will never be requited, though he spreads his sacred chrism pretty much everywhere else. When he secretly weds, Jeanne tips off his powerful enemies—Cardinal Richelieu among them. His Ken Starr is "Witchhunter" Father Barre, who promptly "exorcizes" Jeanne with a cast-iron douche the size of a jackhammer, with worse to come for Grandier. ▶

Ironically, it's only after Barre starts casting out devils that the nuns start taking off their clothes and moaning in ecstasy. What's it like to be up to your neck in nuns? No big deal, because Barre gets his kicks out of tearing and burning the flesh and watching it decay. Rather than fulfill the desires tantalized and repressed in *The Bells* and *Heaven*, *The Devils* subjects them to diabolical punishment. ■

O Fantasma
Different strokes

Directed by João Pedro Rodrigues;
starring Ricardo Meneses (2000)

by Nathan Lee

A MENU OPTION ON THE DVD OF O FANTASMA (PHANTOM)
invites you to sample a selection of "Eye Candy." Under titles like "Helping
Hand," "Hose Man," and "Bite Me," the feature highlights ten "specially isolated moments" from the movie—in other words, the naughty bits. As
cinerotic delicacies go, these are for specialized palates; not every viewer will
relish a second helping of the erotic misadventures of Sergio (Ricardo Meneses), a pathologically horny garbage man who prowls the early morning landscape of Lisbon to satisfy his increasingly extreme fetishistic compulsions.

Nevertheless, if you're so inclined you may jump directly to the scenes
where Sergio masturbates with a pair of soiled motorcycle gloves; receives an
aggressive (unsimulated) blow job in a public toilet; sodomizes a man from
behind while sheathed in full-body latex; or rubs soapsuds into the groin of
his mangy Speedo before yanking a metal shower hose twice around his neck
and choking himself to orgasm. On the less pungent side, there is a lovely
night-swimming vignette: After lowering himself to an indoor pool via a
rooftop skylight, Sergio strips down to nothing but his six-pack, then sports
in the water like a randy, furless otter, lolling on his back so that the tip of
his cock peeps up above the cool blue chlorinated surface.

Among other notable accomplishments, *O Fantasma* is surely the only film
shown in competition at the Venice Film Festival that wound up explicitly

packaged as highbrow gay porn. On the occasion of its release in a New York art house, a critic for the *Village Voice* declared it "the artiest queer stroke movie of the year." Different strokes for different folks: A heterosexual at the *New York Times* saw the picture as "fascinated by perversity [but] utterly indifferent to pleasure."

An experimental narrative of overt sexual and formal transgression, *O Fantasma* is perverse by design, but whose pleasure is it indifferent to? Surely not the sniffing, licking, growling protagonist, whose indiscriminate animal libido is unleashed on half a dozen willing and unwilling partners. (Like most eighteen-year-old men, Sergio is horny as a dog, sometimes literally—in one scene, he marks his territory with urine.) To be sure, Sergio never makes a display of amorous rapture; his characteristic expression—his *only* expression—is an insolent, lock-jawed glare. But I find the *implicit* pleasure he takes from his abject exploits highly arousing. Genuine pornography aside, the explicit spectacles of *O Fantasma* rank among the most stimulating I know, and not merely because they're so explicit.

I have a confession to make. No, I'm not into latex, bondage, or autoerotic asphyxiation. And while Meneses is plenty easy on the eyes, he's not exactly my type. The truth of the matter is, nonnarrative turns me on. Conventional storytelling is the missionary position of cinema: satisfying when skillfully performed, but ultimately a little routine. Don't get me wrong, I wouldn't think twice about going to bed with *The Wrong Man* or *My Darling Clementine*, but what really gets me hard are marginal movies, abnormal aesthetics, cinema that dares to queer things up. And *O Fantasma* is about as queer as it gets, in every sense of the term.

Rigorous and dispassionate, structured along severe geometrical lines, *O Fantasma* doesn't telegraph its emotions or satisfy the expectations of storytelling; it diagrams with fantastic originality the forms and trajectories of lust itself. Everything is nonstop (sometimes over-the-top) metaphor. The opening shot is of a crazed Doberman sprinting down a hallway to claw desperately at a locked door—a wild image of hysterical lust. In a later scene, Sergio's carnal frustration is rendered as a burning plastic garbage cart, a sticky blob of toxic sludge venting its acrid dissatisfaction.

Writer-director João Pedro Rodrigues filmed *O Fantasma* in low-light conditions in and around his own neighborhood, transforming familiar residential Lisbon into a twilight landscape of radical strangeness. His locations are dislocations. Taken literally, the plot—like that of David Cronenberg's

Crash—is apt to seem preposterous. For all their tactility of surface, both of these uncanny, deeply oneiric visions are essentially interior narratives, developing their ideas less through a plausible sequence of events than a succession of internal modalities indicated through abstractions of sound and image. As the title suggests, *O Fantasma* is made up of intangible things, phantom figures traversing ghostly landscapes.

Rodrigues has organized every inch of his debut feature film around the insight that eroticism is a matter of boundaries—physical, psychic, social. Nearly every scene stages the delineation, blurring, or transgression of a border. Sergio's operative mode is to confound. Like the Coyote of Native American lore, he is a trickster figure, as mythologist and literary critic Lewis Hyde has defined the archetype: "the mythic embodiment of ambiguity and ambivalence, doubleness and duplicity, contradiction and paradox." Possessed of a "hyperactive sexuality [that] almost never results in any offspring," Sergio represents "the spirit of the doorway leading out . . . the crossroad at the edge of town . . . the road at dusk, the one that runs from one town to another and belongs to neither."

The emblematic sexual set-piece in *O Fantasma* takes place precisely at such a crossroad. Accompanied by his demon-dog, Lorde, Sergio stalks the quasi-rural outskirts of the city and spies an erogenous opportunity on the far side of a broken stone wall. A car has been abandoned at the edge of a freeway. Inside, a police officer lies gagged and handcuffed. Sergio approaches the prostrate enigma, brings him to erection and climax. Glimpse of nudity notwithstanding, the eroticism of the scene lies not in what we see of the largely obscured hand job, but in the heady ambiguity of the encounter (what's up with that cop?), its transgressive circuit of power, and the geographic frisson created by its setting in the nexus of wilderness and civilization.

Sergio is perpetually traveling from one zone to another. Slipping through doorways, scrambling over hills, scaling fences, creeping through bushes, climbing up trees, crawling out windows, clambering over rooftops, descending through skylights. Much of this movement is impelled by his desire for Joao (Andre Barbosa), a hunky, presumably heterosexual swim jock whose indifference proves an inviolable boundary. Sergio's thwarted attempts to penetrate Joao's space propel the entropic narrative of the film, climaxing in an aborted rape and a descent into madness. Donning his latex suit, our jilted antihero passes the hallucinatory final reel vomiting through the Martian landscape of a vast garbage dump. What, you may ask, the fuck?

Perhaps *O Fantasma* isn't as sui generis as it seems. After all, it's basically the story of a teenage crush, albeit an unusually raunchy, outrageously stylized one. "No one can live without love!" ran the film's laughable, not entirely inappropriate, tag line.

Regardless of sexual (or aesthetic) orientation, the spectacle of Sergio literally digging through the garbage heap of his own predatory sexuality may be a little too emphatic. Rodrigues risks hyperbole in his wholesale rejection of the literal. His audacious imagination is reaching for what Samuel Beckett called "the power of the text to claw." As he says of his phantom on the DVD commentary track, "The way he licks, you really feel his tongue."

Ossessione
Troubling sex for fascists

Directed by Luchino Visconti; starring Clara Calamai, Massimo Girotti (1943)

by Peter Brunette

WHILE IT'S NOT LIKELY TO RAISE BLOOD PRESSURES THESE days, Luchino Visconti's Italian classic *Ossessione* (*Obsession*) scandalized the few who were lucky enough to see it when it came out, all too briefly, a few months before the collapse of Mussolini's government in 1943. It still has its moments.

A steamy tale based on James M. Cain's hard-boiled crime novel *The Postman Always Rings Twice*, the film resembled nothing that had ever been seen on Italian screens. Unlike the Nazis, who regarded cinema as a potent weapon for the advancement of party goals, Italian fascists were content if filmmakers simply avoided showing any displeasing aspects of contemporary Italian life. The fascist goal for cinema was a modest one—to foster the myth of how fortunate Italians were to be living in the best of all possible countries, one in which the trains ran on time. Movies, consequently, tended toward frothy bedroom farce: Fred Astaire and Ginger Rogers minus the high-quality dancing and singing. They were known collectively as "white-telephone films" in honor of the ubiquitous prop found on the screamingly artificial sets.

In a few years, all that would disappear with the advent of Italian neorealism, which first blossomed in Roberto Rossellini's groundbreaking *Open City* in 1945. Visconti's role in the destruction and transcendence of previous

Italian cinema helped pave the way for neorealism. *Ossessione* contains little in the way of overt social critique (though it's strongly implied), yet early viewers found its no-holds-barred depiction of lust and murder almost too much to bear. Vittorio Mussolini, the Duce's film-loving son, stood up, outraged, at the end of the premiere and shouted, "This is not Italy!" At some of the venues where the film was shown, local bishops sprinkled holy water to cleanse what had been defiled so obscenely.

One thing that must have bothered the younger Mussolini was that the female lead, Giovanna (Clara Calamai, whose slovenliness denotes an intense sexual charge), is everything fascist women shouldn't be: a childless adulterer who plots to murder her fat and greasy husband, Bragana (Juan de Landa). While he is always careful to show the economic exigencies that determine Giovanna's choices, Visconti, who went on to make revealing studies of decadence such as *Senso* (or *Livia*), *The Damned,* and *Ludwig,* also clearly enjoys portraying the degraded, hidden hothouse life of the countryside. Giovanna overtly reveals her own sexual desire when she first encounters Gino (the complexly hunky Massimo Girotti) in a striking double take that is accompanied by a fast track inward on Girotti's gorgeous face (it's the first time *we* see his face as well). Like Dido contemplating Aeneas in Virgil's *Aeneid,* Giovanna wants sex, not babies and a white picket fence.

Far more upsetting to the Fascisti was the addition of an ambiguously homosexual character named *Lo spagnolo* (The Spaniard) to Cain's already sordid tale. He's called the Spaniard because Visconti's clandestinely leftist screenwriters were making a surreptitious reference to the communists who fought Franco a few years earlier. Visconti, an aristocratic bisexual (later he would become solely homosexual), is aiming for something more, although it's not clear exactly what. On the overt level, *Lo spagnolo* represents to Gino the call of the open road, and thus becomes a threat to Giovanna. But with hindsight and an additional six decades of cinema during which gay characters proliferated, we can more easily read several of the scenes with the Spaniard and Gino as veiled expressions of homosexual desire. It's doubtful that many viewers in 1943 would have caught on, but the pervasive ambiguity in those scenes may have registered subliminally.

What was most troubling, and which clearly contributed to the outrage that greeted the film, was the portrayal of the macho stud Gino. Male viewers are usually assumed to be heterosexual, then as now, and are almost always offered strong, sexually unambiguous male characters with whom to identify. Gino does his share of strutting and pushing people around, but he is also the object of the desiring gaze of *others*, a recurring gesture that tends to put him in a "feminized" position—that is, the traditional position of the desirable *object* of the (male) gaze. This is a double whammy for the "normal" male spectator. Giovanna contemplates Gino with naked lust, speaking lovingly of his "shoulders like those of a horse," thus threatening Gino's traditional male right to make judgments about *her*. When they are reunited in a café after a long separation, it is Gino who is far more emotionally dependent. ("Tell me, did you think of me sometimes?" he asks, like a girl left behind by a soldier.) He explains his fateful bond with Giovanna to Anita, the prostitute he later meets, through the feminine gauze hanging over her bed. Toward the end of the film, Girotti's already high-pitched voice pushes higher, and his close-ups render him more youthful, ethereal, and angelic—even blonder!—as though Visconti is implying that Gino is a transcendent victim (like a woman?) of a fate beyond his control.

The Spaniard likewise makes Gino the object of his desiring gaze, forcing him further into the role of the passive female. In a powerful scene in which Gino and *Lo spagnolo* share a rented bed while on the road, Gino gets a softly filtered glamour close-up, a shot reserved for many Visconti pretty-boy protagonists (notably Alain Delon in 1960's *Rocco and His Brothers*) and a powerful contrast to the hard edges of *Lo spagnolo* who, if gay, is clearly the macho half of this pair-up.

All of which was a great deal to process for a conventional Italian male in those innocent days of 1943, or even today.

Pandora's Box
Oops! . . . I did it again

Directed by G. W. Pabst; starring Louise Brooks (1929)

by Kevin Thomas

IN G. W. PABST'S **PANDORA'S BOX**, THE INCANDESCENCE OF Louise Brooks never fades. Her freshness combines with a gift for projecting innocent sexuality incarnate, rendering her in this enduring film a uniquely powerful femme fatale. Her Lulu is instinctively a survivor, but not a cold calculator. Since she doesn't set out to destroy men, she seems oblivious to their fates. She is kind and affectionate, also thoughtless and unreflective, her smile as radiant as it is devastating.

It is easy to see why the Cinémathèque Française's Henri Langlois was moved to rescue Brooks from oblivion. In 1955 while staging his "60 Years of Cinema" exhibition, Langlois famously exulted: "There is no Garbo! There is no Dietrich! There is only Louise Brooks!"

On the evidence of *Pandora's Box,* Lulu's sheer innocence is more blinding than the seductive European world-weariness of those other icons. Two years later, Langlois presented his widely acclaimed "Homage to Louise Brooks," cementing Brooks's status. Yet when *Pandora's Box* premiered in Berlin, the critics, like Brooks's peers, misinterpreted Lulu's passivity as proof that Brooks couldn't act. Brooks herself never made any claims to acting ability, explaining that a key reason Lulu was ultimately appreciated was that Pabst, intuiting that Brooks was primarily a dancer, choreographed her more than directed her.

It's no wonder then that Pabst, one of the great triumvirate of the Golden Age of 1920s German cinema along with Fritz Lang and F. W. Murnau, passed over Dietrich in favor of a native of Cherryville, Kansas. Brooks started out with the Denishawn dancers, one of the first modern-dance troupes in the United States, then became a Ziegfeld Follies beauty before getting a contract with Paramount. Her performance in 1928 in Howard Hawks's *A Girl in Every Port,* for which she was loaned from Paramount to Fox, caught Pabst's eye. In that first of the Hawks buddy pictures, Brooks plays a gorgeous American high diver performing in a Marseilles carnival. As thoroughly amoral as she would be in *Pandora's Box,* Brooks captivates thick-headed sailor Victor McLaglen. That threatens the sailor's friendship with pal Robert Armstrong, who knows the girl from back in her Coney Island days as "Mam'selle Godiva."

Pandora's Box was fashioned from two Franz Wedekind plays, *Erdgeist* and *Die Büschse der Pandora.* The perfect casting of Brooks allowed Pabst, with his firm grasp of human emotion and social conventions, to transform lurid melodrama into high art. That in turn enables the film, like other Pabst works, to act as commentary on the instability and decadence of the Weimar Republic. *Pandora's Box* is all the more potent for its outré elements, which for Pabst are neither sensational nor exploitative, merely a means to a revelatory realism.

Pabst doesn't tell us much about Brooks's Lulu, nor does he need to. She is a flapper who is mistress to a powerful newspaper owner, Dr. Peter Schön (Fritz Kortner). Schön has ensconced her in an elegant Art Deco flat, but when he announces this arrangement will end upon his marriage to an aristocratic beauty, Lulu sets him straight. Smiling and matter-of-fact, she conveys that it may not be so easy to do without her.

As it happens, Lulu is acquainted with Schön's handsome son, Alwa (Franz—later Francis—Lederer), who's staging a Ziegfeld Follies–style revue. Alwa's father encourages him to cast Lulu, but when he makes the mistake of bringing his fiancée backstage, Lulu refuses to perform. This is an intense, hectic sequence that attests to Pabst's economy, energy, and dexterity. By the time it is over, Lulu has replaced the fiancée on the arm of the elder Shön, who now anticipates the ruination he feared all along. He arrogantly demands that Lulu shoot herself "to save us both." However, it is Schön who is fatally shot while struggling with Lulu over the gun. A puritanical prosecutor likens Lulu to the seductive Pandora of ancient Greek myth, to whom was entrusted a casket containing all the evils of the world.

Lulu has presumably unleashed these ills on her husband. When a specta-tor at her trial hears the guilty verdict, he sets off a fire alarm, and Lulu es-capes among the fleeing crowd.

Rather than face a five-year sentence for manslaughter, Lulu aims for Paris, accompanied by the still-smitten Alwa and armed with a passport from Alwa's costume designer, Countess Anna Geschwitz (Alice Roberts), who is the cinema's first fully developed lesbian character. She too has fallen under Lulu's spell. But on the train, a sleazy passenger (Michael von Newlinsky) recognizes Lulu and manipulates the couple into joining him at a more "dis-creet" sanctuary than the City of Lights—a gambling boat in an unnamed port city.

With trademark economy, Pabst allows the audience to assume that Lulu has leaked her getaway plans to her disreputable pals. She is pleased to see the ancient, insinuating Schigolch (Carl Goetz), Lulu's first "friend," whom she loves like a father even though he exploits her, and the beefy, crude ac-robat Rodrigo Quast (Carl Raschig). But she will soon have to be saved from the whole rotten lot by the lesbian costumer, who fetches Lulu and Alwa back to London by boat.

On Christmas Eve, Lulu, on her first try at streetwalking, invites a shyly handsome young man (Gustav Diesel) to her garret, even though he is pen-niless. Their encounter is tender but brief, for Lulu has picked up Jack the Ripper, as tormented a figure as the compulsive child-killer of Fritz Lang's masterpiece M (1932).

So intense is Pabst's vision, so sure his understanding of what makes peo-ple tick, and so total his command of the medium that Pandora's Box remains a supreme example of how psychological validity can triumph over poten-tially sensational material—e.g., when the sleazy man on the train attempts to sell Lulu to an Egyptian cabaret owner. Indeed, it matters not that Jack the Ripper hadn't terrorized London for forty years. It's all of a sublime piece, in keeping with the movie's sure and steady interior logic.

Louise Brooks died in 1978. Between 1924 and 1938, she made other no-table films. Even if she had never made another movie, Pandora's Box alone would have—in fact, has—secured her position as an icon of the cinema.

Peeping Tom
Shudder bug

Directed by Michael Powell; starring Carl Boehm,
Anna Massey (1960)

by Peter Keough

THE FIRST FEW MINUTES OF MICHAEL POWELL'S HERALDED
and hated *Peeping Tom* provide a trenchant education on film theory. In extreme close-up, an eye opens. A cut is made to a city street, to a woman in the shadows, and to a camera. The rest is seen from the point of view of the camera's cross-haired viewfinder: the negotiation, the walk upstairs, the disrobing, the look of horror preceded by a curious light in the eye. With a dissolve to a projector, it's all repeated again in silence and in black-and-white for a lone viewer in the darkness. Then the title: *Peeping Tom*.

Freud and a generation of deconstructionists would have a field day. Cinema as sublimated sexual aggression and death wish, the camera as phallus, photography as violation, film as ritualized voyeurism—or as a jolly psychiatrist later describes it in the film, "scopophilia, the morbid desire to gaze."

The emphasis is on morbid, not desire. Like many films exploring the nature of eroticism, *Peeping Tom* is not very erotic itself. The film's most attractive, undraped character turns her face to reveal a disfiguring scar. Mark Lewis (Carl Boehm, with Jon Voight's cherubic looks and Peter Lorre's creepy voice), the Peeping Tom of the title, makes the audience watching him share his discomfort as he photographs the objects of his morbid gaze. Nothing like self-reflection to throw cold water on the pleasures of voyeurism. Especially since what most turns on this Peeping Tom is not naked bodies but naked fear. Voyeurism, the film suggests, does not so much involve pleasure as it does loss and anxiety; it's a vain attempt to outstare transience and mortality. "Everything I photograph I lose," Mark laments. What remains is only a movie, a fetish meant to distract the audience from its own terror of death.

What a turn-on. Perhaps predictably, the British press denounced the film upon its release in 1960. They probably didn't ponder such pointy-headed concepts as scopophilia, but they surely suspected the film was saying something unsavory about the art of cinema and the motivations of audiences and critics. Maybe they felt implicated in the crimes and perversions depicted therein, enlisted as involuntary witnesses to what would later be called a "snuff film." ("It's just a film, isn't it?" pleads a viewer of Mark's handiwork in *Peeping Tom*. He insists it is not.)

It must have touched some kind of nerve to get such hyperbolic reviews. "The only really satisfactory way to dispose of *Peeping Tom* would be to shovel it up and flush it swiftly down the nearest sewer," wrote Derek Hill in the *Tribune*. "Even then, the stench would remain." "I have carted my travel-stained carcass to some of the filthiest and most festering slums in Asia," wrote Len Mosley of the *Daily Express*. "But nothing, nothing, nothing, neither the hopeless leper colonies of East Pakistan, the back streets of Bombay, nor the gutters of Calcutta, has left me with such a feeling of nausea and depression as I got this week while sitting through a new British film called *Peeping Tom*."

Nothing, indeed. Because of (or despite) such histrionic notices, the film was pulled from theaters and buried by its distributor. Powell, honored for such previous films as *The Red Shoes* and *The Life and Death of Colonel Blimp*, was virtually finished as a filmmaker.

Powell's auto-da-fé parallels that of his protagonist. Mark is the focus puller for a movie studio and a part-time photographer of girlie pictures for a corner news shop. (In a nod to the Master of Suspense, whose *Psycho* came out a little later the same year, a Hitchcock look-alike appears in cameo to purchase some "views.") A loner except for the constant companionship of his film camera, Mark suffers the legacy of his biologist father, who used him from infancy as a guinea pig in a study of fear in children, continually filming and recording him and subjecting him to sadistic experiments (*The Truman Show* via B. F. Skinner).

Mark shows some of these films to his winsome neighbor, Helen (Anna Massey): Mark as a child awakening to a lizard tossed on his bed; spying on a pair of lovers; his farewell to his mother on her deathbed; his father (played, ominously, by Powell himself) cavorting with his mother's "successor"; and images of Mark's face with that mystery light in his eyes. It's a good first-date ploy, shocking Helen but arousing her maternal instincts and perhaps her own morbid gaze (she is writing a children's book about "a magic camera and what it photographs"). Could this budding courtship cure Mark of his lethal hobby? Together they evoke the aw-shucks innocence of the couple in David Lynch's *Blue Velvet* (1986). However, Helen's blind, Sybil-like mother (Maxine Audley) is suspicious. In a scene of confused Oedipal dynamics, Mark confronts Helen's mom in his darkroom and they engage in a coded, sexually ambiguous exchange. Deprived of sight, the mother is immune to Mark's camera and can see into his disease. She refuses to let him see her daughter until he gets help.

Mark has come to the same conclusion himself. "It will never see you!" he tells Helen when she offers to pose for his Bolex. Helen remains a virgin to his gaze, which he continues to turn on other objects. In addition to prostitutes, aspiring actresses fill the bill, such as sportive Vivian (Moira Shearer, the doomed dancer of *The Red Shoes* in a sinister allusion), an understudy on *The Walls Are Closing In*, the film Mark is working on at the studio. They find her body in a trunk while shooting on the set in a scene of ruefully funny, self-reflexive black comedy. But the rushes from that liaison fail to satisfy, and meanwhile, the police have begun snooping close to home.

For Mark, though, this is all according to his script. He records the ongoing investigation blithely, for he has one last killing in mind, the images of which will be "so perfect" that even "he"—his father, presumably, or God, or Powell, or the audience—will be satisfied. "Do you know what the most frightening thing in the world is?" he asks Helen near the end. The answer to that question is anticlimactic, as is the origin of the flickering light that torments Mark's victims. What is more frightening is that we cannot tear our eyes away.

Persona
Two women

Directed by Ingmar Bergman; starring Liv Ullmann, Bibi Andersson (1966)

by Michael Wilmington

THE MOST SEXUALLY AROUSING MOVIE SCENE—AT LEAST FOR me—takes place in the first half of Ingmar Bergman's angst-ridden masterpiece *Persona*. You know the sequence I mean. Liv Ullmann, playing Elisabet Vogler, a great actress who has stopped speaking and is being treated for a breakdown, is sitting in her bedroom with Bibi Andersson as Alma, a nurse who can barely stop talking.

Those two Scandinavian blondes, Norwegian Liv and Swedish Bibi, are in their nightgowns, bathed in Sven Nykvist's eerily lucid black-and-white lighting, both of them throat-twistingly beautiful yet disturbingly alike. It's late in the day and Elisabet's room is grayish, clean, somber. Elisabet, still silent, watches Alma begin talking about a sexual adventure she had on a beach with an acquaintance named Katarina and two strangers.

Alma is the nurse, but Elisabet here has the critical look of a doctor examining a patient. Because of the lateness of the hour and the women's undress, there are lesbian undertones that are never unleashed. Alma describes this episode in which anonymous sexual passion overwhelmed her and broke down her defenses, and although the episode had consequences, it obviously still turns her on, as it does us.

At first, the story seems like a *Penthouse* Forum fantasy. But it gains tremendous plausibility. She lingers over each detail: Alma and Katarina were lying on the beach, nude but for straw hats, when the boys came along. One began talking with Katarina, who openly began masturbating him. In moments, they were screwing in the sun, while Alma and the other boy watched. Soon, all four were making love. The boys left, never, apparently, to meet their unexpected partners again.

Alma then reveals that as a consequence of the orgy, she had another intense sex session that evening with her lover Karl-Henrik, which resulted in pregnancy and an abortion. Guilt permeates the scene, and yet we have no doubt that the orgy was somehow worth it.

Alma is totally absorbed in the recollection, and an atmosphere of tremendous sexual tension builds as she recites it, consumed with the memory and radiating, as Bergman admiringly noted, a perfect attitude of shameful lust.

Why was the scene so exciting to me? For one thing, when I saw it, I happened to be in love—in my imagination—with both actresses, and consequently with the characters they play here. This kind of vicarious passion isn't idle lust. The stars of our youthful obsessions—the James Deans or Marilyn Monroes, the Brad Pitts or Gwyneth Paltrows—affect us deeply like no other figures of fantasy in our lives. In my case, Liv and Bibi, along with Shirley MacLaine, Leslie Caron, Catherine Deneuve, and Françoise Dorléac, were the mad crushes of my moviegoing youth and adolescence. I never got over any of them.

But there is more bubbling under the *Persona* scene than my private fantasies. Pauline Kael, who rarely wrote better than when discussing sexuality and sex fantasy in movies, called it "one of the rare truly erotic sequences in movie history." This was in 1966, before the sexual film deluge of the late '60s and early '70s, including Kael's favorite, *Last Tango in Paris*. But it's still true. The reasons are many: mood, sense of revelation, the beauty and sexuality—and theatrical brilliance—of the two actresses, that feeling of psychological and physical disrobing, Nykvist's perfect lighting and composition, the way Bibi curls up in the easy chair like a trembling cat. Most of all, there's the sudden erruption of fierce, out-of-control sex into a film that had seemed to be going in a very different direction—and later goes in a different direction still. *Persona* is a horror movie in which all the horror—the chaos of the world that has silenced Elisabet—is offscreen or implied. Yet the mood, especially when the two women's halved faces later merge in that famous "mask" shot (composed of their "bad" halves, Bergman reminds us in his book *Images*), is one of awful unease, something terrible about to happen, a hint of madness.

Persona, famously, is a film within a film, where the celluloid itself breaks and burns. That remembered orgy seems the most real thing in it, even though it's something we never see. Like many memorable sexual episodes of the '60s and '70s, it happens suddenly, unexpectedly, and leads nowhere but to a memory—or an abortion. Love is one thing, lust another; sometimes, luckily, they commingle. But nothing I ever experienced in the summer of love or afterward remains as exciting to me as that moment in *Persona*.

Bergman made *Persona* at a time of intense psychological trauma and turmoil in his own life. Overworked and caught in the searing international media spotlight, he had unwisely accepted the directorship of Sweden's Royal Dramatic Theatre, which was on the verge of collapse, while at the same time meeting a schedule of a new film every year for Svensk Filmindustri. He had just finished making the two most boldly erotic movies of his career: *The Silence,* with Ingrid Thulin and Gunnel Lindblom as two sisters in a war-torn foreign country, with a little boy (played by Jörgen Lindström, the same actor who appears in the precredit sequence of *Persona*), and *All These Women,* a ribald comedy about a great cellist who is also a Casanova and lives in a chateau with most of his mistresses and ex-mistresses, including Bibi Andersson, Ingrid Thulin and Harriet Andersson.

The Silence, bleak and terrifying, was one of Bergman's biggest financial hits. *All These Women,* sunny and randy, was a failure critically and commercially. So, in the hospital, after working on a rough sketch called *The Cannibals,* Bergman detoured into *Persona,* the movie which, along with *Cries and Whispers,* he has long insisted is his best, deepest work. I agree.

It is itself a sexual fantasy, rooted in sexual reality. Elisabet and Alma were played by Bergman's current lover, Ullmann, and a past lover, Andersson. He cast them together after he saw these two friends on the beach comparing hands, and noted their similarity. The image of Liv and Bibi on the beach merges with the film image of Bibi and Liv in the bedroom sharing the memory of Bibi on the beach, the sunlit sex, the revelation in darkness, the confession: all clasped together in the shared tale of the orgy. Perhaps that's why it remains so arousing. If Bergman showed us the scene in flashback or in present time, it would be diminished. It is the words, the memory, the "shameful lust" on Bibi's face that generates its quenchless heat.

Persona has another hold on me. When I first saw it in 1966, I was in New York City, far from home. I was visiting there because I was in love with a fellow student and actress from the University of Wisconsin–Madison, a girl who always struck me as looking like Catherine Deneuve from her (slightly) worse side. After our sophomore year, my classmate said yes to a proposal of marriage I made almost recklessly one night. But then she transferred to NYU, and to win her, I would have had to relocate and face formidable big-city competition. I didn't have the guts.

So, visiting her but knowing I was losing her, I roamed the city's bookshops, the art-film theaters, all the places I had read about in my small town. Bergman was one of my heroes, *Wild Strawberries* (with Bibi) one of my favorites. As I watched *Persona* that first time, my heart was breaking. I was in the midst of a love, a sexual passion, that didn't work out.

But *Persona* always will.

Picnic
Women on the verge

Directed by Joshua Logan; starring Kim Novak, William Holden, Rosalind Russell, Susan Strasberg, Cliff Robertson (1955)

by Emanuel Levy

JOSHUA LOGAN'S **PICNIC** IS ONE OF THOSE RARE FILMS THAT vividly capture the zeitgeist of the 1950s, particularly the issues of gender, desire, and sexuality. The movie employs narrative and themes that reflect the dominant ideology of that conservative and conformist decade.

Over the years, William Inge's play, upon which the movie is based, has assumed the status of classic Americana. Premiering in New York in 1953, *Picnic* won a Pulitzer and the production became famous for featuring Paul Newman's Broadway debut. Logan's film version was nominated for five Oscars, winning two: color art direction and set decoration (William Flannery, Jo Mielziner, and Robert Priestley), and editing (Charles Nelson and William A. Lyon). *Picnic* is better known as the movie that made Kim Novak a star and convinced Hitchcock that she was capable of playing the complex dual role in *Vertigo*.

Set over Labor Day weekend, indicating that it's no ordinary day, the tale begins with the handsome Hal Carter (William Holden) jumping from a freight train and landing in a small town on the Kansas plains. A college dropout, Hal is not a bad guy, just a bum searching for his identity, drifting from one job to another and from town to town.

A screen test in Hollywood promised a "big career" under the alluring stage name of Brush Carter; Tennessee Williams used the same type of man in *Sweet Bird of Youth*. However, when Hal realized "they were going to have to pull out all my teeth and get me new ones," he refused. Then Hal was arrested after hitchhiking in a car driven by women who wanted to party, then robbed him. "I'm telling you, women are gettin' desperate," says Hal, anticipating the movie's chief issue: desperate (single) women.

Hal now hopes that his college friend Alan Benson (Cliff Robertson), heir of the town's richest family, will help him find a job. An outsider who wants to become an insider, Hal, like most screen heroes of the 1950s, wishes to be "somebody," settle down, and live a respectable middle-class life. The bulk of the narrative shows how a stud like Hal sets in motion a chain of events that have shattering effects on the town's residents.

Picnic is a women's film, statistically if not ideologically, since most of its characters are female. Moreover, each of the five women represents a type. The central figure is Madge (Novak), the "prettiest girl in town," sensitive but not very bright. Madge is the eldest daughter of Mother Flo (Betty Field), who hates Hal because he reminds her of the swaggering husband who deserted her, leaving her the responsibility of raising two girls. Flo's dream is to marry off Madge to Alan, perceiving marriage as her daughter's only avenue to a stable life and upward mobility.

Madge's younger sister is Millie (played by Susan Strasberg, daughter of Lee Strasberg), a tomboy of the bookish type. Mrs. Helen Potts (Verna Felton), the Owens's middle-aged neighbor, lives with her sickly mother. The point is made: None of the women has a steady man in her life.

The most pathetic figure is Rosemary Sidney (Rosalind Russell), a spinsterish teacher who rents a furnished room at the Owens's house. "Anybody mind if an old maid schoolteacher joins the company?" Rosemary says in her first scene. Neurotic and fearing that life is passing her by, Rosemary makes a last desperate grab at marital bliss: She is willing to compromise and marry Howard (Arthur O'Connell), a dull and selfish traveling salesman. Rosemary's hysteria-prone preparation for her meeting with Howard reduces her to a teenager waiting for her first date, while her old-fashioned morality dictates that she be treated as a lady.

By standards of the dominant culture, the unmarried Rosemary perceives herself—and is perceived by others—as a failure. Unlike teachers in the usual small-town films, Rosemary is not particularly concerned with career or students; she's never seen in a classroom. Obsessed with singlehood, she intends to give up her profession as soon as she gets married. Reflecting the decade's conservative mores, Rosemary reproaches Flo for letting her daughter read "filthy" stuff like *The Ballad of the Sad Cafe,* a book that "many wanted banned from the public library."

The introduction of each character provides a field day for semioticians, who study signs and symbols. Each female character is associated with an object that signifies her distinct lifestyle: Mrs. Potts is holding a cake, Flo is seen in the kitchen with eggs, Rosemary applies cream to her wrinkles, Millie is reading a book, and Madge holds a hair dryer, a phallic object signifying unfulfilled desire. Millie tells Madge, "Dry your silly hair over somebody else," to which Madge replies, "Why don't you read your silly book under somebody else?" Flo is horrified when Madge says of her hair: "I wish it didn't take so long to dry—I think one summer I'll cut it short." That long hair, a symbol of Madge's beauty, is her most womanly asset.

In contrast, the men in *Picnic* represent types that are associated with "masculine" activities: golf for Alan, heavy lifting for Hal, drinking for Howard. Stripped to the waist, Hal is the quintessential outdoor man who feels more comfortable in nature. When Mrs. Potts offers to wash his shirt, Hal wonders, "Anybody mind?" "Of course not," she says. "You're a man, what's the difference?" But there is a difference, and for the rest of the story Hal remains shirtless, proudly exhibiting his muscled chest.

Early on, Rosemary describes Hal as "naked as an Indian," revealing sexual starvation as well as racial bias. "Who does he think is interested?" she asks. Everyone, apparently. In the film's dramatic climax, Rosemary, her inhibitions dulled by alcohol, makes a pass at Hal and is brutally rejected. Forcing him to dance with her, Rosemary tears his shirt (with a ferocity that recalls Vivien Leigh's similar act with Brando in *A Streetcar Named Desire*). "You won't stay younger forever," says the vengeful Rosemary. "Did ya ever think that? What'll become of you then?" In *Sweet Bird of Youth,* Geraldine Page echoes the same feelings with her stud (Paul Newman).

Hal is an uninhibited spirit, as Mrs. Potts says after his departure: "He clumped through the house like he was still outdoors. You knew there was a man in the house!" Hal and Alan represent complementary sides of a desirable male. Hal was the physical type in school, excelling in football and chasing girls, whereas Alan, the rich kid, excelled in academics but was lousy with girls.

The five women take different ideological stances toward love and marriage that indicate the inherent tension between those values. Commonsensical Mrs. Potts believes in the superiority of feelings over reason, and she's the first to give her blessings to Madge's romance with Hal. Rosemary knows that marriage—even an unhappy one—will redeem her from inferior spinster status.

Perceiving marriage as an economic transaction in which Madge's youth and beauty would be exchanged for Alan's economic security and prestige, Flo is utterly pragmatic. She tells Madge: "A pretty girl doesn't have long, just a few years, but if she loses her chance when she's young, she might as well throw all her prettiness away." When Madge protests that she is only nineteen, her mother responds cruelly: "And next summer you'll be twenty, and then twenty-one, and then forty!"

Conforming to classic Hollywood cinema, *Picnic*'s coda offers a hopeful resolution by celebrating romantic love. Flo pleads with Madge to stay, arguing that her passion for Hal is transitory, that he'll no doubt become a good-for-nothing drunk and unfaithful, just like Flo's errant husband. But Madge is determined to leave, and as Hal jumps on a passing train, she boards a bus to Tulsa. That last image was perceived as a happy ending, but when viewed today, it is possibly ambiguous. Heading for an unknown but potentially exciting future, will Madge follow in her mother's footsteps?

In his book *America in the Movies,* Michael Wood points out that the film's "persistent, insidious hysteria" and its "undercurrent of alienation and loneliness" went unnoticed at the time. Indeed, *Picnic* is about the heavy price paid for conformity and repressed sexuality. No woman in the film is sexually or emotionally fulfilled. Hal, a stud surrounded by sex-starved women, is the only desirable male. It's worth pointing out that William Inge and Tennessee Williams were homosexual playwrights who might have been expressing their fears of aging and loneliness through their heroines.

Poison Ivy
Welcome to the dollhouse

Directed by Katt Shea; starring Drew Barrymore, Sara Gilbert, Tom Skerritt, Cheryl Ladd (1992)

by Peter Travers

YOU CAN THINK OF **POISON IVY** AS B-MOVIE TRASH, WHICH sometimes it most deliciously is. You can also think of it as the movie in which Drew Barrymore kicked her *E.T.* image over the rainbow. As the teen fatale of this low-budget, high-style find, the former child star slips the tongue to a tomboy school chum, plays footsie with a man's crotch, fucks on the hood of a Mercedes (in the rain yet), and kills . . . well, more on that later. *Poison Ivy* moves beyond wickedly erotic fun to become both an acutely unsettling psychological thriller and a treatise on how women think men think about sex. Which raises a question: Who made this wild thing?

Her name is Katt Shea, an actress turned director who cowrote the *Ivy* script with her former husband, producer Andy Ruben. As protégés of Roger Corman, the Rubens turned out such bimbo-and-slasher cheapies as *Dance of the Damned, Streets,* and *Stripped to Kill I* and *II.* Movie snobs can laugh, but Shea has a gift for transcending pulp. The emotional resonance, visual sophistication, and feminist subtext of her work create a distinctive style worth monitoring.

Although *Poison Ivy* prompted a few noisy walkouts at the Sundance Film Festival, the *New York Times* acclaimed it as a "commercial art film" and the Museum of Modern Art held a Shea retrospective. B movies give new directors a chance to exercise their subversive talents; look at Jonathan

Demme's *Caged Heat* or Martin Scorsese's *Boxcar Bertha*. Shea does that tradition proud.

From the first scene of *Poison Ivy*, Shea shows remarkable assurance. Sylvie Cooper, deftly played by Sara Gilbert (she was Darlene the dis queen on TV's *Roseanne*), is sketching a cross entwined with ivy. The model for her drawing is a tattoo on the leg of the new girl at Oakhurst High School, who is gliding dangerously, languorously over a ravine on a rope swing. The atmosphere is hypnotically sensual as Phedon Papamichael's camera takes in this mystery creature from her pouty mouth to the peekaboo hole in her boot. "She's definitely a turnoff—too overt," says Sylvie in voice-over. "I mean, most girls don't fly through the air with their skirt around their waist."

Sylvie, who describes herself as a "politically, environmentally correct, feminist, poetry-reading type," dresses down with a vengeance. She is fascinated with the new girl's mouth; lips, she has heard, are the perfect reflection of another part of female anatomy. "Not that I'm a lesbian," says Sylvie. "Well, maybe I am." As ever, Sylvie is conflicted. She dismisses the sexy stranger as skanky, then devoutly wishes they were friends.

An accident makes them so. Sylvie stares helplessly when a dog is hit by a car, but the new girl coolly (and tellingly) whacks the animal on the head with a pipe to end its misery. Sylvie is impressed. They share confidences; the girl is a scholarship student who has been living with an aunt since her cokehead mother died. Her father split even though she tried to hold on to him by dressing like "the chicks in high heels" in her dad's *Hustler* collection. Sylvie, meanwhile, is a rich kid rattling around an L.A. mansion. She's impatient with her invalid mother, Georgie (a vividly edgy Cheryl Ladd), and in deep shit with her reformed-alcoholic father, Darryl (a touchingly beleaguered Tom Skerritt), ever since she called in a bomb threat to the TV station he manages. The two loners form a bond, and Sylvie dubs her new friend Ivy, after the tattoo, and Ivy's androgynous name for Sylvie also sticks—Coop, short for Cooper.

Shea gets the sexual confusion of female adolescence just right. And Barrymore nails Ivy's every carnal, comic, and vulnerable shading. Sylvie likes that Ivy makes her parents cringe, but when Ivy moves in with the dysfunctional Coopers (even the maid is uncommunicative) and starts sucking up to them, Sylvie grows alienated. In a darkly comic scene, the girls fight over the affections of Sylvie's mutt, Fred. "The fact that Fred hated every human except me really meant something," mourns Sylvie.

Things quickly turn sinister. Georgie sees Ivy as a reminder of happier times, like when she drove her red Corvette in the rain with the top down. "One day with the top down is better than a lifetime in a box," goads Ivy, encouraging Georgie's suicidal thoughts. Darryl, whose sex life ended with his wife's illness, is aroused when Ivy wears Georgie's low-cut dress. One night they find Georgie passed out from Percodan and champagne. Sitting on the edge of the bed while Darryl retrieves broken glass from the floor, Ivy rubs his crotch with her high-heeled foot. He nuzzles between her legs. The only sound is Georgie's tortured breathing.

Shea uses tantalizing eroticism to reveal the film's emotional undercurrents. When Georgie is pushed from her balcony, feelings reach a fever pitch. Though *Poison Ivy* can be read on several levels, it plays most provocatively as Sylvie's guilty nightmare over her mother's death, with Ivy as an imaginary evil twin. Only through Ivy can Sylvie express repressed longings for her father and hostility for her mother. Ivy's tattoo, miniskirt, and black fuck-me pumps are the fetishes of a naïve, neurotically insecure girl. The film builds to Sylvie's mature realization that she can't replace Georgie in Darryl's life. That this doesn't come off as dime-store moralizing is a tribute to Shea's layered direction and the dynamic teamwork of Gilbert and Barrymore. Sylvie's last words about Ivy—"I miss her"—become a poignant farewell to childhood.

Shea is examining the differences in how women and men define intimacy and the ways those differences can splinter families, lovers, and friends. That's rare for an erotic thriller. Though *Poison Ivy* is more than whoopee, audiences may find the movie easier to get off on than to get into. But why settle for the usual walk around the exploitation block when Shea takes you into uncharted territory on a wild ride with the top down?

My Own Private Barrymore

by Gerald Peary

Talk about embarrassed pleasures. I recall seeing *The Wedding Singer* at a matinee of giggly teenagers. They loved it. I liked it. Adam Sandler, a Jewish Jughead with a pinch of Stan Laurel, *was* *The Wedding Singer*. But I was there for the female lead, because I am a Drew Barrymore groupie.

Shouldn't you be?

If your warped constellation of favorites includes Mary Magdalene, Lucretia Borgia, Tokyo Rose, Pam Smart, Heidi Fleiss, and the great Tonya Harding, then early Drew is for you. Swear allegiance to what a friend succinctly called "the dark Drew." All negative energy! Sharp-tongued, snotty, I-was-a-Teen-Hussy-on-Rehab. Author at fourteen of the hard-luck bio *Little Girl Lost*. Impertinent flasher on *Letterman* unveiling her boobs—"Happy Birthday, Dave!"—while standing on his desk!

"Drew's bisexual," claimed the e-zines. One website offered close-ups of her myriad tattoos; the best is the butterfly sitting pretty below her navel.

Also, Drew is a survivor. She'd been a wild girl forever, saying "Yes!" through the "Just Say No" Reagan era, and still only in her twenties.

But back to 1998, *The Wedding Singer*. Drew was fine, a perky little girlfriend for Sandler. Yet this veteran Drew watcher felt uneasy. The new Drew was *sweet*. Beneath her heaving bosom, she had a *heart*. She got *dewy-eyed with emotion*. ▶

She kept her clothes on.

These un-Drew elements weren't unprecedented. *Boys on the Side* (1995) was sappy. She was a goody-goody in Woody Allen's *Everyone Says I Love You* (1996). *Scream* (1996) had possibilities, but she was killed off before she could go bad. Or to bed.

What to do? I rented a deluge of early Drew. I had to know: Had I been blinded by Drew's sexiness to her career failings? A couch-slave week later, I was sad to realize: what a crummy oeuvre!

Here are some Drew movies that are no fun at all: *Cat's Eye* (1985), *Far from Home* (1989), *No Place to Hide* (1992), *Doppelganger: The Evil Within* (1993), *Bad Girls* (1994), *Batman Forever* (1995).

Then there's a tiny middle ground of okay road movies. In *Guncrazy* (1992), Drew goes American indie as a pistol-loving trailer park chick on a spree with a paroled ex-con; despite cool moments, Drew lacks the homicidal charisma of Peggy Cummins in the 1949 original, a noir masterwork. In the mild *Mad Love* (1995), Drew's manic-depressive teenager rides off with gentleboy Chris O'Donnell through the Southwest; the story isn't much, but Drew plays some emotionally raw scenes in which she breaks down without her meds.

You know about *E.T.* There are only two other early Drew Barrymores which, though schlock genre movies, I heartily recommend:

Firestarter (1984). Drew at eight commands the screen with pyrokinetic powers. Don't get her mad! Burn, baby, burn! There are swell scenes between Drew and a nefarious, ponytailed George C. Scott.

Poison Ivy (1992). If only all Drew movies could match this lurid, primal trash. As a haughty little tramp, she seduces her best friend's dad and plots to murder her best friend's mom. Nowhere has Drew been so uninhibitedly unwholesome, and the sex scenes with the middle-aged Tom Skerritt are smolderingly soft-core. In this Nabokov knockoff, an underage Drew shows the petulant range of a young Bette Davis.

Oh, she's very, very bad, my private Drew Barrymore! ■

Rebecca

Girl, you'll be a woman soon

Directed by Alfred Hitchcock; starring Laurence Olivier,
Joan Fontaine, Judith Anderson (1940)

by Jami Bernard

SHE DREAMT SHE WENT TO MANDERLEY AGAIN. SHE'S NOT THE
only one. This Hitchcock movie (his first in America), adapted from the
Daphne du Maurier gothic with its rage, obsession, and thick psychological
case files, holds a weird fascination for me. Like the second Mrs. de Winter
processing the terrible secrets of the Manderley estate only after it has
burned to the ground, I now realize that I too am in love with the ghost of
the first Mrs. de Winter, who is never seen.

More accurately, I am in love with the idea of the first Mrs. de Winter and
her brooding husband Maxim as the exciting couple that the second Mrs. de
Winter (wrongly) imagines them to have been. As the teenage heroine
Frankie does in *Member of the Wedding*, I have a crush on another couple's
union. And, like the sinister Mrs. Danvers (Judith Anderson), the holdover
housekeeper from Rebecca's staff who makes life hell for the second Mrs. de
Winter, I am annoyed that the shy and awkward replacement wife through
whose eyes we (mostly) see the movie, and who unfortunately more resembles me than that wild, fearless, now drowned Rebecca, has gotten in the way
of my fantasy.

"Manderley—Manderley—secretive and silent." Joan Fontaine narrates
the opening of the film, harking back to when she was such a naïve non-
entity of a girl that her character doesn't even have a name, and then, as the

second Mrs. de Winter, not even her own name. She's a paid companion for crotchety old Mrs. Van Hopper, a vulgarian who sees to it that the hireling will never have a sense of her own self-worth. While enduring Mrs. Van Hopper on a trip to the Riviera, this unnamed, unimposing girl meets the elegant, wealthy widower George Fortescu Maximillian de Winter. He is vacationing—wandering dazed, really, perhaps suicidally—in an apparent attempt to get over the drowning death of his wife, Rebecca. "They say he simply adored her . . . he's a broken man," Mrs. Van Hopper says helpfully, thus ensuring that her charge will never think herself worthy of Maxim. And Max continues the girl's education in poor self-esteem: Even as he courts her, he belittles her. "Stop biting your nails!" he snaps, and when he reduces her to tears, he hands her a handkerchief. "Care to blow your nose?"

Nevertheless, for reasons totally mysterious to the girl, Max proposes. "I'm asking you to marry me, you little fool!" Thus, the girl with no prospects gets a classic romance-fiction windfall—the house, the money, the handsome husband. But there's a catch. She, and they, are in thrall to the ghost of the first Mrs. de Winter, a fiery spirit who could "hunt, ride, or rhumba dance," whose masquerade balls were the toast of the coast of Cornwall, who feared nothing and died tragically.

Max is no help in easing his new wife's transition to the ancestral estate of Manderley. Like all heroes of gothic romance, Maxim's initial behavior suggests hatred and disdain, even sadism. He infantilizes his child bride ("Promise me never to wear black satin or pearls, or to be thirty-six years old"). He turns on her with inexplicable rages. He never notices her clothes or hair, despite having showered his first wife with furs and gowns, all still in Rebecca's closet and lovingly tended by Mrs. Danvers. As Mrs. Van Hopper had warned, this girl hasn't "the faintest idea of what it means to be a great lady," and she's frightened by her bridegroom and intimidated by the stiff, hostile Manderley staff. Everywhere she goes in that house, with its locked-off west wing and its sighing secrets, there's a reminder of the more beautiful, more accomplished Rebecca—the dead woman's monogram is on everything from handkerchiefs to pillowcases. The shadow of the love rival hangs over her every waking moment. "You must have made a mistake," trembles the new Mrs. de Winter when a servant calls her on the house phone. "Mrs. de Winter has been dead for over a year."

Her life would be tolerable if only she had a hint of love or tenderness from her husband. She even offers to demote herself to companion and friend, knowing that Max can never love her as he loved Rebecca. "You thought I loved Rebecca? You thought *that*?" thunders the lord and master when the truth finally spills. "*I hated her!*" Dah-*dum*!

It turns out Rebecca was a no-good, two-timing slut. Whatever. At least she had fire, libido, charisma, independence—all the things lacking in her timid, inept successor. You can hardly blame Mrs. Danvers, the scariest housekeeper in the movies, for her Rebecca fetish. As played by the piercing-eyed Judith Anderson, with her hair drawn back so severely her skull might pop, Mrs. Danvers is self-appointed curator at the shrine to her dead mistress. Everything is still in its place, from hairbrush to transparent negligee. She recalls brushing Rebecca's hair for twenty minutes at a time; who wouldn't? Rebecca had a pet name for this warhorse—Danny—and the implication is that they were lovers. Danny, at least, still carries the torch.

At the end of the movie, she carries the torch too far, setting Manderley ablaze. But if Rebecca wasn't bisexual, it's clear that at least she was a sexual predator without conscience. She married Max for his money and used her affairs as both sport and blackmail. In the novel, Rebecca goads Max into killing her, but in the movie Rebecca trips and conks her head before he can get to it. In any case, Max behaves criminally, covering up the death by stowing Rebecca's body aboard a leaky sailboat, then opportunistically misidentifying another body that washes ashore to forestall an investigation. Although it turns out Rebecca had fully intended to go down in flames, this is still a black splotch on Maxim's resume. Yet the only reaction from the second Mrs. de Winter on discovering the truth is relief bordering on ecstasy: "*You didn't love her? You didn't love her?*"

The psychological lure of the gothic romance—starting with the seminal *Jane Eyre,* which involved another scowling older man with a difficult first wife and a mansion gone down in flames—is that it reassures its female audience that Daddy doesn't hate them after all. The cold, aloof father, or a replacement in the form of an older, likewise distant husband, may appear to be dismissive, even brutal, but he has good reason. The satisfaction of the genre depends on the degree of stretch from which the rubber band snaps back from hate to love. *Rebecca* reconciles the logistics and anxieties of the Electra complex—how can he respect me as a grown-up woman when I still bite my nails, and won't he always love the first Mrs. de Winter more? At the end of *Rebecca,* Maxim's only regret—and this from a possible murderer—is that he has caused his bride to lose her childish innocence: "It's a pity you have to grow up." No black satin and pearls for her, but at least the second Mrs. de Winter can finally assume her place as mistress of the house, even if the house won't be Manderley. ("We can never go back to Manderley again.")

Maxim's apparent disdain for his new bride came naturally. Laurence Olivier had pushed for his wife, Vivien Leigh, to get the role, and didn't want to work with the twenty-two-year-old Fontaine. The belittling effect was amplified by Hitchcock's own offscreen preference for Olivier, plus Fontaine's knowledge that producer David O. Selznick had wanted Loretta Young for the part; Margaret Sullavan and Anne Baxter also tested for it. Fontaine had her own ghosts to deal with—her lifelong competition with older sister Olivia de Havilland. The negative chemistry and Fontaine's insecurity worked; out of eleven Oscar nominations, *Rebecca* won for picture and cinematography. But Fontaine must have felt very much like the second Mrs. de Winter, dwarfed by the shadow of other, more preferable women, and perhaps anticipating that future viewers like me will always long for the Rebecca of our dreams, the one who danced with Maxim at their masquerade, whirling and whirling around the ballroom of a still magnificent Manderley.

Secretary

A woman's work

Directed by Steven Shainberg; starring Maggie Gyllenhaal, James Spader (2002)

by Jami Bernard

THE SECRETARY, SERENE AND CONFIDENT, DRESSED SMARTLY, crisply, in black tailored skirt and white ruffled blouse, makes her morning rounds, moving through her routine expertly, fetching her boss his coffee and mail. Kneeling elegantly in front of her desk, she places her chin—just so—on the hammer of a stapler, pressing it firmly to bind some documents. Rising, coffee in one hand, newly bound papers in the other, she turns with a brisk clack-clack of her heels toward her boss's inner sanctum to start her day. Her efficiency is all the more impressive in that she's shackled by the wrists to a heavy wooden yoke that lies across her shoulders and the back of her neck. She doesn't spill the coffee or break stride; this is a woman who takes pride in her work.

Secretary is one of the few films—actually, the only film—that treats BDSM with humor, respect, and a reasonable grasp of what that off-road lifestyle entails. There's a lot going on in the BDSM acronym—bondage and discipline, dominance and submission—but most filmmakers lump it all under the umbrella of sadomasochism, capitalizing on the common perception of kinky sex as the province of psychopaths and perverts. The benign, quotidian nature of most BDSM relationships wouldn't have the same cinematic kick, the thinking must go.

And then along came *Secretary*, a departure from coy, tittering comedies like Garry Marshall's ludicrous spankfest *Exit to Eden,* and a corrective to dramas like the harrowing *The Piano Teacher* and *The Night Porter,* whose kink-leaning female protagonists are sick and sad, if not cursed. Without resorting to a lecture from *Miss Abernathy's Concise Slave Training Manual, Secretary* gently and disarmingly separates itself from the police-blotter S&M that characterizes so many movies on the subject, portraying instead a joyful dominant-submissive partnership that serves its participants well—and not only sexually. The D/S lifestyle that evolves between the secretary and her boss liberates the hireling from her hollow, self-destructive past, and eventually liberates her boss from his need to compartmentalize his emotions and suppress his desires.

Secretary occasionally ventures into issues like whether BDSM can be a substitute, even a cure, for pathological behavior. But for the most part, it's a blithe black comedy. Director Steven Shainberg adapted Mary Gaitskill's bleak short story with the help of producer Erin Cressida Wilson, and while the movie touches on the psychology of the secretary (but not of her boss, who in many ways is the more troubled of the two), it's far more interested in the story's sweet ironies than in any possibly wider (and, in Gaitskill's view, darker) implications. Some critics wrongly concluded that this is a movie about the joys of spanking or about how pink-collar workers are metaphorically demeaned by their jobs. Instead, it's about a timid young woman's unexpected sexual and personal awakening through the structure and tenderness she discovers in a D/S relationship.

Lee Holloway (Maggie Gyllenhaal), newly released from a psychiatric clinic and walking on eggshells around her concerned family, applies for her very first job so she can get away from her abusive, drunken father (Stephen McHattie) and her nervous, unbearable mother (Lesley Ann Warren). She skims past a help-wanted ad headlined "Be a Leader!" in favor of a listing for plain old secretary. Lee isn't a leader, she's a follower, and, as it turns out, a good one.

When Lee shows up at the small, eerily quiet law firm of E. Edward Grey (James Spader), the last woman to use a steno pad there flees past her in angry tears, but Lee is unfazed. The remote, watchful Mr. Grey grills Lee with a series of personal questions while struggling to contain his mounting sexual excitement. Is she single? Is she planning to get pregnant? Does she have sex with her boyfriend? Lee answers without guile, not knowing any better, and we sense that the lawyer is testing Lee for her suitability—but not as a secretary. He wants someone he can shape and mold, someone who will obey his every command, anticipate his whims. Someone he can spank.

Although Mr. Grey isn't fully in touch with his needs and desires, what he basically wants is a submissive. They're not so easy to come by; as the movie slyly notes, the merely meek are apt to flee in tears. A good submissive is flexible, inventive, determined, quick-witted, adventurous.

And obedient.

After a series of seemingly random tests—at one point Lee dives into a dumpster in search of a missing file, the point being not the task but her degree of compliance—Mr. Grey is ready to get down to business: He spanks her. Under the pretext of punishing Lee for making typos, Mr. Gray issues a string of specific commands, starting with: "Miss Holloway, bend over." He has her stretch out her arms, palms down on his executive desk, and read aloud the letter she has mistyped. As she reads, he spanks. Initially, she registers fear and confusion, but there's curiosity too. And sensation. As the spanking becomes more urgent, the camera stays on Gyllenhaal's face, whose hint of innocent baby fat flushes into erotic fleshiness. New ideas struggle to take root there. When Mr. Grey is spent, he falls forward, steadying himself over Lee's body, one hand near hers, as Lee tentatively extends a pinkie to touch him, a gesture of astonishing intimacy. Later, in the ladies' room, Lee examines the angry welt on her bottom in the mirror, and she is transformed. She likes the tingle and endorphins of the spanking, the concentrated attention from the remote boss she can never please, the red stripe that brands her as property of Mr. Grey. She likes that *he* likes it.

Lee's world opens up. She dresses better, carries herself more erect. Vanilla sex with her boyfriend (Jeremy Davies) doesn't cut it. She begins to make errors on purpose, bouncing down the hall to confess them and collect her punishment. She proudly frames the typo-riddled letters and hangs them in the corridor like trophies, charting the progress of this strange new relationship that leaves her glowing with pleasure and self-worth.

The relationship retains its oddly formal structure—she calls him Mr. Grey, he calls her Miss Holloway. But they are lovers. They never see each other outside the office, yet their relationship transcends office hours; Mr. Grey calls Lee at home to dictate what she should eat for dinner, right down to how many peas she should put on her plate. Like the hothouse orchids Mr. Grey tends, Lee blossoms under the attention. She takes her first solitary walk without her mom watching over her for signs of suicidal behavior because Mr. Grey tells her to; "he had given me permission to do it," she explains in voice-over narration.

For Lee, BDSM isn't just about sexual pleasure, although she's so sensually attuned to her unleashed lust that she orgasms in the ladies' room just thinking about Mr. Grey's hand. She learns to organize herself around BDSM, substituting healthy new rituals for destructive old ones (she stops cutting herself with sharpened toys from an undoubtedly painful childhood). The key to Lee, and to the movie, comes early on when she talks in narration about not wanting to leave the psychiatric clinic because of the comfort of its schedule and routine. "Life was simple; for that reason, I was reluctant to go." She can only thrive within a structured environment.

Late in the movie, Mr. Grey bathes Miss Holloway tenderly while she happily explains every scar on her body. It's a scene of quietly erotic joy by way of Fragonard, with every inch of Gyllenhaal's naked skin aglow, adored. And yet, the sexy poster for *Secretary,* all black-stockinged legs and a butt poised for spanking, is misleading. The real turn-on of the movie lies in power exchange. Lee is submissive, but far from passive. One of the jokes of *Secretary* is that Lee takes to the arrangement so enthusiastically that her boss can't handle the demand; she's *exhausting* him. "We can't do this twenty-four hours a day, seven days a week!" he scolds her. "Why not?" she counters.

It's that simple "why not" that jolts the repressed Mr. Grey into entertaining, for the first time, his own possibilities as a dom. In a postscript, Lee has been promoted from secretary to full-time sub in her new role as Mrs. Grey. As she proudly sees her husband off to work in the morning from the porch of their suburban house, she notes in voice-over: "We looked like any other couple." Only happier.

The Servant

I'm your man

Directed by Joseph Losey; starring Dirk Bogarde,
James Fox (1963)

by David Ansen

Sexual intercourse began
In nineteen sixty-three
(Which was rather late for me)—
Between the end of the Chatterley *ban*
And the Beatles' first LP

—Philip Larkin, Annus Mirabilis

In all the pieces written about *The Servant*—Joseph Losey's acclaimed first
collaboration with screenwriter Harold Pinter—nobody talked about how
sexy it was. Maybe because the men writing about the film (I have yet to
see a woman's take on it) weren't eighteen when they first saw it, as I was.
Or maybe not. This was a very serious film, after all, dealing with complex
issues of class and power and gamesmanship, reflected in the ever-shifting
relationship between the supposed master, Tony (James Fox), a blond,
upper-class fop blindly entrenched in his own sense of entitlement, and
Barrett (Dirk Bogarde), the conniving manservant he hires to run his London flat and attend to his every need. There was plenty of sex in the
movie, but it was not, supposedly, intended to arouse: Sex was a tool in
the intricate game of one-upmanship in which the roles of master and servant were subtly, sometimes brutally, overturned. To acknowledge this as a

turn-on would implicate one in the nasty subtexts of this elegant booby trap of a movie.

The Servant reaches its climax, in which the degradation of Tony becomes complete, in an aborted orgy organized by Barrett and populated with various "decadent" stereotypes (older women with cigarette holders; musclemen, druggies). The tawdry goings-on were meant to shock the 1963 audience, even though nothing really happens at this orgy: It's all expectation and innuendo. "In years to come," Andrew Sarris concluded in his memorable rave review, "The Servant may be cited as a prophetic work marking the decline and fall of our last cherished illusions about ourselves and our alleged civilization."

I was more titillated than horrified. We were not yet free and clear of the sexually repressive Eisenhower era. It was still startling to see a guy with long hair: "The Sixties" wouldn't officially begin for several more years. In 1963, London was, in my imagination, the sexiest city on earth, and I wasn't alone in thinking so. The city was in the process of becoming "swinging" London, a place of Mods, Rockers, long-haired guys, and birds in miniskirts, best symbolized by the androgynous beauty of Mick Jagger. (Larkin's poem, for all its irony, gets at a metaphorical truth about that watershed moment in England.) That Carnaby Street revolution isn't overtly referenced in Losey's movie, but it was part of its aura, and certainly in the back of my mind. (Seven years later, James Fox would be memorably partnered with Jagger in that hallucinogenic apotheosis of '60s sexual ambiguity, Performance.) The Servant's implicit social criticism—its assault on the class system, which was finally crumbling—was very much part of the zeitgeist.

The Servant percolates with a fettered eroticism. It's a dance of avoidance: The strong homoerotic tension between Tony and Barrett is played out in code, never quite breaking to the surface. (The movie's sexiness was not lost on Matthew Bourne, who transformed Losey's work into his 2004 dance piece Play Without Words.)

The Servant was, thematically if not stylistically, a Fassbinder movie before its time: a study of sexual power wielded like a weapon, enacted in a ritualistic atmosphere of vaguely sadomasochistic connotations. By the middle of the movie, Tony and Barrett are enacting an unconscious parody of a bickering marriage, the bathrobed Tony and aproned Barrett arguing over domestic chores. In two of the film's most famous set-pieces, the aggressive ball-throwing the two men play on the stairway of the townhouse, and the game of hide-and-seek, Tony is reduced to a giggly infantilism that's barely distinguishable from sexual panic. He's titillated, yet unable to admit to himself the sexual attraction lurking beneath their games. Losey, whose sensual, sinuous, circular style is as fluid as Fassbinder's was deliberately cold and rigid, masterfully creates the insular, hothouse atmosphere of the flat itself, where Tony seduces his fiancée (the miscast Wendy Craig) with booze and jazz (Cleo Laine sings variations of the same torch song throughout the movie) and a tumble on the wall-to-wall carpet. The flat is a rich man's pleasure palace, as safe from the outside world as a nursery—but not safe from the inside, as it turns out.

The blond, smooth-chested, pretty-boy Fox and the angular, hard-edged Craig made an odd couple: He was the sex object, the more feminine presence. Barrett systematically tries to destroy their relationship. First he "accidentally" interrupts their lovemaking. Then he practices seduction by proxy, using Sarah Miles, whom he falsely introduces as his sister, as sexual bait. It's not long before she's straddling the young master in his big swivel chair. Little does Tony know that in fucking her, Barrett is fucking him, in more than one sense.

The Servant still looks good today. Bogarde's and Fox's performances are superbly nuanced, and Pinter's insinuating wit has a delicious, if familiar, snap. But it can't have the same charge as it had then: Too many movies have subsequently mined this territory. The unspoken power games that seemed exquisitely subtle and ambiguous in '63 now seem almost heavy-handed. They're old artistic news. But when I was an uncertainly bisexual eighteen-year-old college boy, *The Servant* cast a voyeuristic, kinky spell that left me dry in the mouth and feeling slightly and deliciously guilty. The guilt worked on several levels: I had no trouble admitting to myself (though not yet to others) that I found James Fox hot; what made it harder to accept was that his character was such a weak, snobbish, aristocratic twit. (It was easier to explain my even stronger lust for Michael York in the next sexy/chilly Losey-Pinter collaboration *Accident*—but that's another story.) Tony's despoilment at the hands of Barrett—a man more crude and clever than he—was politically and erotically satisfying. Far from being shocked by his decline and fall, I was aroused by it. (And between you and me, I think Losey—whose movies have always carried a strangely displaced erotic energy—was too.) I knew perfectly well what *The Servant* was about and what it "meant." But what no-body else seemed to feel (or admit to) was how glamorous it all was. I wanted to be in that overheated London townhouse going to the decadent dogs, smoking and drinking Scotch on the rocks and having sex with both men and women. And pretending to feel really, really bad about it. If this was the decline and fall of Western civilization, I wanted in.

Shampoo
All the leaves are brown

Directed by Hal Ashby; starring Warren Beatty, Julie Christie, Goldie Hawn (1975)

by Stephanie Zacharek

HAL ASHBY'S **SHAMPOO**, A COMEDY AND AN ELEGY, IS THE most autumnal movie about Southern California ever made. Set in 1968, just as Nixon rose to (or swooped down on) the presidency, *Shampoo* captures the shimmery peak of an era and looks ahead, anxiously, to its shivery end. But let's not rush winter: Autumn is also a season of plenty, a time of year where there seems to be lots of everything to go around. The '60s are often called an era of excess, usually by those who didn't partake of them or who did and now regret it. But what exactly is the difference between "excess" and "plenty"? *Shampoo* doesn't bother with such distinctions: It may be brushed with feathery strokes of sadness, yet it's anything but a cautionary tale. This is a story about the blurry line between sexual generosity and selfishness, about pleasure and its flip side, wistfulness, about not realizing the value of something until it has slipped away from you. The aura around *Shampoo*—you can almost feel it in the teeming molecules of Southern California light captured by László Kovács's camera—is of melancholy dappled with joy, the feeling of sleeping with someone you love for what you know will be the last time.

Warren Beatty is George, a cocksure hairdresser who makes his clients look and feel so beautiful that he can't help desiring them, and they want him too. Beatty may hop from bed to bed, but you can't call him a womanizer. He doesn't prey on women, but rather kick-starts a kind of self-love in them, a sense of well-being that's thrummingly erotic but also has virtually nothing to do with him. He needs these women more than they need him: Their confidence and sexual power are the engines of a vast feminine universe that he finds so dazzlingly seductive he wants in at any cost. In the movie's pivotal scene, Beatty stammers an explanation of why he can't sleep with just one woman at a time, spinning out a kind of blank verse about the incomprehensibility of sexual desire, and about our instinctual but misguided belief that we can use sex as a shield to stave off death: "I go into the shop, and they're so great-looking, you know? And I'm doing their hair, and they feel great, and they smell great. Or I could be out in the street, you know, and I could just stop at a stop light or go into an elevator or there's a beautiful girl—I mean, that's it, it makes my day. I mean, makes me feel like I'm gonna live forever."

There's something about Los Angeles too that can make you feel you're going to live forever, which is part of the seduction of *Shampoo*. Even by the year the picture was made, the '60s seemed like a distant epoch. (Ashby is well aware of that distance, which is part of what makes the picture so wryly haunting.) The Los Angeles of *Shampoo* is a city of ghosts, a snapshot of people who may have lived once but who have now moved on to other worlds, and though we're aware of their flaws and heartaches and dunderheaded mistakes, we wish we could have been around to see them in action. The specter of love hangs over this particular Los Angeles heavier than fog: Inside *Shampoo* there's a gothic romance, a tale of a doomed love that plays out between two of the most beautiful actors who ever strutted through the '60s— Beatty and Julie Christie.

At the beginning of *Shampoo*, Beatty's George and Christie's Jackie are already over as a couple. He's moved on to other women (he keeps the married, insecure Lee Grant and the ambitious Kewpie-doll of a go-getter Goldie Hawn in simultaneous rotation), and she's decided she likes to have her rent paid: She's become the mistress of a hotshot businessman (the wonderful Jack Warden), who also happens to be married to Grant. When Jackie and George reconnect after an absence, they feign indifference. George informs her authoritatively that her hair is all wrong—it makes her look like a hooker, he says, betraying his childish jealousy that she now belongs, almost literally, to someone else. She agrees to let him do her hair, and so he shows up at her swank, sunny cottage—on his motorcycle, naturally, hairdryer tucked into his belt like a pistol. They go into the bathroom; she sits before him, a steam-room queen wrapped only in a towel. He begins fussing around her, barely able to hide his nervousness. It's not long before they half-flutter, half-stumble into each other's arms in a moment that's both uncomfortably funny and heartstoppingly erotic. We hear the bump of their elbows and knees against the bathroom floor, but can we also hear that most intimate sound, the fluttering of eyelashes brushing against and into each other like clumsy moths, or do we imagine it?

We've imagined it, but so what: What we know now is that George and Jackie are meant to be together, the Heathcliff and Cathy of the Canyon, but something beyond their control is going to keep them apart. George can't keep his hands off other women, and Jackie likes money far too much, yet their problems run deeper. George is intensely vulnerable, but he's also blindly in thrall to the women around him, and it's a bad combination: Even in the midst of his sexual generosity (his emotions are expressed far less freely), he can't see how deeply he hurts the people he cares about. Jackie is a tougher soul, but her glimmers of vulnerability are devastating: When she and George fall into a discussion of his restless habits and he tells her bluntly, "I don't fuck anybody for money, I do it for fun," you have to watch Christie's face carefully for the crestfallen look that flickers across it. Suddenly, it's gone, replaced by her usual crisp composure.

Beatty and Christie had played lovers a few years before in *McCabe & Mrs. Miller*, and they'd also been real-life lovers for a time. In both *McCabe* and *Shampoo*, the beauty of them together—Beatty, with his meltingly direct gaze and faint air of physical goofiness, and Christie, with her cut-crystal cheekbones and regal, Sphinx-secret smile—is almost more than we can bear. Braving snow in *McCabe* and relentless sunshine in *Shampoo*, Christie and Beatty are lovers for the ages and for all seasons. They're California dreamin' in the ramshackle mining town of the heart.

Shanghai Express
Decamping

Directed by Josef von Sternberg; starring Marlene Dietrich, Clive Brook, Anna May Wong, Warner Oland (1932)

by Armond White

JOSEF VON STERNBERG TOOK SEX SERIOUSLY. WORKING IN THE first half of the twentieth century, when the cinematic art was more closely identified with the photographic process of capturing nature and glorifying the human face, Sternberg explored the sensuality of experience. His recreation of experience—his art—was not a simple matter of erotic presentation. Sternberg sought to understand the psychology behind erotic behavior. If a prime Sternberg artifact such as *Shanghai Express* is frequently mistaken for camp, it is only because that is the easiest response. Laughter is a trouble-free reaction to this story of Magdalen/Shanghai Lily (Marlene Dietrich), a white female bon vivant. Laughing is a simpler turn-on than arousal, because it ignores the complications of a subtly behaved yet undeniably sexual creature passing through a politicized landscape. She's a Westerner among a motley assortment of train passengers traveling through China during a civil war—a context for better understanding how private behavior relates to public life.

Confusion about Sternberg comes from his collaboration with screenwriter Jules Furthman, more famously identified for his subsequent screwball comedies with Howard Hawks. There is wit in Furthman's Sternberg scripts ("It took more than one man to change my name to Shanghai *Lily*," Dietrich intones), but Sternberg's visualization of this sophisticated banter is never smirky. *Shanghai Express* transcends the realm of the bawdy joke in order to reach a spiritual understanding of its characters as they gesture roughly, anxiously, toward love. To think Sternberg is burlesquing sex is to miss how he philosophizes about destiny. Preferring to see his films as comedy only traduces his drama, the most exquisitely visual and sensual drama in cinema history. Its profundity begins with its glamour, which is more than the swanky kitsch associated with Dietrich's singular, androgynous icon.

Sternberg accepted the sexual image his characters took on, and the attraction they held for each other, as glamorous. But this is glamour as the French erotic philosopher Georges Bataille later defined it—the conscious melding of sex and mortality. In *Shanghai Express*, you can admire Dietrich with her wide-brim hat and feather boa, and Clive Brook as her former lover in his strict military gear, as projections of the sexual ideal—they epitomize our culture's notions of the feminine and the masculine. Yet Sternberg queers their images, going beyond mere Hollywood idolization.

To be turned on by Sternberg's sexual archetypes is to be keyed in to their humanity. *Shanghai Express* uses an adventure plot that analyzes Western morality (it is a forerunner to his 1941 masterpiece *The Shanghai Gesture*). Through the use of exoticism, Sternberg seduced his Depression-era audience past conventional American puritanism (which received his more delirious critique in *Blonde Venus*). In *Shanghai Express*, Sternberg took the kitsch attitude associated with Chinoiserie (the French appropriation of Chinese culture for use as superficial design motifs) as the basis for examining the West's desire to depart from moralized habit and enjoy the liberation of a foreign culture. (The white passengers listen to the blues—sex music—while in foreign climes.) His cosmopolitan sensibility is apparent in the scene where a cow on railway tracks impedes the train's progress. It recalls the opening scene of a donkey in the road blocking the march of the foreign legion in *Morocco*. These incidents emphasize the point of Sternberg's exoticism. (In *Morocco* he introduces Amy Jolly's act with a backstage view of her theatrical cross-dressing preceded by Chinese and African dolls—the latter prefiguring the "Hot Voodoo" in *Blonde Venus*.) Sternberg chose exotic locales to better unleash the sexuality that Western custom has pent up. It surges forward, like the Shanghai Express itself, as a natural, important part of human instinct and social experience.

By placing his films in mysterious or theatrical settings, Sternberg conveys worldliness and relates it to sexual knowing. Then his plot complications shake up that knowing. East and West clash in *Shanghai Express* sexually and politically, enabling Sternberg to use his characters and incidents as metaphors expressing the excitement and danger and thrill of sexual behavior. The image of the train's mail catch symbolizes the sexual click (the hookup) between Dietrich and Brook. Although there's no actual sexual activity between them (not even indicated through the usual Hollywood euphemisms), the atmosphere is erotically charged. This incident became a movie staple; even David Lean repeated it decades later in *Doctor Zhivago* with the trolley car's electrical spark when Omar Sharif first meets Julie Christie—a tribute to Sternberg's film vocabulary of serious sexual emotion.

During the '60s sexual revolution, Sternberg got stuck with the camp label because the era's loosened-up approach to sex also trivialized it. Modern audiences inclined to wink at sex need to adjust to Sternberg's grave vision of sexual morality. Eternally modern, not judgmental, he saw sexual behavior as evidence of human spiritual struggle. That's the significance of Dietrich's Shanghai Lil striking a great glamorous pose while confessing, "I suffered quite a bit. I probably deserved it." It's an archetypal love-goddess posture in which her fur collar forms a sensuous halo around her face. Going further, she cries to Brook, "When I needed your faith you withheld it. Now that I don't need it and don't deserve it, you give it to me." This isn't a campy lamentation but an exquisitely expressed spiritual conflict.

Turn-on becomes uplift when you fully appreciate Sternberg's vision. Shanghai Lil realizes "Love without faith, like religion without faith, doesn't amount to much." Sternberg's lovers are wounded by such sophistication— they live with both sexual brazenness and shame. Weighing the complexity of feelings and morality, Sternberg makes that spiritual struggle almost palpable. When Dietrich stands in a train corridor, dressed in black with a shaft of light illuminating her face, the camera dollies in, bringing us closer to her character's passion. Yes, the shot is sexy but it's also full of emotion, an apotheosis. Sternberg's fantasies remind us we are more than the animals that rut.

The Song of Songs
Pre-Code lunacy

Directed by Rouben Mamoulian; starring Marlene Dietrich,
Brian Aherne, Lionel Atwill (1933)

by Andy Klein

DURING THE FIRST DECADE OF SOUND, DIRECTOR ROUBEN
Mamoulian had an almost unbroken string of critical and/or commercial suc-
cesses. But sandwiched between the musical triumph of *Love Me Tonight*
(1932) and Greta Garbo's box-office smash *Queen Christina* (1933) was the
nearly forgotten Marlene Dietrich misfire *The Song of Songs* (1933), a lulu of
twisted pre-Code sexual circumlocutions.

This was during that brief golden period (1929–1934)—between the
ramping up of sound production and the Breen Office's enforcement of the
Code—when movies dared to be daring. In context, the presence of Spencer
Tracy's naked buns (*Man's Castle*), Mae West's double entendres (*She Done
Him Wrong*), and Barbara Stanwyck's cynical amorality (*Baby Face*) still pack
a wallop.

Many of Mamoulian's early movies appear to be designed as answers to
technical questions. With *Applause* (1929), he found ways around the static
staging that the bulky new talkie cameras seemed to demand. In *Dr. Jekyll
and Mr. Hyde* (1931), he extended the possibilities of sound beyond the util-
itarian. In *Love Me Tonight* (1932), he explored what the screen could do for
musicals that the stage couldn't. In *The Song of Songs*, Mamoulian seems to be
addressing a different question: "Just how much can I get away with?" The
movie is full of outrageous sexual implications and dialogue that drips with

double meaning, not all of it clear. It's the kind of thing Ken Russell might have made had he been born thirty years earlier.

Mamoulian throws all credibility out the window with the very first scene, in which Dietrich is introduced as a blushing, religious teenager named Lily. "Evwy night I wead to Papa fwom the Bible," she tells us after the old man's funeral, "fwom the Song of Songs." If you're wondering what pushed Papa's heart to the breaking point, take a good look at the Song of Songs (aka the Song of Solomon)—as charmingly erotic a piece of work as you're likely to find in the Old Testament, the New Testament, *and* the Apocrypha. In a civilized country, Daddykins would have been locked up and Lily hustled to the nearest therapist. But the Germany of Mamoulian's imagination must not have been civilized, because here no one bats an eyelash.

The now-orphaned innocent heads for Berlin, where she moves in with her Aunt Rasmussen (Alison Skipworth), a nasty old woman with a thirst for Jamaican rum and an unkind word for all. Aunt Rasmussen insults the memory of Lily's father within seconds, and Lily leaps to his defense by mentioning his taste in Biblical lit: "He loved the Bible, and he loved the Song of Solomon best of all!"

Aunt Rasmussen instinctively confirms our worst suspicions about Dad: "I don't remember the Song of Solomon, but knowing your father, I imagine there was something dirty in it." Her remark suggests some really interesting possibilities for a backstory, but it's never followed up; the movie breathlessly rushes on to the main plot.

To free up more time for drinking and dissing others, Aunt R. puts Lily to work at the bookstore she runs. Lily's first day on the job, a sculptor named Richard (Brian Aherne) walks in and slyly asks her to retrieve a book from the top shelf, which would require our maiden to climb a ladder. Lily smells a libidinous rat and balks; country girl or no, she's not totally naïve, yet she agrees to sneak out that night and pose for Richard, whose bachelor pad/studio is conveniently across the street. Slipping something in Auntie's tea to help her sleep more soundly, Lily keeps the appointment, but is aghast when Richard asks her to get naked. It takes at least ninety seconds to wear down her resistance. "Don't think of me as a man," he tells her. "A model means no more to me than a tree." Given how the story develops, we can conclude that Richard suffers from some sort of rare arboreal sex kink.

Over a series of sittings, Richard replicates Lily in clay. Since Mamoulian couldn't show Dietrich completely naked, the camera, in a clever sleight-of-hand, focuses on clothed parts of her anatomy, then pans over to the corresponding parts on the naked statue. This persistent tease affects Richard as well as us: In one unforgettable scene, he stares at Dietrich's shadow while groping and rubbing up against her clay counterpart.

Lily finally admits she's crazy about Richard. They go hiking in the country, where Lily wildly rubs her face in the grass—Richard isn't the only one with a thing for flora—and sensuously advises, "You've got to bury your nose in it," an instruction with wider implications. But Lily's ardor scares Richard, so he essentially fobs her off on the fabulously wealthy Baron von Merzbach (Lionel Atwill, so villainous he seems to have a self-twirling mustache), an art patron who buys Lily's statue. Von Merzbach bribes Aunt Rasmussen to evict Lily, and soon the poor girl has no option but to become his trophy wife.

Bringing her home to his grotesque mansion, the baron introduces Lily to the smirking house staff, including "Fräulein von Schwertfeger, the . . . uh . . . housekeeper," allowing that meaningful pause to sink in. He also introduces her to the groundskeeper, von Prell, with a jovial, "His father carried the sword, but he chose the plow"; they all enjoy a hearty laugh at *that* bit of coded sexual innuendo, whatever the hell it's supposed to mean.

We are briefly led to believe that the baron truly loves our Lily. But before the ink is dry on the marriage certificate, he inexplicably turns into a hammy Erich von Stroheim imitator. As Lily cries in her room over the fate-worse-than-death she is about to endure, the baron cackles outside the door and polishes his monocle.

Things just get more overwrought until a moment of passion literally sets a house on fire. Then Lily becomes Marlene's more typically jaded self, and von Merzbach goes berserk and disappears from the story without explanation. At the end, Lily smashes the top half of her statue (which still leaves some of the best parts) and reconciles, sort of, with Richard. "We'll begin again," he tells her. "Do you remember long ago when we climbed a hill into the sky? Well, we'll climb again now . . . and find the sky. [pause] Perhaps."

Splendor in the Grass
Let Nature be your teacher

Directed by Elia Kazan; starring Warren Beatty,
Natalie Wood (1961)

by Michael Sragow

WATCHING THAT GREAT BUT MISCAST ACTOR LIAM NEESON
glower his way through *Kinsey*, I kept thinking how much more fun Warren
Beatty would have had with the part. Throughout Beatty's career, his innate
erotic confidence has empowered him to play impotence (in *Bonnie and
Clyde*), abstinence (in parts of *Reds*), and middle-aged panic (in *Bulworth*).
Sexual befuddlement is not beyond his range.

In fact, it's with a combination of ardor and confusion that Beatty began his
film career and became an instant star in Elia Kazan's *Splendor in the Grass*. He
played champion high school athlete Bud Stamper, the "biggest catch in
town," in this tale of teen love foundering on sexual prohibition in small-town
Kansas, 1928. It's the kind of picture so emotionally supercharged that people
are often embarrassed to admit how much they treasure it. Yet its very title (a
quote from Wordsworth) has entered the vocabulary as a synonym for explo-
sive adolescent passion. The February 2005 *Harper's* used "Splendor in the
Grass" to headline a column about a canine dating service.

With Kazan's movie, Beatty immediately became, in Hollywood terms, a
made man, and his costar (and future lover) Natalie Wood was never more
tremulously affecting than as Deanie Loomis. When Deanie's mother tells her
that nice women don't have sexual desires, for a moment the film becomes a
precursor to *Kinsey*—and just as tragicomically clumsy. But *Splendor in the*

Grass is much more. It's a touchstone for generations that grew up when young love on screen was airbrushed into Gidget or Tammy, and sex education consisted of scare films about VD.

Beatty's most prominent role before Bud Stamper was the ridiculous high school aristocrat Milton Armitage on TV's *The Many Loves of Dobie Gillis*. But director Kazan saw that Beatty, a student footballer himself, was perfect for the big-man-on-campus son of oil tycoon Ace Stamper (Pat Hingle). Beatty plays Bud as a good guy genuinely devoted to Deanie despite his dad's condescension to her family's lower status. Deanie, in turn, worships Bud.

Working from an original script by William Inge, *Splendor in the Grass* was Kazan's attempt to break with mainstream proprieties about the sexual component of love, just the way director Jack Clayton did two years before with the affair between Laurence Harvey and Simone Signoret in *Room at the Top*. But Kazan and Inge were using teenagers—and not juvenile delinquents, but kids most likely to succeed or be crowned at the prom. The wholesomeness of Bud and Deanie's rapture is one reason why hipsters like Pauline Kael denigrated the movie: She thought it should support all "sexual experimentation," not merely the consummation of a boy and girl who are "tenderly in love." What would she think in the new millennium? Even a provocateur like Camille Paglia, a self-described "pro-sex feminist," admitted to Bill Maher on HBO that today's teen world of "hookups" made her renew her advocacy for the rites of courtship.

Although *Splendor in the Grass* is about two high-schoolers who can't sustain a relationship because they're forbidden to consummate their love, it's an engulfing romance. Kazan brings magical fervor to the sight of his glowing couple parting the crowd in a school hallway. Wood's mingling of pride and yearning and Beatty's fresh, unsmug virility make these simple images memorable, even lyrical. But furtive, limited embraces no longer satisfy these two. At one point, Bud walks Deanie home and they find they have the house all to themselves. Desperation clashes with delight as Deanie shuts the shades. It's emotionally authentic and thus still shocking when Bud slides Deanie down his body to the floor and compels her to kneel before him and vow she'll do anything. You know this courtship is doomed unless it gets fulfilled quickly. To his credit, Bud wants to marry Deanie, attend an agricultural college, and work the family ranch. But he can't thwart his father's ambition to send him to Yale and groom him for the Stamper oil business.

Beatty is superb at making Bud an old-fashioned manly man undone by his erupting feelings. Bud can't differentiate between the wildness of his flapper sister (Barbara Loden, Kazan's mistress and second wife) and her fate as the victim of a gang rape; the trauma makes Bud feel as if making love with Deanie would lead to *her* ruination too. The movie is startlingly acute about middle-class attitudes toward "good" and "bad" girls. Bud eventually follows the adult male advice to blow off steam with the other type of girl, the school's resident floozy. But by the end you see the hypocrisy behind it all; even the nice girls are willing to park with their beaux by the waterfalls as long as they can keep their reputations. Bud's sexual initiation lacks oomph. Yet it's fitting that Kazan never gives you a more torrid sense of flesh and desire than when Bud and Deanie are all over each other, fully clothed—unless it's when Deanie dreams of Bud and caresses her pillows, or later when she thrashes out her anger, anguish, and frustration in a bathtub. The most buttoned-up or banal episodes explode, until you realize that banality and learned behavior, and the chaos beneath, are the movie's true subjects.

Splendor reaches an early apex when Deanie loses Bud to his own righteous perplexity and, dazed and confused, sits behind the floozy in English class. The dried-up, insensitive teacher asks her to recite lines from Wordsworth's 1807 "Ode, Intimations of Immortality from Reflections of Early Childhood": "What though the radiance which was once so bright / Be now for ever taken from my sight / Though nothing can bring back the hour / Of splendour in the grass, of glory in the flower; / We will grieve not, rather find / Strength in what remains behind." Deanie, of course, *feels* those verses, and breaks down. Her collapse has no actressy bravura. Wood still has reservoirs of emotion for when Deanie goes to her graduation dance with another guy only to throw herself at Bud, whose rejection drives her to attempt suicide. At her hospital bed, Bud declares, too late, that he'll marry her, then breaks down at the sight of her lying unconscious in delirium. Wood then has a moment as devastating as any in Tennessee Williams: When Deanie hears Bud sob in the corridor, her mind clears and she murmurs, to an empty room, "Who's there? Who's there? . . . Somebody was here. Somebody was here."

Deanie recovers at an asylum. Bud, after flunking out of Yale and witnessing the ruination of his family, recovers in the arms of a waitress from a New Haven pizza joint. But when both are on their feet, Kazan and Inge offer a killer closer. Deanie, now elegant and engaged to a doctor in Cincinnati, visits Bud and his warm, kind wife (and young Bud, Jr.) at the Stampers' old ranch. The surface action depicts adult resignation and "maturity." Bud and Deanie are worlds apart. But how contented can they be when each admits that they don't think much about happiness? Deanie repeats those Wordsworth lines to herself, but they offer no salve to the audience. *Splendor in the Grass* is a plea for men and women to honor intensity of feeling. It salutes the "glory in the flower," not the "strength in what remains behind."

Talk Dirty to Me

The lonely housewife and the handyman

Directed by Anthony Spinelli; starring John Leslie, Juliet Anderson, Jessie St. James (1980)

by Charles Taylor

FOR MOVIE CRITICS, THE TRAP OF WRITING ABOUT PORN IS that it makes the question we're supposed to ask—"Is it any good?"—irrelevant. When critics dismiss porn because of shoddy production values, silly scripts, or bad acting, they're dodging the question: "Did it turn you on?"

Aesthetics are beside the point more often than critics care to admit. There are plenty of movies we enjoy that aren't good movies. Part of the dishonesty of the "guilty pleasure" concept is the implication that we should feel obliged to justify everything we enjoy (as if we should feel guilty about what brings us pleasure). Sometimes you can make an aesthetic case for a dumb comedy or a B action movie. But we should be able to laugh at one or enjoy the revenge mechanics of the other without having to pretend that we're necessarily watching a good movie. Having to make an aesthetic case for a picture that turns you on is just as dishonest.

It is possible—but not necessary—to commend Anthony Spinelli's 1980 porno *Talk Dirty to Me* for the way it integrates the sex scenes into the plot, as most of Spinelli's pornos do, and note its thread of movie fandom and the clever way its characters correspond to some genre archetype—the brash masculine hero (John Leslie); the gentle, dimwitted sidekick (the appealingly boyish Richard Pacheco); the brassy bad girl (the inimitable Juliet Anderson); and the blond goddess heroine (Jessie St. James).

Talk Dirty to Me puts a porno buddy-movie gloss—a nontragic one—on *Of Mice and Men*. Two drifters, Jack (Leslie) and Lenny (Pacheco), float around San Francisco subsisting on odd jobs, beer, and, in Jack's case, women. When Jack spots Marlene (St. James) walking along the beach, he tells Lenny he can have her in three days. He discovers that Marlene loves old movies just as he does (scenes of very bad impersonations follow), then gets himself hired as her handyman.

Marlene's kick is that she likes to be talked dirty to during sex. Her husband is too uptight to oblige, but Jack has no such hang-up; when he and Marlene finally make it, he takes delight (and so does she) in goading her into a spiel of exuberant rot. But Jack isn't so single-minded that he stops there. Along the way to Marlene's bed he has encounters with the doctor (Chris Cassidy) who treats Lenny's sprained ankle, the real estate agent (Juliet Anderson) on whose property Jack and Lenny are squatting, and the good-time girl (Shirley Wood) who promises no-strings-attached nooky. Like the flimsy plots of the '30s Paramount comedies that were simply excuses for songs and comedy routines, the plot of *Talk Dirty to Me* is an excuse for sex. And, as in those revue comedies and strung-together musicals, the (sexual) set-pieces exist to showcase the appeal of the performers.

People think they're being killingly witty when they make fun of the bad acting in porn. It never occurs to them that the sex *is* the performance. To be blunt, we enjoy porn stars (or not) because of how they look and how they fuck, or how they look when they're fucking.

For viewers whose idea of porn was formed by the current crop of buffed, plucked, surgically enhanced bodies, the performers of the "golden era" (roughly the mid-'70s to the early '80s) may come as a surprise. Certainly Jessie St. James and Annette Haven and John Leslie would turn heads on any corner, but their beauty and bodies do not look like the result of lab work. I'm not making some moralistic condemnation; if porn stars function as fantasy figures, then there's logic to the way they make themselves over to fulfill that fantasy. The problem is that the fantasy itself—Pepsodent smile, big tits, long blonde hair—has become so uniform. (That the men in straight porn are mostly anonymous and unappealing is a separate issue.)

I sing the praises of classic porn not to pretend that my lust has been consciousness-raised to the level of a Naomi Wolf–whistle, but for the very reason that the sheer variety of performers contributed to the low-down, horny fun. There's no sense of discovery when a girl in six-inch Lucite heels and shorts cut halfway up her rump, with boobs spilling out of a halter top, gets down and dirty. It's what you expect her to do. But even with the predictability inherent in a porn scenario, put a gal in the sensible blouse and skirt that Juliet Anderson's real estate agent wears in *Talk Dirty to Me,* and the moment she lifts that skirt to reveal she's not wearing underwear carries a real erotic thrill.

The dirty fun of porn lies in the way every encounter holds the potential for sex. And the women (and men) who populated the movies of the golden age were nearly impossible to characterize by one image or stereotype. Anderson was thirty-nine when she made her porn debut, an age at which Hollywood actresses are already being shunted into mommy roles. (Sometimes that democratizing impulse went too far: Watching the bearded, balding, scrawny Aaron Stuart, who plays Marlene's husband, in action is about as thrilling as being privy to the erotic fantasies of your high school science teacher.)

John Leslie was born to fuck on camera. Olive-skinned and curly-haired, Leslie might seem threatening if it weren't for the huge grin that frequently splits his face. When Chris Cassidy's uptight doctor is so turned on by Leslie's gutter-stud come-on that she goes down on him, Leslie, with perfect timing, provides the capper by declaring, "You're an animal!" All that's missing is the ba-da-bump. He's a dirty-minded satyr (especially when he's wagging his erection in the direction he wants it to go), and the slyest, funniest, most appealing man ever to work in porn movies. Leslie's characters swagger; he's out to show that *he's* in charge. Which would be unbearable if it weren't for the sense of humor which, as with the early Gable, tells you he doesn't take himself too seriously, and for the way he's delighted when his partners meet his challenge and throw down their own.

Those challenges work in different ways here. With Anderson, whose ballsy, no-nonsense persona makes her the Joan Blondell of porn, the encounter is a draw. Leslie's leer matches Anderson's filthy grin, and neither cedes any ground. Something more submissive happens during Leslie's scene with Cassidy, a tall, wavy-haired, strawberry blonde with the "natural" look that, for a time in the '70s and '80s, was the legacy of the '60s counterculture to American erotica. With some performers, it's the face or the voice that carries the most expression. With Cassidy, it's her hips. The way she squirms

with Leslie is insistently, incessantly erotic. She's so turned on that her submission becomes a way of demanding "more!"

With the wonderful Jessie St. James, it is the face and the voice. Slim and
small-breasted, with long platinum-blonde hair and fine-boned features, St.
James was, like her contemporary Annette Haven, one of the adult performers whose beauty denoted class. With Haven, there was at times a distancing
regality; St. James lacked a comparable defense mechanism. What makes her
touching is also what makes her sex scenes so sexy, that she is vibrantly *present*. Her distinct eroticism in *Talk Dirty to Me* comes from a particular combination of shyness, shame, and sexual hunger. She blushes, eyes closed, as
Leslie details where he intends to kiss her, but her shallow, heavy breathing
is the sound of someone happy to get past an inhibition. There's a snarl in
her voice as she tells Leslie what she wants him to say, and you sense that
she's getting off on this newfound aggressiveness.

Pauline Kael once argued that some of the performers we enjoy most are
more personalities than they are actors. Which is why I have no hesitation in
saying that Jessie St. James is terrific in *Talk Dirty to Me,* vulnerable and sexy,
with the warm charisma that draws us to people on the screen.

Talk Dirty to Me is a good example of how porn once allowed its performers to convey distinct personalities. It may sound as if I'm edging into the
aesthetic arguments I disdained earlier, but Anthony Spinelli's desire to tell a
story with characters points up what today's porn lacks—not "production
values," but a sense of fun and play and what-the-hell abandonment. What's
most depressing about contemporary porn isn't the interchangeable fuck-
doll personas but the pervasive joyless professionalism that turns every encounter into a transaction. The plotless gonzo structure has returned porn to
a level that doesn't even approach the old loops shown at smokers' and men's
clubs. *Talk Dirty to Me* comes from an era when porn stars and filmmakers
could still at least daydream that one day porn movies would be like any
other movies. You can be a heartless bastard and ridicule their ambition, or
you can be touched by their determination to try.

Annette Haven: What's a Classy Girl Like You Doing in a Movie Like This?

by Charles Taylor

It's a casually ladylike gesture: A stylish, impeccably groomed woman rests her chin on folded hands as she takes in the scene before her. That she's watching her maid give head to a male visitor doesn't alter the woman's air of cool bemusement. She's orchestrated this scenario, and although she's turned on, she patiently waits her turn. In Annette Haven, good breeding meets the experienced sensualist who prolongs pleasure with a long simmer before reaching full boil.

"You've got more class than the other girls," Kay Parker's madam remarks to Haven in *V: The Hot One*. It's still true. Almost two decades after her '70s and '80s heyday, Annette Haven remains the classiest actress ever to work in adult movies. She was certainly the most classically beautiful: tall (or perhaps it was her bearing that made her seem so), with long auburn hair, high cheekbones, porcelain skin, and a mouth more generous than her exquisitely modulated features would lead you to expect. She was ready to make her mainstream debut in Brian De Palma's *Body Double,* but the studio, Columbia, would not cast a porn actress in the lead role. Cowards.

Haven was to porn what Grace Kelly was to Hollywood, a distinctly American beauty, but one who seemed to exist in a realm far removed from the one most Americans inhabit. You could believe Haven was the prettiest girl in town (or the prettiest teacher, as she is in *High School Memories*), or a sophisticate from some exotic, rarefied place. She was stunning enough to seem right at home as Scheherazade in *A Thousand and One Erotic Nights*. Even as a Southern madam in *Memphis Cathouse Blues*, coaching a novice on how to service a client, there was something regal about her, something untouchable. Haven was such an erotic presence because her classiness was exactly what you didn't expect to find in skin flicks. She never condescended to the movies she was in, never felt she had to tart herself up to suit them. Her classiness didn't come off with her clothes. Haven was God's gift to the lingerie industry; all porn shows actresses stripping, but Haven's movies made a virtual fetish of the moment she peels down to reveal a garter belt and, ever so briefly, panties.

Where Grace Kelly was the ice queen who eventually melted, Haven wore her sophistication like the supplest armor. She didn't come down off the pedestal and, amazingly, almost never provoked the macho revenge that the mechanics of porn dictate awaits such a woman.

During sex, Haven was in effortless control. She keeps her eyes closed, a subtle smile telling you she's shut out everything but sensation. Haven concentrates on the cock, a toy that exists for her alone, as if it were somehow separate from her partner. It was fine if the men got pleasure in the bargain, but they were there mainly to serve. In "Annette's Interview," one of the *Swedish Erotica* loops, when she instructs the young journalist she's seduced to keep doing what he's doing, she barely raises her voice. She knows she doesn't have to; no one would defy such bearing and presence. For Annette Haven, it was good to be the queen. ■

The Tango Lesson
Quick, quick, slow

Directed by Sally Potter; starring Sally Potter, Pablo Verón (1997)

by Stuart Klawans

APPROPRIATELY ENOUGH FOR A MUSICAL COMEDY ABOUT THE disruptions of eros, *The Tango Lesson* really gets moving only after an intrusive splat. Writer-director Sally Potter, portraying herself, is at her table in London drafting the treatment for a film when the marks she's been making begin to dissolve beneath her fingers. The ceiling above her, it seems, has sprung a leak of some sort, "seems" and "some sort" being key for the curious viewer.

At the beginning of the story, Potter's work area is spotless—maybe too spotless—just as the movie she's writing, titled *Rage,* is a bit too diagrammatic in its view of sex and power. (It represents femininity with three preening fashion models, masculinity with a legless, whistle-tooting man, and their interaction with a gunshot.) Something is needed to smudge this desiccated idea for a film, and sure enough, something does. Water erupts through the floorboards, which needed to be torn up for repairs, so that Potter's immaculate table becomes an island teetering amid the debris. Now the ceiling starts to drip on her *Rage.* Her home—her old life—is officially uninhabitable, not just because of bad plumbing, but perhaps because Potter's own psyche has forced moisture to the surface.

As the viewer knows by now, the moisture is associated with a suitable cause for arousal: Pablo Verón. Potter had first seen him in Paris, the world capital of love, when she wandered without a ticket into the rear of a theater

266

(Paris doesn't restrain you with tickets) and glimpsed him performing a tango with a severe-looking young woman. In a close-up of herself watching the dance, Potter smiles slightly and relaxes forward with an exhalation. She wears the dreamy look of someone gazing across a dark space toward the light of a possible self, wrapped in happiness and a man's strong legs.

After the show, she seeks out Verón in a bar and asks whether he gives lessons. An awkward question, not only because she is transparently asking for something more, or because she is perhaps a dozen years older than this dark-goateed satyr in his black trousers, but because she and Verón share no language. She speaks almost no Spanish; he can manage only a few words of English. For this first meeting, then, they use French, in which they are equally clumsy.

Nothing much happens at that first encounter. But with the loss of her home, Potter decamps to Paris to resume dancing lessons with Verón, after which their most important conversations will be carried out in body language.

Bodies moving together: tentatively, impulsively, in tension, at cross-purposes, with missed cues and melting ease, right on the beat, in a pulse so fluid there's no beat at all. Since this is the essence not only of sexual union but also of a certain ideal of cinema, many Fred-and-Ginger movies can be said to have inspired *The Tango Lesson*, and many romantic melodramas of the silent era. Still, I feel that Potter's film is novel, for reasons that begin with her making explicit the theme of two people striving for harmonious movement. What's more, she addresses the subject from a viewpoint seldom offered in the movies, that of a mature, sexually active woman.

Potter's physical characteristics make the theme all the more striking. She's no Susan Sarandon. Her features, though pleasant, are milder than need be because of the masking effect of a bland, habitual smile. Her pale skin is almost bloodless in Robby Müller's black-and-white cinematography. Although her body is trim and her bearing upright, her movements initially are tentative; even later, when the hot flush of anger contorts her face, there's no muscle behind her gestures. She's a lead actress without star power, and here she's competing against Verón, who is as cocky as James Cagney and fills the frame almost as expansively.

Potter's detractors think she was self-indulgent (or blindly mistaken) to cast herself this way. I think no other choice would have given her, as director, such a vivid embodiment of the risks of infatuation. Desire opens up the protagonist to looking foolish, as it does to us all. It prompts her to swallow her words, or lie, in hopes of currying favor. (To get closer to Verón, a thoroughly secular man of Jewish background, she even claims to "feel like a Jew"—as if he were searching for a woman who could give him a lifetime of kosher dinners.) Most unsettling for the director is the loss of control she experiences when she's with him, and yet, being not only a director but a feminist, she fights this self-abandonment and therefore messes up her principle vehicle for communicating with Verón, the tango. If she really wants to dance with him, she needs to follow.

But she cannot give herself up so completely to a man, and so the two of them push and pull, negotiating with their bodies what they cannot resolve with words. It's not so much an erotic struggle as a struggle for eros. Since it takes place in Müller's sparkling light, in settings that are simultaneously everyday and glamorous, to some of the most soulfully pulsing music of the twentieth century, the protagonist (and her audience) gets plenty of sensuous rewards even when the struggle goes poorly. When the protagonist gets beyond the struggle—gradually taking more pleasure in the whirl of the dance until she at last has a literal breakthrough that sends her dashing and spinning across seemingly endless space—*The Tango Lesson* provides that well-centered giddiness, that sense of spiritual release within the body, that sex forever promises but does not always deliver.

I come back to *The Tango Lesson* again and again because it is ultimately about freedom, as compared with the Pavlovian compulsion that's the substance of most other erotic films. Not that I mind being a doggie. Show me the right material—a current cinematic love object exposed to best advantage—and I, like anyone, will reliably become aroused. It's a pleasure, but it's also just hydraulics.

The Tango Lesson, by contrast, is a gamble, whose payoff is all the greater for being made in an unexpected currency. It takes Potter from *Rage* to joy, from dryness to an Argentinean downpour. Very cool. Very hot.

Tarzan and His Mate
Bwana hold your hand

Directed by Cedric Gibbons; starring Johnny Weissmuller,
Maureen O'Sullivan (1934)

by Charles Taylor

THERE HAS NEVER BEEN A PORTRAIT OF MARRIED BLISS TO
equal *Tarzan and His Mate*. In the second of the six Johnny Weissmuller–
Maureen O'Sullivan Tarzan and Jane pictures, marriage is a perpetual holiday,
and the chores and routines of matrimony haven't dulled the erotic edge of
the union between the Mayfair beauty and her jungle lord. When we see the
couple in the morning, waking up in the tree house Tarzan built, Jane is
sprawled naked under a blanket fashioned from fur, and the muss of O'Sullivan's curls, the way she luxuriates in her bed while Tarzan, who has awakened
her by blowing in her ear, hovers over her, is the movies' most glorious image
of postcoital contentment.

For all the ways in which the phrase "Me Tarzan, you Jane" has been used
to signify primordial male possessiveness, the Weissmuller-O'Sullivan Tarzan
series is the saga of a wild man's domestication, as well as—and this is what
gives the film its special kick—a well-brought-up young lady's discovery of
her own sensual appetites.

You could, at first, make the mistake of thinking that Tarzan is whipped.
Jane has trained him to start each day with the words "Good morning, I love
you." In later entries in the series, the makeshift shelter they share turns into
a treetop duplex, complete with elephant-operated elevator and kitchen that
includes table and crockery—of a fashion. When Jane tells Tarzan it's time to

do the marketing, he takes to the jungly tendrils (as the late Peter Cook once called them), returning with enough fresh fruit and catch-of-the-day to feed whoever has dropped in. The introduction of Boy, the plane-crash orphan they raise as their own, completes the domestication.

The Tarzan series is perhaps the sweetest and most charming set of adventure movies Hollywood ever produced. But it's *Tarzan and His Mate,* directed by Cedric Gibbons, that remains the best of them, the series' erotic jewel.

For all the ways in which she trains Tarzan, Jane knows enough not to finesse all the jungle out of him. It's not just that he always shows up to protect her from every rhino or alligator or tiger that happens upon her when he's taken to the trees and left her for a few minutes. It's that she's got this jungle hunk all to herself and has no intention of messing up a good thing.

In *Tarzan and His Mate,* an old friend of Jane's (played by Neil Hamilton, later Commissioner Gordon on the '60 TV hit *Batman*) shows up to persuade her to return to London. He's brought all the latest Paris fashions and perfumes to woo her back to civilization. The bounder (Paul Cavanagh) accompanying him asks Jane if she wouldn't like having a few more men around to keep her mate in line via some competition. Jane, laughing off his suggestion, reminds him of *her* enviable position, with no other women on the scene to turn Tarzan's head.

The exchange is a great joke on male cluelessness. Who would Jane look at with Tarzan around? Next to him, even the most virile Lothario is a weed. And here's this simp, swaggering around the jungle in his pleated linen shorts and pith helmet, the Little Lord Fauntleroy of the wild, while Weissmuller—thick, wavy hair swept back, Adonis build swathed only in loincloth—displays casual mastery over every beast and knows the location of every swinging vine and glorious swimming grotto where he and his beloved can frolic. The other guy is deluded to think a woman is even going to pretend interest in another man when she's landed a partner who is protector, provider, and, judging by the delight on Jane's face each morning, a good man to have around the tree house.

As portrayed by Weissmuller, who was graceful and confident enough to bring out the gentle comedy in his character, Tarzan is the most ardent and faithful of lovers. Reciting his morning endearments (which he pronounces as two words with his own special inflection: "Goodmorning? Iloveyou"),

Tarzan is completely, hopelessly smitten. Weissmuller looks at O'Sullivan like a silky cat adoring the human he's adopted as his mother.

Tarzan and His Mate takes full advantage of being made before the Production Code smothered the raciness that still flourished in movies of the early '30s. There are some still-grisly passages involving a subplot of ivory hunters looking for a sacred elephant burial ground. But most of the adventure scenes—a chimp mourning over the body of his mother, a hippo who submerges in a lagoon and reemerges bearing the wounded Tarzan on its back—have the distinctive mixture of savagery and transcendent sentimentality that makes Edgar Rice Burroughs's original novel read in passages like Dickens. (Burroughs is one of those "nonliterary" writers who have lasted, as have Alexandre Dumas and Arthur Conan Doyle, as will Stephen King.) You could get steamed about the movie's depiction of "darkest Africa" and the alternately compliant and savage natives, but that would mean being foolish enough to believe the picture was intended or taken as a realistic portrayal.

What the Production Code would soon change for good in American movies is evident in the love scenes, with their unaffected, unembarrassed eroticism. Best is the underwater sequence where Tarzan frolics with a fully nude Jane (now restored after being cut out of prints for years). It's a dreamy interlude of lyrical foreplay, with Jane (Olympic swimmer Josephine McKim acted as O'Sullivan's body double) holding Tarzan's ankles, undulating waves of movement working their way down from him to her. In later installments of the series, O'Sullivan's costume would become a ragged-edged dress. Here it's an animal-skin halter and matching loincloths for front and back that leave her thighs delightfully bare. (In the last shot, she leans back against Weissmuller as they ride atop an elephant, and the sight of their naked thighs next to each other provides perhaps the sexiest moment in the movie, an image of erotic contentment and comfort.)

In *Tarzan and His Mate*, O'Sullivan's Jane has been given a trilling little cry to match Tarzan's famous full-throated yell (she's like the Lily Pons of the jungle). You'd think that the sound of these two, their devotion to and desire for each other echoing across the jungle, would have shamed Nelson Eddy and Jeanette MacDonald into silence. *This* is the real Indian love call.

Trouble in Paradise
The art of the steal

Directed by Ernst Lubitsch; starring Herbert Marshall,
Miriam Hopkins, Kay Francis (1932)

by Joe Morgenstern

THERE MAY BE NO HONOR AMONG THIEVES, BUT THERE'S
plenty of passion between the larcenous lovers of *Trouble in Paradise*—a sexual pull rarely seen before or since Ernst Lubitsch brought this comic masterpiece to the screen. Today we have phrases for the ties that bind Herbert Marshall's suave Continental crook, Gaston, and Miriam Hopkins's blithe American pickpocket, Lily. One might say, however glibly, that they get off on each other's love of danger, that they turn each other on with their daring. Such expressions didn't exist three-quarters of a century ago; such notions had no place in the common lexicon of love. Even now these phrases barely hint at the intricacies of a film that still seems startlingly new in its playfulness and quicksilver moods.

Another phrase automatically attaches itself to *Trouble in Paradise,* just as it does to other peerless comedies directed by Lubitsch in the decade that followed: *Ninotchka, The Shop Around the Corner, To Be or Not to Be, Heaven Can Wait*—the Lubitsch Touch. This is now understood, at least by those who try to understand anything about Hollywood's golden age, as shorthand for sparkling sophistication with a bracingly cynical European flavor. But wit and worldliness are only part of the potent cocktail; another key ingredient is emotion. As we see in *Trouble in Paradise,* Lubitsch can swing, leap, or glide with ineffable ease from brittle game-playing to intense ardor.

The games begin immediately, and they play out giddily. Gaston, who has just pulled off a hotel robbery, waits in his lavish suite at the same Venice hotel for the glamorous countess who is to dine with him. At least she claims she's a countess, just as he claims he's a baron. We know he's scamming her. Then we learn that she's scamming him. Is this an impediment to love? Anything but. Deceiving each other, puckishly picking each other's pockets—or more intimate areas of apparel—they excite each other, seduce each other, discover that they're made for each other. It's an astonishingly agile scene that ends with mutual pleasure—not the pleasure of the flesh, since that's more fragrant when unseen, but of adventure. "Darling!" she exclaims when he reveals that he's stolen her garter. "Tell me all about yourself! Who are you?"

As for ardor, it isn't only the province of Lily and Gaston. He breaks into the private life of Mariette (Kay Francis), the wealthy widow of a French industrialist, by stealing her expensive handbag, and then, after she has offered a public reward, returning it with shameless aplomb and silver-tongued flattery. Soon he's her secretary-cum-confidant, and, with Lily's connivance, poised to take over her financial affairs. But Gaston seems to be falling for Mariette, and no wonder, since Francis plays her with a dazzling admixture of warmth, insouciance, and desire. (With good roles for women in such desperately short supply today, it's exciting and dismaying to see a movie with two such sensational ones.)

I say that Gaston seems to be falling in love because *Trouble in Paradise* is a moment-to-moment thriller as well as a romantic comedy, and we're never quite sure, in the intense heat of many moments, whether his intentions are pure, impure, or muddled, whether it's Mariette's money, body, or lyrical soul that draws him and keeps him when prudence tells him to take her money and run. (Made and set at the start of the Great Depression, the movie explores, among other things, privilege and class.) All we know for certain, until the very end, is that Lily is fiercely jealous, and that any outcome is possible: Lubitsch and screenwriter Samson Raphaelson play their game for all it's worth, confident the audience will follow every social or sexual nuance.

The very first image—after the star-surmounted Paramount mountain—is a sexual cue. "Trouble in" the title begins over an elaborately canopied double bed. By the time the word "Paradise" appears, the movie's territory has already been surveyed and staked out. *Trouble in Paradise* was made a year and a half before the Production Code, which turned Hollywood's studios and producers into grudging Puritans. Lubitsch's film is hardly licentious—he was too subtle an entertainer for that—but it's suggestive in ways that are still striking. The camera takes note of a nude sculpture on the stairs of Mariette's home, of a neon sign of a bare-breasted woman, her nipples flashing. As Lily begins to suspect that Gaston's interest in Mariette is not exclusively pecuniary, she says, in clear reference to her rival's breasts, "They're all right, aren't they?" In a lively commentary that accompanies the Criterion Collection DVD, Peter Bogdanovich claims that Mariette's two comic-relief beaux—one, known only as The Major, is played by Charlie Ruggles, the other, François, by Edward Everett Horton—are eunuchs as far as sexual interest is concerned. That's not true. It's obvious from one open-coded exchange between Gaston and François (who, not coincidentally, is Gaston's mark in the initial hotel robbery) that François is gay; he talks about visiting the ancient city of Constantinople to savor more than its scenery.

Shock was never the point, and the notion of titillation can't begin to convey the movie's delights. Lubitsch, working with the cosmopolitan Raphaelson, was a virtuoso entertainer who conjured with surprise, contradiction, ambiguity. Yet he was also open, as he knew his audience was, to the power of sexual excitement. When the lovers in *Trouble in Paradise* scheme their schemes and run their scams, they feel gloriously, libidinously alive.

Troy

When sex appeal needs a leg up

Directed by Wolfgang Petersen; starring Brad Pitt, Peter O'Toole,
Julie Christie, Eric Bana, Diane Kruger, Orlando Bloom (2004)

by Joe Morgenstern

TROY DOESN'T HAVE A LEG TO STAND ON AS A WORK OF ART, OR
even of efficient commerce, but it does have its very own Achilles heel—the
flat-footed silliness of its Bronze-age hero, played by a blond, deeply bronzed
and muscled Brad Pitt in Greco-martial miniskirt. This legendary warrior
coulda, indeed shoulda been a contender for all-time classic hunkdom,
whether in the annals of gay or straight hero worship, just as the movie
should have been what it was obviously meant to be—a big, bright vending
machine dedicated to dispensing sex appeal. (And not just Pitt's: Eric Bana's
Hector and Diane Kruger's Helen of You Know What were essential parts of
the merchandising equation.)

Instead, we have a clankingly mechanistic plot and a hero who spends inexplicable amounts of time pouting, grousing, grumbling, or blathering
about fame ("They'll be talking about this war for a thousand years!"). He
makes a noisy spectacle of himself when he parks his chariot outside the
walled city of Troy and howls "Hector! Hector! Hector!" in a voice—a hec-
toring voice—reminiscent of Marlon Brando howling "Stella!"

It's tempting to lay the failings of the movie at Pitt's sandaled feet. He's vulnerable to derision even when he shakes his character's semitorpor and,
sword in hand, leaps into action—literally leaps, in a weirdly spasmodic
martial-arts style that suggests Hong Kong wire-fighting on a short leash.

With the right material, though, and the right directorial tone, Pitt has been charming (*Ocean's 11*), powerful (*Fight Club*), or intense and surprising (*Twelve Monkeys*). Measured in the crass but concrete terms of revenue, he's a genuine superstar, and a smart one: I have it on the authority of a superstar architect who knows and likes him that Pitt is genuinely knowledgeable about architecture, and a devoted collector of art and furniture.

In fairness, he does have his shining moments in *Troy*. I have it on equally good authority, from a woman of trustworthy taste as well as intelligence, that many women found him—and Bana—extremely sexy, even though they were bored by the movie as a whole. In fact, the extraordinary boredom quotient of *Troy* is due not to Pitt's deficits—we'll never know what he might have done with the right material and tone (and we will somehow survive without knowing)—but to a series of bizarre failures perpetrated by the people who put this would-be epic together at a cost of a quarter-billion dollars or more. (For real-world context, that's what NASA spent on the entire Mars Pathfinder mission, including the rocket launch. The movie will, in the end, earn its money back and then some, but mainly thanks to overseas audiences; domestically it didn't do well at all.)

The basic failure has to do with star treatment, or the lack of it. Stars are fragile, perishable commodities. Long ago, in an industry far away, Hollywood studios knew how to protect their stars from overt foolishness (including their own), and how to mount and display them in calculated circumstances that served or enhanced their talents. Judging from what is and isn't on the screen in *Troy*, the calculation was simply that Brad Pitt's well-oiled bod, plus plenty of action amplified by digital effects, would be the needed formula for success.

To this end, the producers hired an action director, of sorts: Wolfgang Petersen, who, after making his name with a claustrophobic German film about life aboard a Nazi U-boat, succeeded in getting a standard Clint Eastwood performance from Clint Eastwood in *In the Line of Fire,* and a standard Harrison Ford performance from Harrison Ford in *Air Force One,* but who has never betrayed any aptitude for moving armies around, let alone moving audiences with the subtleties of dramatic acting.

Then there's the failure of the script by David Benioff, a writer whose ear is attuned to the Tin Age. Never mind that the structure allows Achilles to be conspicuously underemployed; he drops out of the story completely for a significant length of time. Never mind that Mr. Benioff has others blathering about fame just as annoyingly. ("You came here because you want your name to last through the ages," Agamemnon tells his troops. "If you go to Troy," Achilles's mother tells him, "people will remember your name for thousands of years, but I shall never see you again.") Most of the dialogue deals Achilles an unplayable, if not quite unspeakable, hand. "You sack of wine!" he shouts ineffectually at Agamemnon. "We men are wretched things," he grumbles in his tent.

On the rare occasion when Pitt is given something interesting or affecting to play, he plays it well. Back in his tent after rescuing the beautiful Briseis, who takes him for a violent brute, he leans into her, intimately, and says: "I'll tell you a secret, something they don't teach you in the temple. The gods envy us. They envy us because we're mortal. Because any moment might be our last." Although the speech continues in a grab-bag-existential way, it's a pretty good speech, and Pitt puts it over. Yet the most memorable scene belongs not to him—not to the very special mortal on whose sex appeal that quarter-billion dollar investment depends—but to Peter O'Toole, the wonderful and wily old virtuoso who plays Priam, the Trojan king.

It's a scene that should be studied in film classes of the future, both as an example of how a great actor can create his own occasions, and how a sex symbol can be marginalized, even miniaturized, by writing—and, of course, direction—that fails to give him the emotionally resonant material he needs; in fact, that gives him little to do but react. The situation is this: Achilles has just slain Priam's son, the courageous Hector, and now, late at night, a disguised King Priam comes to Achilles's tent to ask for Hector's body. "I loved my boy from the moment he opened his eyes to the moment you closed them," Priam says, his own eyes glistening with tears, and suddenly you realize what's been missing throughout the film: Eloquence! Feeling! Intimations of grandeur! The close-ups in this scene yield exactly the sense of character depth and intimacy that Brad Pitt's fans would have welcomed, but they're close-ups of a seventy-two-year-old man.

Sex-symbolic stars, unlike the suns that sizzle silently in the real firmament, can't operate in a vacuum. Just as they need to be fawned over by their fans, so they need to be burnished and nourished by their support troops—directors, writers, costumers, cinematographers. Everyone knows this is true for female stars, but it's equally so for men, from John Wayne to Kirk Douglas, Marlon Brando to Sylvester Stallone to Brad Pitt. Only when the proper elements fall into place can sex appeal flourish. It's the icing on the beefcake.

Twentynine Palms
Bad sex among the succulents

Directed by Bruno Dumont; starring David Wissak,
Katia Golubeva (2003)

by Ella Taylor

DAVID (DAVID WISSAK), A PHOTOGRAPHER SCOUTING DESERT LOCATIONS
for a magazine shoot, is a wiry, restless young man, dark and unkempt with an
imposing curved nose and a helmet of shiny brown hair that flops into his ex-
citable eyes. His tag-along girlfriend, Katia (Katia Golubeva), a pale, Russo-
French blonde of the Michelle Pfeiffer school, is as quiet and supple as a cat, and
comes burdened with no more useful occupation than to gaze into her lover's
eyes and murmur "Je t'aime" at regular intervals. Basing themselves in a bare-
bones motel down the road from the pricier Twentynine Palms Inn, they trawl
the Joshua Tree area in a red Hummer, pausing to wander naked through the
cruelly beautiful terrain and engage in varieties of less-than-imaginative soft-
core sex—filmed in something approaching real time by writer-director Bruno
Dumont—after which they lie like sated lizards on the hot rocks, contemplating
armies of yucca trees and churning white windmills. They have some more explicit sex in their room and—twice—in the motel pool. "Do you love me?" Katia
asks, and is rewarded with an invitation to fellatio that sounds more like a command and evolves into something approaching rape. Then, over ice cream
cones at the local Foster's Freeze, the couple starts quarreling in earnest. He
worships, he sulks, he hits. She giggles, she pouts, she offers up a string of non
sequiturs with a faraway look in her eyes. Then, more fighting, more fast food,
more sex of the kind that's a turn-on in the same way that pornography is—
short, sharp, and followed by immediate boredom, embarrassment, or ennui.

Over and over in *Twentynine Palms*, Dumont rubs our noses in every detail of this tumultuous, yet oddly inconsequential, relationship. ("Someday I want to see you pee," David tells Katia. She balks, but Dumont turns us into voyeurs instead.) This is not a new strategy for Dumont, whose *The Life of Jesus* and *L' humanité* both used obsessive repetition to probe the potential for extremity in the cumulative banalities and thwarted desires of a stunted psyche. But he's explored this to much better advantage in his wonderfully elliptical *The Life of Jesus*, the story of a cramped and meaningless life that finally explodes in a shocking act of racism.

Shot in gorgeous CinemaScope, *Twentynine Palms* at least has the virtue of savage beauty. Dumont has a wonderful feel for spatial contrast—he sets the tawdry amenities and constriction of the motel against the magisterial, unspoiled openness of the desert, which properly dwarfs the two lovers—and he's a master at creating a slow burn of premonitory terror. Willfully, microscopically descriptive, *Twentynine Palms* demands to be understood on its own terms, and like Dumont's other work, it flatly refuses to make those terms clear until the end of the movie. Fair enough, but in the meantime we have to put up with the most annoying pair of movie lovebirds since Tom Cruise and Nicole Kidman fucked and fought their way through *Eyes Wide Shut*. You couldn't call either of them a personality, and their endless, indefatigable coupling, with its grunts and squeals and cataclysmic orgasms—perhaps intended as a kind of shorthand for predatory male aggression that is somehow uniquely American—adds up to little more than textbook porn.

Dumont clearly means to explore the roller-coaster ups and downs of the intense love affair, very likely one he's had himself. He may even intend us to find David and Katia, or at least David's orgasmic moans, funny. In truth, like most lovers who see nothing beyond themselves and each other, they're a terrible bore to spend time with. The bursts of mutual rage, adoration, and carnality seem grounded in little more than a director's memory of a trip when he got royally laid. They're all Promethean instinct, but their state of nature is more ridiculous than grand. Perhaps because he senses this himself, Dumont unleashes on us a B-movie climax of studied and perverse depravity involving a male rape (what else is left?), capped by another that looks like something swept up from the cutting-room floor of *Psycho*. There's something pinched and moralistic in Dumont's stance, even sadistic—an orgy of punishment for the crime of being a couple of airheads chasing pleasure.

Radley Metzger, Soft-core Auteur
by *Gerald Peary*

When the burgeoning porn industry of the mid–'70s demanded penetration, Radley Metzger chose the nom de plume of Henry Paris with which to direct such hard-X classics as *The Private Afternoons of Pamela Mann* (1975) and *The Opening of Misty Beethoven* (1977). But Metzger devotees prefer his earlier period of creativity, 1966–1973, when the New York filmmaker, under his own name, was the (uncrowned) king of soft-core eros.

A Korean war vet, Metzger learned movies by editing trailers—Antonioni, Bergman, Truffaut—for the early art-house distributor Janus Films. Then he and Ava Leighton formed Audubon Films, importing low-budget European smut. They made money with *I, a Woman* (1965), a Swedish sexual confessional starring pouty Essy Persson. Metzger had a typically self-reliant-American idea: Why not manufacture his own European-style erotica?

Shooting abroad, he cast steamy-looking continentals who, uninhibited and unclad, traipsed through Xanadu-like castles by the Mediterranean blue. With Metzger, art direction was everything; that, plus bold, genuine Technicolor. Influenced by the 1960s European masters, his mise-en-scène was fairly inspired. Unfortunately, his scripts were often leaden, as with *Carmen, Baby* (1967), a dreary nonsinging version of the Prosper Mérimée story, and *Little Mother* (retitled *Woman of the Year*), a dull 1973 tabloid telling of Eva Peron (called Marina Penares) sleeping her bosomy way to the top, shot in Yugoslavia.

Here are four far better Metzgers, all bearing the filmmaker's "auteur" signature: an extended close-up of the writhing, frenzied face of his female star in orgasmic ecstasy:

Score (1973): Metzger's best work, from a cleverly scripted off-Broadway drama. It's a *Who's Afraid of Virginia Woolf?* variant in which a George-and-Martha couple in their thirties (Lynn Lowry, Gerald Grant) seduce an uptight Nick-and-Honey in their twenties (Claire Wilbur, Calvin Culver); they do it girl-girl and boy-boy. It's the first fairly mainstream American feature to jolt its audience, presumably buying tickets for the female action, with overt celebrations of male orality. The only member of the original theater cast who didn't make the cut was Sylvester Stallone; too stiff for a soft X?

Therese und Isabell (1968): Metzger's box-office hit offered sex highlights from Violette Leduc's scandalous autobiography, *La Bâtarde,* set at a French girls' boarding school. Lesbianism! That's why voyeurs raced to savor Essy Persson from *I, a Woman* rubbing clumsily against a female classmate to a mismatched voice-over from Leduc's purple-prose porno: "A saint was licking away my soils!"

The Lickerish Quartet (1970): Three decadents who live in a castle—a man, his wife, their moody son—discover at a carnival show that a daredevil motorcycle rider (Silvana Venturelli) resembles the actress they've been watching obsessively in a 16mm stag movie. She's invited back to the castle and then, as these things go, she seduces each of the trio. It's a decent tease of a sex film despite pretentious dialogue: "In the dark. That's where we start and where we finish. In between, it's a game of hide-and-seek."

Camille 2000 (1969): Second to *Score* in Metzger's oeuvre, this is his most opulently conceived and also most underrated film. The nineteenth-century French melodrama from Alexandre Dumas *fils* is transported to *La Dolce Vita* contemporary Rome, and fetching performers (Danièle Gaubert, Nino Castelnuovo) do all right as the fated lovers. Warning: There's no deathbed coughing à la Garbo's clothed Camille. ∎

The Unbearable Lightness of Being
The erotics of Being

Directed by Philip Kaufman; starring Daniel Day-Lewis,
Lena Olin, Juliette Binoche (1988)

by Richard Schickel

"TAKE OFF YOUR CLOTHES," THE HANDSOME DOCTOR SAYS TO
the pretty nurse. She does, more wry than appalled. She's been there before,
with this sly, perpetually horny brain surgeon. In an adjoining room, two
doctors and a patient watch through frosted glass. Soon enough, a pair of extremely attractive breasts pop into their view. And ours.

Thus, the opening of Philip Kaufman's *The Unbearable Lightness of Being*. It
is not the last time Tomas (Daniel Day-Lewis) will make this demand. And it
is not the last time an attractive woman will comply. It is part of the "lightness" of his "being" that will, eventually, become "unbearable" to him—to
everyone—in this seductive film. Sabina (Lena Olin), one of two women
whose lives are entwined with his (the other is Juliette Binoche, playing
Tereza) tells Tomas it is simple curiosity that drives his womanizing. He
wants to learn the secrets of the bedroom—including how women verbalize
passion, their cries and whispers—and he does not deny it.

He does, however, deny her love. It may be that the sheer joy of their cou-
plings is enough. Sabina, an artist, is less rooted in the conventional; she's an
escape artist who will happily set up shop in three different countries. When
a rather square lover decides to move in, she simply decamps. It is she, paradoxically, who carries the burden of the film's "lightness," she who most
lacks commitment to places and persons.

She stands in vivid contrast to Tereza, a quiet, fiercely monogamous woman—entertaining enough sexually, but determined to ground the lightness of Tomas's being in responsible adulthood. She meets him at a provincial spa, falls for him at first sight, and follows him to Prague. Appearing on his doorstep, she reports a sniffle. Naturally, he tells her to disrobe (the film is slyly aware that women are obliged to be naked in front of male doctors). They are soon making passionate love, and not long after, they marry. She takes up a camera. He continues to stray.

We can, if we wish, see Tereza and Sabina as halves of the eternal feminine—the nurturer and the sensualist. To the film's credit, this is a matter it does not stress. At fairly regular intervals it offers us frank sex scenes, the best and longest of which has Tereza photographing Sabina in the nude. Sabina is surprisingly shy, but by the end of the sequence both women are naked and heading for a lesbian encounter (interrupted by Sabina's lover). The energy and conviction of these scenes—and Kaufman's direction of them—are integral to our pleasure; we look forward to them.

To digress, I think these scenes are exemplary. Movie sex should be handled as it is here—with frankness and good nature. We don't necessarily have to see pussies and pricks (though some of the former, if none of the latter, are briefly on view). But we must have the sense that the actors and actresses have stripped for these scenes, that they are at least that much into them. When people make love, they do not normally keep their underwear on. So if the camera catches a glimpse of bra, panties, or undershorts, we know thespian modesty has trumped reality. We also don't want a lot of cuts; we need at least a few shots that maintain the relationship between face and naked form or we suspect body doubles, almost as fatal as glimpses of underwear.

I know this sort of thing is hard to arrange, particularly with American actresses, whose stardom is inversely proportional to how much clothing they shed. But that's the imperative of the inherent literalness of movies, which mostly runs counter to their equally inherent eroticism, often resulting in prissiness. This is why I'm generally more turned on by sex in novels, which leave room for randy imagination. But that probably says more about the nature of the two art forms—and maybe my sensibilities—than it does about the successful, even magical, eroticism of *The Unbearable Lightness of Being*.

An adaptation of Milan Kundera's superb novel, the film was released in 1987, well after that curious era when earnest people wanted to know whether the art of cinema and the sleaze of porn might one day merge. A lot of them had ventured forth in the 1970s to see *Deep Throat* or *The Devil in Miss Jones* and hoped to attain the same frisson in venues less threatening to their *amour-propre*. I thought this question had been answered in the first thirty minutes of *Last Tango in Paris,* but that was a rare instance where a sexual metaphor addressed the larger issues of the movie—power and control in human relationships.

Somewhat belatedly, *Unbearable Lightness* offered a comparable kick in a critically approved context. Indeed, it raised some of the same issues as *Last Tango.* Tereza does want to control Tomas's anarchic sexuality. But it is not solely about that, which is in its favor. In John Updike's moving and tender *Villages,* he writes: "Sex is a holiday, a remarkably brief one in our body's budget compared with sleeping or food-gathering or constructing battlement for self-defense, such as the Great Wall of China." Updike's novel is heavily charged with eroticism, but it is rich in personal history too.

The same is true of Kaufman's film, which devotes at least as much time to the Soviet invasion of Czechoslovakia in 1968 as it does to sexuality. To oversimplify: Sex is a metaphor, the means by which Tomas asserts his right to pleasure free of state control. One could speculate that if he did not live in a country where discretion was imposed from above, his need for sexual adventure might be less pressing.

Politics, then, is what imposes heaviness on his (and Tereza's) beings, though the blithe Sabina more easily evades it; an escape to Switzerland works for her as it does not for them. When they return to Prague, Tomas and Tereza lose their careers. She ends up a barmaid, he a window washer. He cruelly responds to the overtures of a married woman. Tereza ripostes with an encounter of her own.

They finally achieve a satisfying escape to a farm owned by a former patient. The new life of hard work and simple food offers no overt pleasures, no "lightness." It is an embrace of what we might call the "real." There is no opportunity for screwing around—except with each other—but also no opportunity for the state to screw them around.

One night at a country inn, they drink, dance, and make love (though the camera now hangs back). The next morning we see them driving home in their rickety truck, with Tomas speaking the film's last words: "I'm thinking how happy I am." We do not see the truck skid off the road, killing them both—the film's final, tragic absurdity. We are left with this thought: That many lives are driven by pursuit of the impossible—whether it be the perfect lay or the perfect ideology—yet, if we are bound to die meaninglessly, why not live that way, nestled in the quotidian?

Be that as it may, this film, like Updike's novel, makes the case for a life of simple contentment. And it stands in powerful contrast to Kaufman's other, failed attempts to solve the sexual conundrum. *Quills* is a frenzy of ill-realized perversity, tarted up with dubious philosophizing. *Henry and June* is a different matter—ostensibly a direct engagement with the costs and pleasures of Henry Miller's youthful sexuality. As played by Fred Ward, Miller is an exemplar of working-class lust, while his wife, June, more or less plays the Tereza role, Anais Nin the Sabina part. But Uma Thurman's June is rather prudish, and the Anais Nin of Maria de Medeiros (whose lack of star status obliges her to be the more naked) has an advanced case of sex-in-the-head. As a result, the sexual encounters—and there are more than in *Unbearable Lightness*—are joyless. Worse, the single-minded concentration on sex gives the movie the feeling of porn without any redeeming prurience.

In contrast, the willingness of *Unbearable Lightness* to take up matters irrelevant to its double-helix plot is really its glory. By putting sex in its proper, Updikian place, it offers a portrait of life that is as real and balanced as we are likely to get in a movie.

At the end of a life of frantic sex, artistic achievement, and ideological quarrels, Graham Greene was heard to murmur that there was a lot to be said for companionship that is merely affectionate. Somehow we imagine him happy in the end—as happy as Tomas is in his final moment—embracing a more bearable lightness of being, one free of the distorting, even dehumanizing, pressures of lust and ideology.

Wuthering Heights
The moor's last sigh

Directed by William Wyler; starring Laurence Olivier,
Merle Oberon (1939)

by Eleanor Ringel Gillespie

*"Cathy, if he loved you with all the power
of his soul for a whole lifetime, he couldn't
love you as much as I do in a single day."*

—HEATHCLIFF (LAURENCE OLIVIER)
TO CATHY (MERLE OBERON)

In the roiling language of William Wyler's 1939 masterpiece *Wuthering Heights,* that's how you say, "I love ya, baby."

Based on the first two-thirds of Emily Brontë's 1847 novel, Wyler's film presents the headlong rush and tumult of Heathcliff and Cathy's grand, doomed passion, so all-consuming it destroys everything in its path, including its star-crossed lovers.

Wuthering Heights is the story of Heathcliff, an orphan brought up at that eponymous estate by a Yorkshire family of good standing (even if they live on moors worthy of the hound of the Baskervilles). As children, Heathcliff and Cathy—the daughter of Heathcliff's benefactor, Mr. Earnshaw (Cecil Kellaway)—become soul mates. Their bond is sealed through playing make-believe m'lady games at the rough-hewn Peniston Crag, a place of wild heather and wilder hearts.

When Mr. Earnshaw dies, Cathy's brother, Hindley (Hugh Williams), takes over the estate. By this time, Cathy and Heathcliff have fallen in love, but

Cathy's head is turned by the conventional world of dances and high tea. She renounces her true love for a life filled with nice clothes, a nice house, and a nice husband, Edgar Linton (David Niven). Heathcliff departs, hurling curses, and much later returns to make good on those curses, and then some.

The main narrative is bookended by a chilling ghost story set forty years later, in which a Mr. Lockwood (Miles Mander) seeks shelter from a howling blizzard at Wuthering Heights—now as wretched and in disarray as its owner, Heathcliff. Lockwood hears a voice calling for his host, then feels the icy grasp of a phantom hand. The faithful housekeeper (Flora Robson) ominously explains that it's Cathy, still wandering the moors hoping to be reunited with her Heathcliff.

Love, death, the whole damn thing—that's what *Wuthering Heights* comes down to. The brooding, demon-ridden Heathcliff and the pretty but changeable Cathy loved with a love that is more than love, to borrow from Edgar Allan Poe's "Annabel Lee." Death and fate frame their romance. Cathy's deathbed scene may be the most erotic farewell in the history of movies, with Heathcliff at her side, muttering, "Take any form, drive me mad, only do not leave me in this dark alone where I cannot find you!"

And then there's all that love-from-beyond-the-grave stuff indicated in the framing device. Heathcliff's heedless, arrogant vengeance dooms Cathy to a ghostly, yearning existence and himself to a life—if you can call it that—of madness and despair. After hearing Lockwood's tale, he rushes into the blinding snowstorm, seeking the ghost of his beloved.

The movie's producer, Samuel Goldwyn, wasn't happy with Brontë's unhappy ending. He proposed a final scene in which the spirits of Heathcliff and Cathy walk hand in hand through Stay-Puft clouds toward a heavenly sunset. Wyler refused to shoot it, so Goldwyn got another director, H. C. Potter, to shoot a pair of doubles headed together for Eternal Bliss.

The atmosphere on Wyler's set during the shoot was more withering than *Wuthering*. Olivier and Oberon got along about as well as Vivien Leigh and Clark Gable did in *Gone With the Wind*. He thought she was a poor actress and was disappointed his lover, Leigh, had not been cast. She felt his disdain. According to one anecdote, Olivier spat at her—twice!—during a love scene, and reportedly tossed aside her protests with, "Why, you amateur little bitch. What's a little spit between actors?" Ironically, their mutual antagonism may account for the eroticism that courses through their scenes together. That subterranean friction brings out a frankly disturbing side to Cathy and Heathcliff's love. For all the grand romance, there's something unholy about its force and flirtation with madness, its hunger and hatred, arrogance and misery. Everything about *Wuthering Heights* is too much: the words, the passion. Even Gregg Toland's Oscar-winning cinematography, with its black-and-white shimmer, is too much.

At times the movie feels feverish, infected with mysticism and a prescient fear that all will not be well for Heathcliff and Cathy. When Cathy bursts out that she doesn't merely love Heathcliff, "I *am* Heathcliff," thunder rumbles ominously across the moors as if to suggest a passion so forbidden it tempts the gods themselves. Again, it's like Poe's lovers in "Annabel Lee." Melodramatic? Absolutely. *Wuthering Heights* feels like no other film. Echoing its lovers, it has a storm-tossed restlessness, a frenzied spirit, a reckless ecstasy.

Yes, it is all too much. And just right.

Young Lady Chatterley

D. H. Lawrence lite

Directed by Alan Roberts; starring Harlee McBride,
Peter Ratray (1977)

by Ty Burr

THE BUXOM, ELEGANT WOMAN UNCOILS ECSTATICALLY IN FRONT
of a roaring fire, drinking in the sight of her unclad, lower-class lover. Outside, the rain pours; inside, it is as if time has stopped. In a daze of lust, the
woman purrs, "Everything about your body is beautiful, a work of art . . . *I
want you to sodomize me.*"

Young Lady Chatterley is a quintessential relic of 1970s soft-core porn, a
genre that flourished in the decade between *Deep Throat* and the rise of home
video and marks the sex-film industry's most sustained lunge for middle-
class respectability. With *Deep Throat* (1972), a gap opened between the new
breed of hard-core movies and mainstream X-rated fare like *Midnight Cowboy*; an unarticulated need arose for comparatively discreet "date-movie" sex
films that brushed an artful patina over the old in-out.

Thus, *Emmanuelle* (1975), the first true '70s soft-core flick and by some
accounts the most financially successful French film of all time. Gauzy and
pretentious as hell, *Emmanuelle* proved the existence of a niche market that
found its most effective delivery medium with the late-'70s rise of pay-cable
channels like HBO and its sister service Cinemax. With bountiful nudity
and simulated sex, soft-core attracted cable viewers without being so explicit as to cause complaints or cancellations. Legions of teenage boys knew
full well what played on "Skinemax" after midnight, and their parents could

rest assured their sons wouldn't be exposed to gaping vulvas and money shots. Even Mom and Dad could watch *Melody in Love* or *Hard Ticket to Hawaii* and get hot but not bothered. Soft-core preserved the original social compact of "dirty movies": arousal under the sanitary wrapping of the Aristotelian unities of time, place, and action.

In other words, you could pretend these were real movies.

That said, not many soft-core films managed the delicate balance of class and smut required by the genre, and I should know. From 1984 to 1989, after graduating from an Ivy League college, I was a Cinemax sex-movie content appraiser, which meant I vetted new releases and film libraries for the cable channel's acquisitions, scheduling, and promotion departments.

The job title was actually "film evaluator," and there were six of us. Jim and Monty handled the big Hollywood movies, Roger the classics libraries, Mary the documentaries, David the art films. Because I was young and male and straight and new, I was handed low-budget action films and soft-core, the stuff that was aired in blocks titled "Drive-In Saturday Night" and "Friday After Dark." In my new field of expertise, it was clear what got the ratings: breasts. Particularly all-American, cheerleader-type breasts, as in the distaff *Porky's* knockoff *H.O.T.S*, or woozily shot Eurobreasts, as in the *Emmanuelle* series featuring the blank-faced, rail-thin Sylvia Kristel and Laura Gemser.

Most of the submitted films weren't remotely up to snuff—there were a lot of triple-X movies whittled down to about twenty minutes each. So we invented rules: Flaccid male nudity was okay, turgid was not. The movie had to pass the First Five Minutes Test, meaning if there wasn't a sex scene by then, the audience was gone. The most happily absurd yardstick of all was the Breasts-Per-Minute Ratio, or BPM—the number of breasts divided by the running time—which triggered endless Talmudic hairsplitting. Did the same breast in two different shots equal one breast or two? At what point did a clad breast become an unclad, and therefore official, breast?

By all these measures, *Young Lady Chatterley* scored off the grid, and in fact was the single most successful "Friday After Dark" film during my Cinemax tenure. First five minutes, high BPM, flagrant but not explicit male nudity— it was all there.

So was a curious (and now hilariously quaint) faux-European gentility that coexisted uneasily with the low comedy and lusty sight gags favored by American drive-in teasers. Directed by Broadway hoofer Bob Brownell under the *nom de soft-core* "Alan Roberts," *Young Lady Chatterley* is a frank hybrid:

a movie that begins in D. H. Lawrence period-film territory but that mostly takes place in "London, England: Today," where it concerns the American descendent of Lawrence's Lady Chatterley as played by Harlee McBride, a pleasant, auburn-haired actress (and future wife of comedian Richard Belzer).

First, the elements of ersatz highbrow need to be established. Unfurling to fake classical music over a background of roses and statuary, the credits read like a who's who of bland Anglo-Saxon pseudonyms: director Alan Roberts, writer Steve Michaels, actors Edgar Daniels and Henry Charles, not a surname in the bunch. The music, by Don Bagley, has been "adapted from the works of Claude Debussy."

The first scene takes place in the spurious location of "Brisbane, England, 1901." Lady Frances Chatterley (Mary Forbes) intones in a potted British/San Fernando Valley accent that life is "too, too pointless," and quickly sets about seducing the gardener (Patrick Wright), who in any event tells her that "when I see a wench's nipples hard and stiff, I likes to think it's me as done it." Discreet shagging follows, the emphasis on his working-class backside rather than her noble nudity.

In the modern sequences, Cynthia Chatterley is an American working in London and engaged to Philip (William Beckley), a ponce who makes it clear on which side of the Atlantic the film's allegiances lie. Upon inheriting the Chatterley estate and told she must sell it for back taxes, Cynthia goes to see for herself and is promptly insulted by Paul (Peter Ratray), the sulky surfer-dude gardener. The lighting is high-key California sunshine; the mansion looks positively Glendale.

The rest of *Young Lady Chatterley* plays out as a silly but amusing vision of British class divisions melting away under the democratic carnality of the American intruder. Lady C. discovers her forebear's randy diary and, under its spell, does the gardener as well as the saucy "Cockney" chambermaid Sybil (Lindsay Freeman). Cynthia also schtups a hitchhiker (Michael Hearne) in the back of her Rolls Royce as the shocked Bavarian chauffeur (Lawrence Montaigne) looks on. And in the movie's dinner party climax(es), Philip's upper-class-twit friends, dressed as eighteenth-century royals, give in to their repressed urges and roger the assembled help for a full-bore comic orgy.

By then the illusion of "class" is hanging on by its fingernails through the music, the fraudulent accents, and a banquet sequence that rips off *Tom Jones*. But *Young Lady Chatterley* feels far more comfortable in its lowbrow moments and ends, incongruously, with a pie fight. This is D. H. Lawrence by way of *Laugh-In* and Benny Hill.

YLC tries to be all things to all soft-core devotees. For its time, at least, it succeeded. Today the movie says more about the tastes of that time, and encapsulates the genre's unstated battle between sleaze and respectability. That battle is long over, thanks to the mainstreaming of hard-core through video and the Internet. How do you keep an audience down on the Chatterley estate after it's ridden the Bang Bus? You don't. In the era of 24/7 money shots, a high BPM is chasteness itself.

The Last X-Rated Picture Show

by Ty Burr

For a while, it was the brave new world we had dreamed of. All the Hays Code's crazy rules—married couples can't sleep in the same bed, gay people don't exist, methods of smuggling should not be presented (Section I.2.d)—had by the late 1960s come to seem not just foolish but harmful, actively standing in the way of the unpleasant truths movies were finally telling.

In 1968, MPAA head Jack Valenti introduced the new "voluntary" ratings system of G, M (later PG), R, and X, and for a while the system worked. Specifically, the X rating allowed serious explicit work to be produced, distributed, and exhibited. In 1969, *Midnight Cowboy* became the first (and, to date, last) X-rated film to win an Oscar for best picture. But there was also Lindsay Anderson's *If. . . .* and Brian De Palma's *Greetings,* as well as *Last Tango in Paris, A Clockwork Orange, Medium Cool, The Killing of Sister George,* and others.

Interestingly, X was the one rating the MPAA chose not to copyright. Anyone could use it, with the result that the aborning adult film industry turned it into a synonym for smut. Newspaper chains began to turn down ads for X-rated films, theater chains stopped booking them (why show something you can't advertise?), and studios stopped making them (why make something you can't show?).

So the era of the Serious X-Rated Movie came to an ignoble end—but not before one flawed gem squeezed through the door. Ironically, *Inserts* (1975) is about an earlier type of sex film, the quickie stag films that flourished in the 1930s. Richard Dreyfuss plays Boy Wonder, a washed-up director of silents reduced to shooting porn loops in his Beverly Hills mansion. Veronica Cartwright and Stephen Davies are his two "stars" (the latter nicknamed "Rex the Wonder Dog"); a young Bob Hoskins plays the mobster money-man; and—the reason to see the film—Jessica Harper is his latest girlfriend: fast-talking, intelligent, ambitious, very sexy.

Written and directed by John Byrum, *Inserts* feels like a play—one set, real time—and Dreyfuss gives a showy, "entertaining" performance that sidesteps the possibility of real pain. The sex scene Boy Wonder shoots with his actors early on is patently, comically fake, even if the nudity is somewhat more raw than we're used to. It's the long dialogue scenes between Dreyfuss and Harper that make up the film's—pardon the expression—climax, as the actress sits there nude and somehow gets you to focus on her brain, and as the relationship between seducer and seduced constantly shifts.

The film even addresses the gulf between desire and fulfillment, implying that "real movies" (the one we're watching) are about the dance, while "dirty movies" (the one they're making) are about the money shot. *Inserts* doesn't show the money shot, and that's both the joke at the movie's beginning and the unexpected tragedy at its end.

No wonder it's so hard to find on video. ∎

Y tu mamá también

Three for the road

Directed by Alfonso Cuarón; starring Diego Luna,
Gael García Bernal, Maribel Verd (2001)

by Kenneth Turan

IN ONE OF THOSE BIZARRE JUXTAPOSITIONS THAT CHARACTERIZE
the Cannes Film Festival, I first heard about Alfonso Cuarón's *Y tu mamá
también* at a mock château in the south of France during a mammoth party
to celebrate the world's first glimpses of *The Lord of the Rings*.

Y tu mamá had been screened earlier that day for an elite group of American specialty distributors, no critics invited. Contrary to later mythology, the
distributors were taken with the film and immediately saw its box-office potential, but none of the companies affiliated with major studios were in a position to acquire it. The film was simply too hot, too sexually explicit for
MPAA signatories to handle without trims, and Cuarón had announced he
had no intention of cutting even a frame.

Outrageous without being offensive, provocatively and unapologetically
sexual (and ultimately released unrated), *Y tu mamá* is alive to the possibilities of life and cinema. It is also a sophisticated film happily masquerading as
something casual and off the cuff.

Nominally a simple road movie about two Mexican teenagers taking off
for a mythical beach in the company of a suddenly available woman of
twenty-eight, *Y tu mamá* manages to be comic, dramatic, political, sociologi-
cal, and, yes, erotic, all without breaking a sweat.

Cuarón's picture, cowritten with his brother Carlos, is also reminiscent of the classics of the French New Wave, echoing their unmistakable freshness and excitement, the sense of joy at being alive and making movies that made those works distinctive and unforgettable.

To turn out something so apparently effortless takes, paradoxically, a background of craft and experience. Cuarón caught Hollywood's eye with his Mexican debut film, *Love in the Time of Hysteria,* which he parlayed into a pair of studio literary adaptations, *A Little Princess* and *Great Expectations.* Wanting then to "go off and get my hands dirty," Cuarón and his longtime collaborator, the gifted cinematographer Emmanuel Lubezki, returned to their homeland to make what turned out to be a sexually candid, deeply Mexican film that pulses with energy and spirit.

Y tu mamá (even its title is a bragging sexual reference) begins with a graphic bedroom scene, set against a huge poster for *Harold and Maude,* between seventeen-year-old Tenoch (Diego Luna) and his girlfriend, who is about to abandon him for a summer in Italy. Tenoch's homeboy Julio (Gael García Bernal), it turns out, is similarly at loose ends.

Formidably self-centered best friends who do everything from getting high to pleasuring themselves together, Tenoch and Julio are dripping with attitude and conceit. Though their humor runs to flatulence jokes and their interest in the outside world is confined to interchanges like "Left-wing chicks are hot"/"Totally," they nevertheless view themselves as the epitome of knowledge and sophistication.

The film's attitude toward these two is one of the keys to its success. *Y tu mamá* is neither complicit with the boys nor hostile to them; rather, aided by a voice-over, it views them from a bemused, interested distance, entertained by their energy and sass but knowing full well what essentially clueless space cowboys they are.

Bored beyond belief by their vapid, druggy summer, the friends perk up at a wedding so establishment the joke is that there are more bodyguards than guests. The boys drool over the beautiful Luisa (Maribel Verd), the wife of one of Tenoch's cousins. When she asks about Mexico's beaches, they make one up out of thin air, call it Heaven's Mouth, and offer to drive her there if she's ever in the mood.

After a phone call from her absent husband, who tearily confesses to what is not his first infidelity, Luisa is suddenly in the mood. The boys have no idea where they're going, but they're too excited by the trip's fantasy potential to back out. Off they go, unready in more ways than any of them realize.

First up is a getting-to-know-you interlude. Luisa is not the ethereal philosopher the boys fantasized, but a lively and down-to-earth dental technician. They like her so much they reveal the existence of their secret society, the Charolastras, which has precepts like "the truth is cool but unattainable."

Gradually, emotional and sexual complications, both erotic and wildly comical, take center stage. These underscore quite a different precept: Be careful what you wish for. Yet no matter how raunchy things get, the film's emotional balance, its ability to avoid the gratuitous and keep everything recognizably human, keeps the material from being anywhere near as off-putting as it may sound in the abstract.

The film's advance word and publicity prepared audiences for the sexual antics, but passion is not this trip's only component. Cuarón and his collaborators are intent on giving us a vivid, kaleidoscopic vision of roadside Mexico, from local festivities to steers blocking the highway. When the Spanish-born Luisa says, "You're so lucky to live in Mexico, it breathes with life," she is speaking for the film as well. Simultaneously, Y tu mamá is making off-handed but pointed comments about the country's politics. Though they rarely mention it, the trio drives through an endless series of police/military checkpoints. The voice-over calmly takes note of a laborer hit by a bus because there is no place to cross a highway for miles, of a fisherman who will soon have to be a janitor because of the construction of a luxury hotel; we are told in a deceptively casual way what an oligarchy means to ordinary lives.

Pointing out the serious aspects risks making this graceful film sound drier than it is. What could be more satisfying than strong characters, a sense of humor, and a handful of unabashedly erotic scenes (including one that climaxes with a wonderful twist)? Jazzed by the medium's potential to tell all kinds of stories in all kinds of ways, Cuarón did more than get his hands dirty. He struck gold.

Contributors

John Anderson's work appears regularly in *Newsday*, *Variety* and the *New York Times*. He has contributed to the *LA Times*, the *LA Times Magazine*, *The Nation*, and *The Christian Science Monitor*, as well as *Film Comment*, *LAWeekly*, *Artforum*, *Interview*, *Out*, *Ms.*, and *The Washington Post*. He is a past member of the selection committee of the New York Film Festival and the author of *Sundancing* (Avon, 2000), *Edward Yang* (University of Illinois Press, 2004), and, with Laura Kim, *I Wake Up Screening* (Billboard, 2006). He is a member and past chair of the New York Film Critics Circle and a member of the National Book Critics Circle. He is based in Los Angeles.

David Ansen is movie critic and senior editor at *Newsweek*.

Sheila Benson began writing at a small paper (the *Pacific Sun* in Mill Valley, California), moved to a bigger one (lead film critic for the *Los Angeles Times*, 1981–1991), contributed to Microsoft's *Cinemania*, and has been published in various magazines and newspapers. Now living in Seattle, she reviews for the *Seattle Weekly*, although, looking back, it seems as though all the important stuff happened in between.

Jami Bernard is a film critic for the *New York Daily News*. In addition to editing *The X List*, she is the author of *Breast Cancer: There & Back*, plus four film books: *Chick Flicks*, *Total Exposure*, *First Films*, and a biography of Quentin Tarantino. Her next book, a humorous weight-loss memoir, will be published by Penguin in 2006. Her work has appeared in the National Society of Film Critics anthologies *The A List* and *Sex and Violence*, and in numerous publications. She is a member and former chair of the New York Film Critics Circle. For more information, visit www.jamibernard.com.

Peter Brunette is a critic for indieWIRE.com and the British trade journal *Screen International*. The author or editor of seven books on film history and theory, including studies of Italian directors Roberto Rossellini and Michelangelo Antonioni, he is also Reynolds Professor of Film Studies at Wake Forest University. His most recent book is on the Hong Kong director Wong Kar-wai (University of Illinois Press).

Ty Burr is the film critic for the *Boston Globe*. Prior to that, he was the video critic for *Entertainment Weekly*, and also covered film, music, theater, books, and the Internet. He began his career at HBO in the 1980s, serving as an in-house "film evaluator" and helping to put Corey Haim movies and soft-core porn on Cinemax. While at *EW*, he wrote *The Hundred Greatest Movies of All Time* (Time-Life Books, 1999) and *The Hundred Greatest Stars of All Time* (Time-Life Books, 1998); he has also written on film and other subjects for the *New York Times*, *Spin*, the *Boston Phoenix*, and other publications. He is currently writing a book about watching classic movies with children. A member of the Boston Society of Film Critics, Burr lives in Newton, Massachusetts.

Jay Carr, a native New Yorker, edited the previous National Society of Film Critics anthology, *The A List*. Former chief film critic for the *Detroit News* and the *Boston Globe*, he now is the film critic for *AM New York* and NECN.

Roger Ebert has been a film critic for the *Chicago Sun-Times* since 1967. Since 1976 he has cohosted a national movie review program on television, first with Gene Siskel and for the past five years with Richard Roeper. In 1975, he won the Pulitzer Prize for criticism. He is the author of an annual *Movie Yearbook* and two volumes of *Great Movies* essays, and the editor of *Roger Ebert's Book of Film*, a Norton anthology.

David Edelstein is a movie critic for *Slate* and National Public Radio's *Fresh Air*, and a commentator for *CBS Sunday Morning*. He has also been a critic for the *Village Voice* and the *New York Post*.

Chris Fujiwara is the author of *Jacques Tourneur: The Cinema of Nightfall* (Johns Hopkins University Press). A regular contributor to the *Boston Phoenix*, Fujiwara has also written for *Film Comment, Cineaste*, the *Boston Globe*, and other publications.

Eleanor Ringel Gillespie has been the lead movie critic for the *Atlanta Journal-Constitution* for twenty-seven years. She is a regular contributor to CNN, MSNBC, CNN Headline News, and the Atlanta NBC affiliate, and a columnist for *TV Guide*. She's served on panels and juries at the Sarasota French Film Festival, Dallas International Film Festival (jury chair), Florida Film Festival, and the High Falls Film Festival in Rochester, New York. She is the author of *Stargazing* and is currently working on a book about business and the workplace in film. Her reviews have won awards from such organizations as Sigma Delta Chi (the Green Eyeshade awards) and the Cox newspaper chain. Her face is currently on a MARTA city bus in Atlanta, just like Carrie in *Sex and the City*.

J. Hoberman is senior film critic for the *Village Voice* and an adjunct professor of cinema at the Cooper Union in New York City. His books include *The Dream Life: Movies, Media, and the Mythology of the Sixties; The Red Atlantis: Communist Culture in the Absence of Communism;* and *Bridge of Light: Yiddish Film Between Two Worlds;* as well as two collections of his work, *The Magic Hour* and *Vulgar Modernism*.

Dave Kehr is an entertainment writer based in New York.

Peter Keough has been film editor at the *Boston Phoenix* since 1989 and has reviewed thousands of movies, though he admittedly often confuses them with X-rated features he snuck into in the late '60s. A member of the Boston Society of Film Critics, he edited *Flesh and Blood: The National Society of Film Critics on Sex, Violence, and Censorship* (Mercury House Press).

Stuart Klawans has been the film critic of *The Nation* since 1988 and writes occasionally on film and literature for the *New York Times, Newsday, Parnassus, Film Comment,* and other publications. He is the author of *Film Follies: The Cinema Out of Order* and *Left in the Dark: Film Reviews and Essays, 1988–2001*.

Andy Klein is the film editor and chief critic for *Los Angeles CityBeat.* He also appears regularly on KPCC–FM *Film Week* and KCET–TV's *Life and Times.*

Nathan Lee is the chief film critic of the *New York Sun* and a frequent contributor to *Film Comment.* His work has appeared in the *New York Times, Filmmaker, Salon,* and *Papersky.* He lives in Brooklyn with the daemon-dog Charlie.

Emanuel Levy has juggled a dual career as film professor (now at UCLA) and film critic. A two-time president of the L.A. Film Critics, Levy was a senior critic for *Variety* and chief critic for *Screen International.* In 2004, he launched EmanuelLevy.com, an acclaimed website of film criticism and commentary. Levy is the author of eight books, including *George Cukor, Master of Elegance; John Wayne and the American Way of Life; Cinema of Outsiders: The Rise of American Independent Film;* the tribute volume *Citizen Sarris, American Film Critic* (editor); and *All About Oscar: The History and Politics of the Academy Awards. Painting With Light,* the first biography of Vincente Minnelli, will be published by St. Martin's in 2006. Levy has served on juries at forty-one festivals, including Cannes, Montreal, Venice, Locarno, Taoromina, San Francisco, Seattle, Vancouver, Sundance, Hawaii, and Shanghai. He has appeared on *Nightline,* NPR, PBS, CNN, NBC, FOX, IFC, and the Sundance Channel.

Joe Morgenstern is the film critic of *The Wall Street Journal* and a Pulitzer Prize winner. He was a foreign correspondent for the *New York Times* before he became the theater and movie critic for the *New York Herald-Tribune* in 1959. He moved to *Newsweek* as movie critic in 1965 and was a columnist for the *Los Angeles Herald-Examiner* from 1983 to 1988. He has written scripts for television, including *The Boy In the Plastic Bubble* and several episodes of *Law & Order.* Morgenstern is cofounder of the National Society of Film Critics. A graduate of Lehigh University, he received a bachelor's degree in English and graduated Phi Beta Kappa and magna cum laude.

Rob Nelson is the film editor and lead film critic at *City Pages* in Minneapolis. His work also appears in the *Village Voice* and *Mother Jones.* He is the recipient of three editorial awards from the Association of Alternative Newsweeklies, and is the curator of Get Real: City Pages Documentary Film Festival, held each November in Minneapolis.

Gerald Peary, a film critic for the *Boston Phoenix*, heads the cinema program at Suffolk University, Boston, and curates the Boston University Cinematheque. He has written eight books on cinema, including coediting *Women and the Cinema: A Critical Anthology*, *The Classic American Novel and the Movies*, *The Modern American Novel and the Movies*, and *The American Cartoon*. His latest book is *John Ford: Interviews*. A University of Wisconsin Ph.D., he was a Fulbright scholar studying Yugoslavian film comedy and was acting curator of the Harvard University Film Archive. Peary has been president of international critics juries (FIPRESCI) at Rotterdam, Karlovy Vary, Vienna, Bangkok, and Turin, and has worked as a story editor for documentarians Errol Morris and Ron Mann. He is currently writing and directing a full-length documentary about American film criticism.

Peter Rainer discusses movies regularly for *Film Week*, aired over Minnesota Public Radio, and for public television station KCET. He was a finalist for the 1998 Pulitzer Prize in criticism and chairman of the National Society of Film Critics from 1989–2004. He has been a film critic for the *Los Angeles Herald-Examiner*, *Los Angeles Times*, *Los Angeles* magazine, *New Times Los Angeles*, and, most recently, *New York* magazine, where he is currently a contributing editor. His writing has also appeared in the *New York Times Magazine*, *Vogue*, *Esquire*, *Newsday*, and *GQ*. He wrote and coproduced *A&E Biography* shows on Sidney Poitier and the Hustons, and has appeared as a commentator on *Nightline*. He is also the editor of the NSFC anthology *Love and Hisses*.

Carrie Rickey is a film critic for the *Philadelphia Inquirer* and writes for many publications on topics related to art and film. Her essays appear in *The Rolling Stone History of Rock and Roll*, *The American Century*, and *The Triumph of Feminist Art*.

Jonathan Rosenbaum is the film critic for the *Chicago Reader* and writes the column "Global Discoveries on DVD" for *Cinema Scope*. His books include: *Essential Cinema: On the Necessity of Film Canons*; *Movie Mutations: The Changing Face of World Cinephilia* (coedited with Adrian Martin); *Abbas Kiarostami* (with Mehrnaz Saeed-Vafa); *Movie Wars: How Hollywood and the Media Limit What Films We Can See*; *Dead Man*; *Movies as Politics*; *Placing Movies: The Practice of Film Criticism*; *This Is Orson Welles* (editor); *Greed*; *Midnight Movies* (with J. Hoberman); *Film: The Front Line*; and *Moving Places: A Life at the Movies*.

Richard Schickel has produced, written, and directed more than thirty documentaries, including *Charlie: The Life and Art of Charles Chaplin; Scorsese on Scorsese; Woody Allen: A Life in Film;* and *Shooting War,* a history of combat cameramen in World War II. His reconstruction of Samuel Fuller's *The Big Red One* won several awards. He is the author of more than thirty books, including biographies of D. W. Griffith, Walt Disney, and Clint Eastwood. His latest title is *Good Morning, Mr. Zip Zip Zip,* a moviegoing memoir, and a study of Elia Kazan, to be published in 2005. He has reviewed movies for *Time* since 1972, and he writes a monthly column, "Film on Paper," for the *Los Angeles Times Book Review.* He has been awarded a Guggenheim Fellowship, the British Film Institute Book Prize, the Maurice Bessy Prize for film criticism, and the William K. Everson award for contributions to film history.

Lisa Schwarzbaum joined *Entertainment Weekly* as a senior writer in 1991, and became one of the magazine's two film critics in 1995. In addition, she contributes book reviews, essays, and cultural criticism. Her work has appeared in the *New York Times Magazine, Vogue, Redbook,* and other publications, and she reviews films on national and local TV and radio programs. Schwarzbaum, who holds a B.A. from Sarah Lawrence College, is also a member of the New York Film Critics Circle.

Matt Zoller Seitz is a film critic for the *New York Press,* a TV critic for the *Newark Star-Ledger,* and was a finalist for the Pulitzer Prize in criticism. His work has been published in the *New York Times, Newsday, The Independent, Dallas Observer, TV Guide,* and *Sound and Vision,* and has been reprinted in *Spike, Mike, Slackers and Dykes; The Making of a Charlie Brown Christmas; Essays for the 21st Century; The A List;* and *Signs of Life in the USA: Readings on Popular Culture for Writers.* His DVD liner notes include the Criterion editions of *Mon Oncle* and *Man Bites Dog.* Seitz is also a member of the New York Film Critics Circle and the Television Critics Association, and is an independent filmmaker, a freelance Final Cut Pro editor, and a cofounder of Brooklyn Schoolyard (www.brooklynschoolyard.com), a New York–based production company. His debut feature, *Home,* was released in 2005.

Michael Sragow is the lead film critic for the *Baltimore Sun.* He edited the Library of America's two-volume collection of James Agee's writing (October 2005), and is working on a biography of Victor Fleming for Pantheon. His reviews and essays have appeared in *The New Yorker, The Atlantic Monthly,* and *Rolling Stone.*

David Sterritt, chair of the National Society of Film Critics, is the film critic for *The Christian Science Monitor* and a film professor at Columbia University and Long Island University. His writing has appeared in the *New York Times, Film Comment, Cineaste, The Journal of Aesthetics and Art Criticism, Cahiers du Cinema,* and elsewhere. He has served two terms as chair of the New York Film Critics Circle, is cochair of the Columbia University Seminar on Cinema and Interdisciplinary Interpretation, has served on the New York Film Festival selection committee, and has lectured at such institutions as the National Gallery of Art and the Museum of Modern Art. Media appearances include *Nightline, The Charlie Rose Show, Morning Edition,* and *All Things Considered.* He has published books on Alfred Hitchcock, Jean-Luc Godard, Robert Altman, Terry Gilliam, and the Beat Generation; his latest is *Guiltless Pleasures: A David Sterritt Reader.*

Amy Taubin is a contributing editor for *Film Comment* and *Sight and Sound.* She also writes frequently on film for *Art Forum,* and her essays have been included in many collections. Her book, *Taxi Driver,* was published in 2000 in the British Film Institute's Film Classics series. She wrote weekly film criticism for the *Village Voice* (1987–2001) and originated the column "Art and Industry," which covered American independent filmmaking. She began her professional life as an actor, appearing on Broadway, most notably in *The Prime of Miss Jean Brodie,* and in avant-garde films, among them Michael Snow's *Wavelength,* Andy Warhol's *Couch,* and Jonas Mekas's *Diaries, Notebooks, and Sketches.* Her avant-garde film *In the Bag* (1981) is in the collection of the Museum of Modern Art. She teaches in New York City at the School of Visual Arts.

Charles Taylor writes a column on popular culture for the *Newark Star-Ledger.* His writing on movies, books, and politics has appeared in *Salon,* the *New York Times, The New Yorker, Newsday, The New York Observer, Sight and Sound, Film Comment,* and other publications.

Ella Taylor is a film critic for *L.A. Weekly.* A former academic, she has also written on film for *The Atlantic Monthly Arts and Entertainment Supplement, Mirabella, Elle, Newsday,* and *The Guardian,* and on television for the *Village*

Voice and *Seattle Weekly.* She is the author of *Prime Time America: Television Families in Post-War America* (University of California Press).

Kevin Thomas has been reviewing movies for the *Los Angeles Times* since 1962, which makes him the longest-running film reviewer on a major U.S. daily. Career highlights include interviewing Akira Kurosawa on his eightieth birthday; writing the eulogy for Mae West's funeral (recently included in *Farewell, Godspeed: The Greatest Eulogies of Our Time*); and interviewing Joseph Losey on his first return to Hollywood after the blacklist. A fourth-generation California newspaperman, Thomas received a distinguished alumnus award from Gettysburg College in 2000, and in 2004 received a lifetime achievement award from the National Lesbian and Gay Journalists Association.

Desson Thomson is a film critic for *The Washington Post,* with an eclectic, widely traveled background, including a stint in the rock band Kaspar Hauser. With a degree in communications and cinema studies from American University, Thomson is also a singer and songwriter; his current band, Cairo Fred, performs in Washington clubs.

Peter Travers has been the film critic and senior editor for film at *Rolling Stone* since 1989. He appears regularly as a film commentator on CNN and MSNBC, and his film analysis has been featured on *The Charlie Rose Show,* HBO's *Spoken and Stirred,* and more. His work can be read online at www.rollingstone.com. Travers is also the author of *The 1000 Best Movies on DVD* (Hyperion) and the editor of *The Rolling Stone Film Reader* (Pocket Books). A former chair of the New York Film Critics Circle, Travers was a film critic for *People* magazine from 1984 to 1988.

Kenneth Turan is a film critic for the *Los Angeles Times* and National Public Radio's *Morning Edition,* as well as the director of the Los Angeles Times Book Prizes. He has been a staff writer for *The Washington Post* and *TV Guide,* and the *Times'* book review editor. A graduate of Swarthmore College and Columbia University's Graduate School of Journalism, he is the coauthor of *Call Me Anna: The Autobiography of Patty Duke.* He teaches film reviewing and nonfiction writing at USC and is on the board of directors of the National

Yiddish Book Center. His most recent books are *Sundance to Sarajevo: Film Festivals and the World They Made* (University of California Press) and *Never Coming to a Theater Near You* (Public Affairs).

James Verniere was born in Newark, New Jersey, and reborn in Manhattan's Criterion Theater at a showing of *Lawrence of Arabia.* A graduate of Rutgers University and member of Phi Beta Kappa, Verniere has a master's degree in English literature and once taught English composition at New Jersey's Clinton Correctional Institute for Women. A film critic since the late 1970s, he has written for *Film Comment, Sight and Sound,* and *Heavy Metal.* Verniere has been the *Boston Herald* film critic since 1985, and his feature stories are distributed by the Tribune Syndicate. Verniere's work has appeared in the NSFC anthology *The A List.*

Armond White is a film critic for the *New York Press* and author of *The Resistance: Ten Years of Pop Culture That Shook the World* (Overlook Press) and the forthcoming *Knee Deep in Great Experiences: A Study of Public Enemy and Morrissey,* to be published in 2006.

Michael Wilmington has been the chief movie critic of the *Chicago Tribune* since September 1993. He also reviews movies and video for CLTV and Metromix.com. He is the editor of the National Society of Film Critics' film and video poll and website. Wilmington was a film critic and reporter for the *Los Angeles Times* from 1984 to 1993; film and video critic and contributing editor for *L.A. Style* from 1987 to 1993; film critic and film editor for *L.A. Weekly* from 1983 to 1985; and contributing editor of the *Velvet Light Trap* of Madison, Wisconsin, from 1972 to 1976. He is coauthor, with Joseph McBride, of the 1974 book *John Ford* (Da Capo) and has contributed extensively to film journals including *Film Comment, Sight and Sound,* and *Film Quarterly.* He was film critic for *Isthmus* of Madison from 1980 to 1993, where he won five Milwaukee Press Club awards for arts criticism, plus three honorable mentions. At the *Tribune,* he has won or shared two Peter Lisagor awards for arts writing and two runner-up citations for broadcast criticism. As a teenager at the Belfry Theatre of Williams Bay, Wisconsin, he acted in the same company with the young Harrison Ford, and, in 1966,won a Brass Bell trophy.

William Wolf publishes the online magazine *wolfentertainmentguide.com*, where his film and theater reviews appear. He is a member of the Online Film Critics Society, the New York Film Critics Online, and is president of The Drama Desk, an organization of theater critics and journalists. He was formerly a film critic for *Cue, New York,* and the Gannett News Service, and served two terms as chair of the New York Film Critics Circle. He teaches in the French and English departments at New York University and at the NYU School of Continuing and Professional Studies. He is the author of *Landmark Films: The Cinema & Our Century* and *The Marx Brothers.* His work also appears in *The A List.*

Stephanie Zacharek is a senior writer for the online magazine *Salon.* Her work has also appeared in the *New York Times, Entertainment Weekly, Rolling Stone, New York,* and *Sight and Sound.*

Permissions

"The Age of Innocence" by Amy Taubin. Portions of this essay were originally published in *Sight and Sound,* December 1993. Reprinted by permission of the author.

"Anatomy of Hell" by Stephanie Zacharek. Originally published in different form in *Salon.com* on October 15, 2004. Reprinted by permission of the author.

"À nos amours" by David Edelstein. Reprinted by permission of the author.

"Ayn Rand: A Sense of Life" by Jonathan Rosenbaum. Originally published in different form in the *Chicago Reader,* March 20, 1998. Reprinted by permission of the author.

"Baby Doll" by Michael Sragow. Originally published in different form in the *Boston Phoenix.* Reprinted by permission of the author.

"Baby Face" copyright © 2005 Dave Kehr. Printed by permission of the author.

"Bad Education" copyright © 2005 Andy Klein. Printed by permission of the author.

"Baise-moi" by Gerald Peary. Portions were published in the *Boston Phoenix,* December 2001, and *Film Comment,* November/December 2000. Reprinted by permission of the author.

"Basic Instinct" by J. Hoberman. Originally published in *Sight and Sound,* June 1992.

"Behind the Green Door" copyright © 2005 Carrie Rickey. Printed by permission of the author.

"Belle de jour" by Michael Wilmington. Originally published in the *Chicago Tribune,* July 14, 1995. Reprinted by permission of the author.

"Beyond the Valley of the Dolls" by Roger Ebert. Originally published in the *Guardian,* April 1, 2005. Copyright © Guardian Newspapers Limited 2005. Reprinted with permission.

"Black Sunday" by James Verniere. Printed by permission of the author.

"Blue Velvet" by Andy Klein. Originally published in different form in the *L.A. Reader,* September 19, 1986. Reprinted by permission of the author.

"Body Heat" copyright © 2005 Peter Travers. Printed by permission of the author.

"Butch Cassidy and the Sundance Kid" copyright © 2005 Lisa Schwarzbaum. Printed by permission of the author.

"Bye Bye Birdie" by Jami Bernard. Originally published in different form in the book *Chick Flicks,* by Jami Bernard. Reprinted by permission of the author.

"Carmen Jones" copyright © 2005 Jami Bernard. Printed by permission of the author.

"Contempt" by Desson Thomson. Reprinted by permission of the author.

"Crash" by Jonathan Rosenbaum. Originally published in different form in the *Chicago Reader,* March 21, 1997. Reprinted by permission of the author.

"Crimes of Passion" copyright © 2005 Peter Travers. Printed by permission of the author.

"Days of Heaven" by Eleanor Ringel Gillespie. Reprinted by permission of the author.

"Deep Throat" copyright © 2005 Emanuel Levy. Printed by permission of the author.

"Don't Look Now" by Sheila Benson. Reprinted by permission of the author.

"Ecstasy" by Kevin Thomas. Reprinted by permission of the author.

"Eyes Wide Shut" by Rob Nelson. Originally appeared in different form in *City Pages,* July 21, 1999. Reprinted by permission of the author.

"Eyes Without a Face" by Kenneth Turan. Copyright © Los Angeles Times. Originally published October 31, 2003. Reprinted with permission.

"The Fabulous Baker Boys" by Jay Carr. Reprinted by permission of the author.

"The Last of the Mohicans" by Matt Zoller Seitz. Reprinted by permission of the author.

"Last Tango in Paris" copyright © 2005 Peter Brunette. Printed by permission of the author.

"Laura" copyright © 2005 Emanuel Levy. Printed by permission of the author.

"Laurel Canyon" by Carrie Rickey. Originally published in the *Philadelphia Inquirer*, April 4, 2003. Reprinted by permission of the author.

"The Long Hot Summer" by James Verniere. Reprinted by permission of the author.

"The Makioka Sisters" by Peter Rainer. Originally published in the *Los Angeles Herald Examiner*, November 6, 1985. Reprinted by permission of the author.

"McCabe & Mrs. Miller" by John Anderson. Reprinted by permission of the author.

"Morocco" copyright © 2005 Stephanie Zacharek. Printed by permission of the author.

"Mulholland Drive" by Peter Travers. Originally appeared in different form in *Rolling Stone*, November 8, 2001. Reprinted by permission of the author.

"The Mummy" copyright © 2005 Charles Taylor. Printed by permission of the author.

"O Fantasma" copyright © 2005 Nathan Lee. Printed by permission of the author.

"Ossessione" copyright © 2005 Peter Brunette. Reprinted by permission of the author.

"Pandora's Box" by Kevin Thomas. Reprinted by permission of the author.

"Peeping Tom" by Peter Keough. Originally published in different form in the *Boston Phoenix*, March 18, 1999. Reprinted by permission of the author.

"Persona" by Michael Wilmington. Reprinted by permission of the author.

"Picnic" copyright © 2005 Emanuel Levy. Printed by permission of the author.

"Poison Ivy" by Peter Travers. Originally published in different form in *Rolling Stone*, May 28, 1992. Reprinted by permission of the author.

"Rebecca" by Jami Bernard. Originally published in different form in the book *Chick Flicks*, by Jami Bernard. Reprinted by permission of the author.

"Secretary" copyright © 2005 Jami Bernard. Printed by permission of the author.

SIDEBARS

Index